PHILIP B. KURLAND is professor of law at the Law
School of The University of Chicago. He is the
author of *Religion and the Law* and the coauthor of
Jurisdiction of the Supreme Court of the United States
and *The Great Charter*. Since 1960 he has been the
editor of *The Supreme Court Review*. He has also
edited *Felix Frankfurter on the Supreme Court, Of
Law and Life and Other Things That Matter,* and *Mr.
Justice*. He was law clerk to Mr. Justice Frankfurter
in 1945–46, and has been chief consultant to the
Subcommittee on Separation of Powers of the United
States Senate Committee on the Judiciary since 1967.

*Politics, the Constitution,
and the Warren Court*

The 1969 Cooley Lectures
University of Michigan Law School

Politics
the Constitution
and the Warren Court

Philip B. Kurland

The University of Chicago Press
Chicago and London

International Standard Book Number: 0-226-46408-3
Library of Congress Catalog Card Number: 74-124734

The University of Chicago Press, Chicago 60637
The University of Chicago Press, Ltd., London

To My Fair Ladies

Contents

Preface

BEGINNING IN 1753, a series of lectures on the law was delivered at Oxford University and ultimately published as Blackstone's *Commentaries on the Laws of England.* In 1880, in Boston, Oliver Wendell Holmes, Jr., delivered the Lowell Lectures that eventually came to a broader audience as *The Common Law.* In 1920, the Storrs Lectures at Yale were delivered by Benjamin Cardozo and resulted in his famous little book *The Nature of the Judicial Process.*

Ever since, law school deans have been enamored of the notion of a lecture series in the vain hope that another classic might thus be born. For the most part, it has been an unfulfilled ambition. Even the incomparable Learned Hand failed this aspiration in his Holmes Lectures, published as *The Bill of Rights.*

I am grateful to Dean Francis A. Allen and his faculty at the University of Michigan Law School for ignoring the empirical data and inviting me to deliver the prestigious Cooley Lectures, which were based on the pages that follow. From 15 September through 19 September, 1969, I was accorded the greatest kindness and courtesy by my hosts, the faculty and students of the law school. It was an exhilarating and enlightening period for me, whatever hardships I may have imposed on them. I am particularly indebted to Dean and Mrs. Allen, Professor and Mrs. Paul G. Kauper, and Professor and Mrs. Roger C. Cramton for their gracious hospitality. The warmth of both the senior and junior common rooms as well as the lecture hall was reminiscent of a civility that has all but disappeared from the halls of academe.

My gratitude has another dimension. The preparation of the Cooley Lectures afforded the opportunity to put into essay form some of the thoughts I have had about the Supreme Court. The congeniality of the essay form for my purposes has been set forth in its definition by Felix Frankfurter: "[T]he essay is tentative, reflective, suggestive, contradictory, and incomplete. It mirrors the perversities and complexities of life" (Kurland, ed., *Felix Frankfurter on the Supreme Court* 203 [1970]).

Once again I am obligated to Mrs. Artie Scott for the dedicated conversion of my unreadable manuscript into a readable typescript and to Mr. Samuel Clapper for digging out and verifying the references that I have used.

Introduction

I DO NOT PROPOSE to express here the point of view of the Warren Court's vituperative detractors. Nor do I come to join the adulatory admirers of that Court. I come neither to praise Caesar nor to bury him. I ask that you forget, if you can, that I am, in the unpublished—but nonetheless immortal—words of Dean Allen, one of those antediluvians from the University of Chicago who purportedly live entirely on the intellectual sustenance of Felix Frankfurter and Adam Smith, instead of enjoying the mental and spiritual nourishment provided by Earl Warren and Kenneth Galbraith. And if you are, as so many are, among the ardent partisans, I ask you to indulge that temporary suspension of disbelief that makes it possible for the novelist, the playwright, and the poet to tell truths even in the context of fictions. It is not that I pretend either to the verbal felicities or the imaginistic capacities of these other arts. That the context of my subject is one of fictions, however, should soon become evident to you. It is to dissipate some of the promulgated romance about the Warren Court that I ask that you try to look at the Supreme Court neither "as the devil incarnate" nor as the Messiah.

Mr. Justice Holmes was fond of telling us that "continuity with the past" is "not a duty" but "only a necessity."[1] The prospect of a Supreme Court with two new members—one of them a new Chief Justice of the United States—appropriately calls for a backward glance at the "Warren Court." For the coming years will bring to the Court a series of cases whose relevance and importance cannot but depend on what

1. Southern Pacific Co. v. Jensen, 244 U.S. 205, 220 (1917).

has gone before. Many of the issues that made the Warren Court the embattled institution it was will again come up for consideration by the newly constituted high tribunal. Problems of criminal procedure will bulk large on the docket. Questions of church and state will call for resolution. Freedom of expression for dissenters will also trouble the new Court, as will reapportionment problems in new guises. Many questions will be raised about the functioning of the Selective Service System and the problem of involuntary loss of American citizenship will again be rehearsed.

If a new Chief Justice is to give his name to the reconstructed Court, however, it is important to recognize that Earl Warren's replacement by Warren Burger cannot be analogized to a change of administrations after a presidential election. The judiciary is different. It has no pecking order. It has no seniority system. No judge, however lowly his court, should be beholden to any other judge, however supreme his designation. No Justice, whatever his place on the high bench, is superior or inferior to any other Justice by reason of that place.

The importance of the appointment of a new Supreme Court Justice depends more on his individual capacities than on his title. As Charles Evans Hughes once told us:

> The Chief Justice as the head of the Court has an outstanding position, but in a small body of able men with equal authority in the making of decisions, it is evident that his actual influence will depend upon the strength of his character and the demonstration of his ability in the intimate relations of the judges. It is safe to say that no member of the Supreme Court is under any illusion as to the mental equipment of his brethren. Constant and close association discloses the strength and exposes the weaknesses of each. Courage of conviction, sound learning, familiarity with precedents, exact knowledge due to painstaking study of the cases under consideration cannot fail to command that profound respect which is always yielded to intellectual power conscien-

tiously applied. That influence can be exerted by any member of the Court, whatever his rank in the order of precedence.[2]

Hughes afforded an important lesson, not because it deprecates the role of Chief Justice—it doesn't—but because it reminds us of the equal importance of the other eight members of the Court. And that the essential test of command is "intellectual power conscientiously applied." This brings to mind the fact that there were seventeen members of the Warren Court. Most of Warren's associates—these included Robert H. Jackson and Felix Frankfurter, Hugo L. Black and William O. Douglas—were at least his peers in the conscientious application of intellectual power. And these sixteen Associate Justices must share with Warren such glory or infamy as the Court may have earned in the last decade and a half.

Certainly there has been enough praise and blame to go around. The rhetoric in this contest over the virtues and vices of the Supreme Court is familiar.

> It is frequently charged that this tribunal is tyrannical. If the Constitution of the United States be tyranny; if the rule that no one shall be convicted of crime save by jury of his peers; that slavery shall not be permitted to exist in any state or territory; that no one shall be deprived of life, liberty or property without due process of law; if these and many other provisions made by the people be tyranny, then the Supreme Court when it makes decisions in accordance with these principles of our fundamental law is tyrannical. Otherwise it is exercising the power of government for the preservation of liberty. The fact is that the Constitution is the source of our freedom. Maintaining it, interpreting it and declaring it are the only methods by which the Constitution can be preserved and our liberties guaranteed.

So goes the argument in defense of the Court's behavior.

2. HUGHES, THE SUPREME COURT 57 (1928).

On the other hand:

> Through its steady expansion of the meaningless mean-
> ing of the "due process" clause of the Fourteenth
> Amendment, the Supreme Court is putting constitutional
> compulsion behind the private judgment of its members
> upon disputed and difficult questions of social policy.

Thus speak those who attack the Court.

For some reason, it is heartening to report that the first
quotation is from a speech by Calvin Coolidge in Baltimore
in 1924.[3] The second is from a *New Republic* editorial in
1926.[4] It is not surprising that they have a contemporary
sound. With only slight modification these themes have been
stated and restated almost daily in the editorial pages of the
public press. The difference between then and now is to be
found in the fact that Coolidge was defending a Court dedicated to the preservation of "liberty of contract" against attacks from the "left" by such radicals as Theodore Roosevelt
and Robert M. La Follette. Controversy has always swirled
around the Supreme Court. The only peace it has known is
the quiet described by Holmes as that of "the storm centre."[5]

Of course, there are always real questions behind these
rhetorical forays. But one must cut below the cuticle of
catchwords to discover what the issues are. And it must be
made clear that the essential question is nothing so simple as
whether the Court is adhering to the commands of the Constitution. For the commands of the Constitution are often
written in Delphic language. Strict construction of vague language is not possible for mere mortals. That is why so many
of us resort to dogma in lieu of reason to explain the "plain
meaning" of abstruse phrases.

3. Quoted in KURLAND, ed., FELIX FRANKFURTER ON THE SUPREME
COURT 158 (1970).
4. *Id.* at 181.
5. HOLMES, COLLECTED LEGAL PAPERS 292 (1920).

In the words of Felix Frankfurter, to whom the "strict constructionists" now look as to a hero, though he was once regarded with somewhat less esteem by these same people:

> Humility, painstaking solicitude for the ascertainable feelings and needs of present-day society, the imaginative effort to reconcile contending claims, respect for the spontaneity and persistence with which groups are established to conserve a social interest—these are the high qualities of discernment, of tolerance, of wise statecraft without which constitutional law is a system of pernicious abstractions instead of the governance of a teeming continent.[6]

Where the Warren Court succeeded, it was because it displayed these qualities. Its failures may well be attributable to their absence.

The Supreme Court is not now, nor has it ever been, the creator of many of the problems that it is called upon to resolve. America's complex society produces the very basic issues that the Court addresses. Probably no other nation in the world—except in mimicry of American institutions—has thrust upon such a judicial body the ultimate responsibility for establishing the fundamental rules for the "governance of a teeming continent."

Admittedly the recent Court has eagerly sought after societal problems that had proved too intransigent for resolution by other branches of government, both state and national. But, if the Court can be faulted for not properly resolving them, it ought not to be condemned for creating them. The conflict between the races; the problems of a suffocating urbanization; a mushrooming growth of crime; the deteriorating scope for freedom of individual action against the expanding demands of society; the anomaly of poverty in a nation of affluence; the pressures for the centralization of power, economic as well as governmental; the horrors

6. KURLAND, note 3 *supra*.

deriving from a self-proclaimed leadership of the free world community; the demands of an engulfing egalitarianism; none of these is of the Court's making. Yet all of them have contributed to its heavy docket. Some of these problems have been exacerbated and some have been palliated by the Court's decisions. But, in either event, usually at the price of adding to the Court's vulnerability to attack.

Those who will can praise or damn the Court for its efforts during the period of the Warren chairmanship. But unless one is interested only in indulging emotions, one's conclusions ought to rest on consideration of the facts, many of which tend to be overlooked.

The first of these that I would call to your attention is that the Warren Court has not been the creator of any of the major doctrines that it has sought to effectuate. The *School Desegregation Cases*[7]—certainly the most important decisions it rendered—were in the making for a decade before the opinion was rendered.[8] Indeed, the seeds of these decisions were sown in the very doctrine that they overruled, the concept of "separate but equal." The seeds were grown when the American people were satisfied to pay only lip service to the Supreme Court's pronouncement: to adhere to the privilege of separation but never to the duty of equality. That the issue came to a head in public education was certainly due to the new importance of formal education and of universal compulsory education in the twentieth century. At least since 1945, there had been no question about the conclusion that the Court would reach when it decided the case. The Court hesitated only about how the change in constitutional canons was to be effected, not whether they would be changed.

Indeed, the Vinson Court's ban on racially restrictive property covenants[9] proffered a more fundamental constitu-

7. Brown v. Bd. of Educ., 347 U.S. 483 (1954).
8. See chapters 3 and 4, *infra.*
9. Shelley v. Kraemer, 334 U.S. 1 (1948).

tional doctrine than that essayed by the Warren Court. Certainly the judgment, if not the opinion, in *Brown* would have been forthcoming in 1954 even had Vinson survived.

So, too, with the concept of commanding state legislatures to reapportion.[10] That notion had been accepted by Douglas, Black, and others at least as early as 1946 when Governor Warren was still rejecting apportionment of the California legislature on a far more modest level. The slogan of one man–one vote has a far more ancient lineage.[11] There was no question that most state legislatures were malapportioned, avoiding the mandates of their own constitutions if not of the nation's fundamental law. An insistence by state legislators on flouting their own laws, more than any novel legal theory, may well be what moved the Court to action. As Paul Freund has written:

> It is sometimes said that when legislatures and executives cannot be moved to advance the cause of liberalism, the opportunity and responsibility devolve on the courts. Stated thus baldly, the counsel is surely a dangerous invitation, dangerous to the standing of the Court and false to the liberalism in whose name it is propounded. But in the context of the Tennessee apportionment case the default of the lawmaking machinery had special relevance, for the very structure and processes that are presupposed in representative government had become distorted.[12]

The ban on "voluntary" public school Bible reading and religious services was announced by state courts more than a half-century before that rule became the law of the land

10. See chapter 3, *infra.*
11. " 'Every man to count for one and no one to count for more than one.' This formula, much used by the utilitarians, seems to me to form the heart of the doctrine of equality or equal rights, and has coloured much liberal and democratic thought." Berlin, *Equality,* in 56 PROC. ARISTOTELIAN SOC. 301 (1955–56).
12. FREUND, ON LAW AND JUSTICE 13 (1968).

by reason of Supreme Court decisions.[13] In the state of Illinois, the Supreme Court, in a suit brought by the Catholic church, prohibited the reading of the Bible or of prayers in public schools in 1910 and was preceded by other state court decisions to the same effect beginning in 1890.[14] The application of the protection of the First Amendment to actions by the state goes back to the time of Holmes and Brandeis.[15]

The essential doctrines of criminal procedure for which the Warren Court received such brickbats and kudos[16] were also "old hat." They may be found stated in Judge Thomas M. Cooley's famous and influential treatise, *Constitutional Limitations,* first published in 1868. Indeed, the list of antecedents for the Warren Court's decisions could be extended almost without limit.

This is not to say that there has been no novelty in the Court's doctrinal creations. Its notion of the meaning of the Eighth Amendment's prohibition against cruel and unusual punishments,[17] for example, is not only novel, it is bizarre. But the fact remains that the areas of judgment for which the Court has become best known essentially were those where it accepted ideas that had long been in circulation. If all of these major areas of the Warren Court's work reflect a shift in ultimate power from the states to the judicial branch of the national government, that too was no novelty but merely the culmination of long years of Supreme Court behavior.[18]

13. See Engel v. Vitale, 370 U.S. 421 (1962); School District of Abington Township v. Schempp, 374 U.S. 203 (1963).

14. See Kurland, *The Regents' Prayer Case: "Full of Sound and Fury, Signifying . . . ,"* 1962 Supreme Court Review 1, 19 n. 76.

15. See Chafee, Free Speech in the United States (1941); see also Levy, Legacy of Suppression (1960), for dissipation of some of the myths about the intentions and actions of the founders.

16. See chapter 3, *infra.*

17. See Trop v. Dulles, 356 U.S. 86 (1958); Robinson v. California, 370 U.S. 660 (1962); *cf.* Rudolph v. Alabama, 375 U.S. 889 (1963).

18. See chapter 3, *infra.*

A second important set of facts that should be observed in passing judgment on the Warren Court depends on following Holmes's famous dictum to think things and not words. One must look to see not only what the Court has said but what its words have accomplished. Both the Court's admirers and its detractors equate the Court's pronouncements with obedience to them as the law of the land. However bad some of the decisions, we might be better off if those were the facts. They are not.

As of the end of the Warren era we had little more real school integration than we did when *Brown v. Board of Education* was decided in 1954, even after Congress ratified the Court's decisions and sought to implement its principles. (The early withdrawal by the Nixon administration of the deadlines for compliance imposed on southern schools is revealing of the complexities and difficulties of bringing about fundamental changes in American life.)[19] School prayers and Bible reading are still the rule rather than the exception in the absence of specific judicial mandates directed to particular school boards.[20]

True, there has been widespread reapportionment of local legislatures. But it must be recognized that the politicians rather than the people have controlled such reapportionment. To the extent that voting power has been shifted, it has been shifted from rural areas, and occasionally urban areas, to suburbia—politically the most reactionary constituencies that this country has to offer. And it should be recalled that the centralizaion of power in the national government has made state legislatures all but redundant.

The *Miranda*[21] and *Escobedo*[22] rules, according to sur-

19. See 37 Cong. Q. W. Rep. 1606 (29 August 1969).
20. *Cf.* Hearings before the Subcommittee on Separation of Powers of the Committee on the Judiciary, United States Senate, on the Supreme Court, 90th Cong., 2d Sess. 53 *et seq.* (1968) (Prof. Bickel).
21. Miranda v. Arizona, 384 U.S. 436 (1966).
22. Escobedo v. Illinois, 384 U.S. 436 (1966).

veys, have changed only the formalities of police behavior and not its substance.[23] This, even though a large number, but a very small proportion, of guilty verdicts have been reversed for failure to comply with the Supreme Court's guidelines.

One must be careful, however, not to overplay the ineffectiveness of the Court's actions. If it has used old doctrines, it has used them in new applications. And the Court must be given its due in helping to spark and sustain the Negro social revolution that engulfs us at the moment.[24] And certainly, too, the Court has made major contributions to the egalitarian ethos that is becoming dominant in our society.[25] The Court is a mirror of vital movements in American life. Even if it is not responsible for initiating them, it is responsible for succoring them. As Nietzsche once put it: "Here is the hero who did nothing but shake the tree when the fruit was ripe. Do you think that was a small thing to do? Well, just look at the tree he shook."[26]

To my mind the Warren Court suffered from three basic failings. First, it was unable or unwilling to adhere to the step-by-step process that has long characterized the common-law and constitutional forms of adjudication. The Warren Court took a more exalted view of its own functions. It was not content to decide the cases before it. It preferred to write codes of conduct rather than resolve particular controversies. Moreover, it seemed to feel that every proposition had to be taken to its logical extreme. Thus, in the reapportionment cases, nothing would suffice except to extend the one man–one vote formula with a mathematical precision that ignored the complexities of political life.[27] The self-

23. See, *e.g.*, Note, *Interrogation in New Haven: The Impact of Miranda*, 76 YALE L.J. 1519 (1967).
24. See chapter 4, *infra*.
25. *Ibid.*
26. 2 HUMAN, ALL TOO HUMAN 137 (1880).
27. See Dixon, *The Warren Court Crusade in Search of the Holy Grail of One Man–One Vote*, 1969 SUPREME COURT REVIEW 219.

incrimination prohibition was read as a doctrinaire formula rather than a rule derived from historical necessity. In protecting the interest it thought valuable, it tended to ignore any countervailing interests that society properly demanded also be given consideration. It thus mandated more than it could accomplish.

Paul Freund, in a recent speech on Mr. Justice Jackson, provided a story that the new Court should ponder:

> As a judge, Robert Jackson displayed what I would call, summarily, a dialectical mind—recognizing principles in collision. His thinking was not one-dimensional, all warp and no woof. He bore no resemblance to the boy who said he knew how to spell "banana" but he didn't know when to stop.[28]

Second the Court has failed to recognize the incapacities that inhere in its structure. It lacks the machinery to gather the data necessary for broad rule-making as distinguished from the resolution of particular litigation. It is still, in form, an appellate court. It is dependent upon the litigants before it and a very small staff to provide it with relevant information. It also lacks the machinery for the administration of the broad rules that it has promulgated. It is dependent largely on lower courts—state and federal—to apply its rules to other litigants who come before them. If its construction of the Constitution is to be enforced on behalf of those who do not invoke a judicial forum, it must look to the other branches of the national government for aid. Such aid is not always forthcoming.

Most important of the Court's major failings has been its unwillingness to accommodate to Mr. Justice Brandeis's wisdom uttered in another context: A judge "may advise; he may persuade; but he may not command or coerce. He does coerce when without convincing the judgment he overcomes

28. DESMOND, FREUND, STEWART, & SHAWCROSS, MR. JUSTICE JACKSON 36 (1969).

the will by the weight of the authority."[29] The Supreme Court, too, cannot compel; it must convince. For its strength ultimately depends on the support of public opinion, as that prescient young man Alexis de Tocqueville recognized in the 1830s. The Court's opinions have tended toward fiat rather than reason. Some of its major opinions have been patently disingenuous. It has distinguished precedents on the flimsiest of grounds and frequently ignored those that it would not bother to distinguish.

There may be good reasons for this. Alfred Kelly has suggested one:

> The Court, almost by definition is ill-equipped to deal with the process of discontinuity in the social order. . . . [I]t is perhaps part of the tragic nature of modern times, that we live in an age of historical discontinuity. . . . [T]he society is fraught with historical discontinuity in technology, in political order, in revolutionary techniques, in racial relations, everything you touch in the society is loaded with historical discontinuity. . . . [T]he very nature of the judicial process ill-equips it to deal with this, and it seems to me, recognizing that sometimes the simple process of stare decisis somehow does not handle this problem of continuity, it looks in a kind of almost frantic way for other techniques, among which are writing very bad history. . . . It falsifies history in order to produce continuity where there is not any.[30]

Perhaps, the Court should have practiced generally what it preached to the states in the reapportionment cases, where it said: "[T]he State must justify each variance, no matter how small."[31] A searching explanation of the reasons for change would have been more persuasive than the

29. Horning v. District of Columbia, 254 U.S. 135, 139 (1920).
30. Hearings, note 20 *supra*, at 73 (Prof. Kelly).
31. Kirkpatrick v. Preisler, 394 U.S. 526, 531 (1969).

patently false claim of adherence either to prior decisions or to "the original understanding."

The results of these failures of the Warren Court are awesome. Because it has taken on such a political mien, it has become more subject to political attack. Contrary to what the papers may have reported, the Fortas affair was not the cause for the weakening of confidence in the Court. It was the weakened confidence in the Court that made possible the Fortas affair. It was the popular mistrust of the Supreme Court that allowed the impeachment and removal of a Justice by methods other than those provided in the Constitution. Any Justice is now vulnerable to a strong attack by the press, supported by pressures from members of the legislative and executive branches of the government. The sword of Damocles hangs over the Court by the thin thread, today a gossamer thread, of public confidence in the integrity of the judiciary.

At the close of Warren's tenure, both the Supreme Court and the law were at low tide so far as public reaction was concerned. The Court's lack of prestige was reflected in data published by the Gallup Poll. The disdain for the law was demonstrated not only by the FBI's crime statistics but by the behavior of all levels of American society. It is revealed no less in the actions of three presidents and five Congresses who have indulged a war not sanctioned by constitutional procedures and in those of organizations and individuals who set themselves above the law.

We were, in the recent past, concerned about the "credibility gap" created by the executive branch when it became apparent that its words and the truth were not necessarily related. There is another credibility gap between the Court's pretensions and its actions. The restoration of public confidence is vital both to the continuance of the Court's powers and to the maintenance of the rule of law in this country.

The Supreme Court has been and must continue to be a strong force in the vital center that provides cohesion for a democratic society. The accomplishment of its mission is not measurable in terms of individual decisions. Its function is to help maintain a society dedicated to the notion that law must be the choice over force as the means of resolving the conflicts that burden society. It must epitomize reason rather than emotion in helping seek justice. Above all it must emphasize individual interests against the stamp of governmental paternalism and conformity. At the same time it must retain the confidence of the American people.

The Court can survive without performing these functions. Courts have survived in other societies that have rejected the concept of law based on reason. They survived in Hitler's Germany, in Stalin's Russia, and in the Union of South Africa. It is not the survival of the Court that is at stake, but the survival of the primacy of individual liberty that is in question.[32] And these values will remain viable only so long as the Court makes its appropriate contributions toward their maintenance.

32. "We started to find some positive content for Liberty, and all we have discovered is that it does not follow because we are not conscious of constraint that we are not constrained. Yet little as that seems, it is not I think an altogether contemptible result, for behind it lies a faith. It is the faith that our collective fate in the end depends upon the irrepressible fertility of the individual, and the finality of what he chooses to call good. It is the faith that neither principalities, nor powers, nor things present, nor things to come, can rightfully suppress that fertility or deny that good. It is the faith in the indefectible significance of each one of us, inherited, if I understand it aright, from One who lived and died some 1900 years ago in Palestine. It is a faith not easy to live by, whose credo is full of hard sayings. If you accept it, it may cast you for the role of Prometheus, a part of whose lines, you will remember, contain a good deal about defying the Powers of this World. Those powers are ruthless, competent, and strong; and among the properties in the play there are real lightning and a real eagle; make no mistake about that. Moreover, the audience is likely to be very small; indeed it is not improbable that there will be none at all. The only curtain calls you will get are those you give yourself. But the lead is a man's part, and perhaps some of us can fill it. Who can tell?" HAND, THE SPIRIT OF LIBERTY 154 (Dilliard ed. 2d ed. 1953).

To do this, the Court will probably have to retreat from its political stance. From now on, it must seek to persuade rather than coerce. Whether it will be able to do this will depend largely on its personnel. And its personnel will depend largely upon a recognition by the president and the Senate of the importance of choosing Justices—indeed all federal judges—by appropriate standards.

What are these standards? One thing is clear. They are not the mechanical demands issuing from Congress in recent years that would require prior judicial experience for some specified period. Some of our best Justices have had no prior judicial experience.[33] Some of our worst Justices have satisfied this criterion. The capacities that must be sought are those suggested by Charles Evans Hughes. A judge of the federal courts must have "strength of character" and "intellectual power." Not one or the other but both. It takes both, if a Supreme Court Justice is to have that breadth of vision, that capacity for disinterested judgment which the task demands.

The question asked today is whether the new Justices will measure up to such standards as are appropriate to their duties. The answer lies in the womb of time. As my colleagues in the Divinity School are wont to say, "Let us pray."

33. See Kurland, *The Constitution and the Tenure of Federal Judges: Some Notes from History,* 36 U. CHI. L. REV. 665, 697 n. 69 (1969).

1
The Tyranny of Labels

TOO MUCH DISCUSSION of the Supreme Court—and it has become a popular subject of debate—has been conducted in terms of comic-strip caricature. The catchwords are "judicial restraint" and "judicial activism." Or "liberals" and "conservatives." Or the argument might be phrased in terms of "neutral principles" against "value judgments." There is the tendency, both of supporters and of critics, to view the Court at polar extremes. On the one hand, it is seen as a political body, essentially not different from a legislature, in which the Justices impose solutions on all problems that come within their ambit solely according to their personal predilections or the interests of their self-selected constituencies. On the other hand, the Supreme Court is considered to be like any common-law court, purportedly limited in its function to applying preexisting rules to the particular factual circumstances presented to it. It must be, they say, either a rule-making body or a resolver of disputes. The one attitude suggests complete discretion—subject, of course, to the recognition that politics is the art of the possible. The other approach allows only a limited role of choice. As Chief Justice Morrison R. Waite put it: "Our province is to decide what the law is, not to declare what it should be. . . . If the law is wrong, it ought to be changed; but the power for that is not with us."[1]

The fact is, as any person with even a slight acquaintance

1. Minor v. Happersett, 21 Wall. 162, 178 (1874).

1

with the business of the Court should acknowledge, that the Supreme Court's behavior does not, in fact, approach either extreme. The Supreme Court has always operated—and operates still—somewhere between the judicial mode and the political mode.[2] Indeed, at different times and with regard to different subjects the Court will find itself closer to one pole or the other, never attaining either. It is prevented from becoming a purely political body by its institutional form and its intrinsic lack of power. It cannot avoid the painful necessity for exercising judgment because the rules that it is charged with administering—certainly at the constitutional level but even at the level of statutory interpretation—lack the certainty that would permit automatic application. As Mr. Justice Frankfurter once noted: "When the legislative will is clouded, what is called judicial construction has an inevitable element of judicial creation."[3] And the Court may find clouds where everyone else sees nothing but sunshine.

The classic expression of the concept of judicial restraint in constitutional litigation is to be found in one of Mr. Justice Holmes's early Supreme Court opinions:

> While the courts must exercise a judgment of their own, it by no means is true that every law is void which may seem to the judges who pass upon it excessive, unsuited to its ostensible end, or based upon conceptions of morality with which they disagree. Considerable latitude must be allowed for differences of view as well as for possible peculiar conditions which this court can know but imperfectly, if at all. Otherwise a constitution, instead of embodying only relatively fundamental rules of right, as generally understood by all English-speaking communities, would become the partisan of a particular set of ethical or economic opinions, which by no means are held *semper ubique et ab omnibus*.[4]

2. See Weiler, *Two Models of Judicial Decision-Making,* 46 CAN. BAR REV. 406 (1968).
3. Andres v. United States, 333 U.S. 740, 752–53 (1948).
4. Otis v. Parker, 187 U.S. 606, 608–09 (1903).

For reasons that will appear, there probably is no equally acceptable statement of the theory of judicial activism by any Supreme Court Justice. Perhaps Justice James Mc-Reynolds put the position most succinctly, when he said: "Plainly, I think, this Court must have regard to the wisdom of the enactment."[5] Or, strangely enough, it may be that we should look to Felix Frankfurter for the proper rationale of the activist attitude:

> Words like "liberty" and "property," phrases like "regulate Commerce . . . among the several States," "due process of law," "equal protection of the laws," doctrines like those of separation of powers and the non-delegability of the legislative function, are the foundation for judicial action upon the whole appalling domain of social and economic fact. But phrases like "due process of law" are, as an able judge once expressed it, of "convenient vagueness." Their ambiguity is such that the Court is compelled to put meaning into the Constitution not to take it out. Such features of the Constitution render peculiarly appropriate a favorite quotation of John Chipman Gray: "Whoever hath an absolute authority to interpret any written or spoken law, it is he who is truly the lawgiver to all intents and purposes, and not the person who first wrote or spoke them." . . . The scope for interpreting the Constitution is relatively wide and the opportunity for exercising individual notions of policy correspondingly free. This is the most active and controversial sphere of Supreme Court litigation. Within it the justices are cartographers who give temporary location but do not ultimately define

5. Nebbia v. New York, 291 U.S. 502, 556 (1934). It is interesting to note the comment of one who would probably speak highly of the Warren Court. "In all the duel between the Supreme Court and Franklin Roosevelt there was perhaps no more arrogant statement than these words of James McReynolds. Not the Court but the people through their elected representatives determine the wisdom of legislation." BAKER, BACK TO BACK 125–26 (1967).

the evershifting boundaries between state and national power, between freedom and authority.

It is plain, therefore, that judges are not merely expert reporters of pre-existing law. Because of the free play allowed by the Constitution, judges inevitably fashion law. And law is one of the shaping forces of society.[6]

Certainly there are times when the Justices, in rendering their opinions, recognize the breadth of the power that they purport to exercise. Yet, there is probably no Justice who has not appealed to the image of the judicial mode, if not to restrain himself, at least in an attempt to check his brethren.[7] There is a recognition by the Justices that the Supreme Court, for all its lofty preeminence among all courts of the world, remains a court and for that reason, if not for that reason alone, is required to behave differently from the purely political branches of government. Mr. Justice Black reflected this concept of restraint in his recent Carpentier Lectures. Black, who has been responsible for some of the most "activist opinions" of the Warren Court era, at least until recently, described his duties thus:

> In these pages I shall discuss specifically "judicial activism," "judicial restraint," "due process of law," and First Amendment rights. In all that I write I shall emphasize my reasons for believing (probably contrary to what you have heard) that the courts should always try faithfully to follow the true meaning of the Constitution and other laws as actually written, leaving to Congress changes in statutes, and leaving the problem of adapting the Constitution to meet new needs to constitutional amendments approved by the people under constitutional procedures.[8]

6. FRANKFURTER, MR. JUSTICE HOLMES AND THE SUPREME COURT 6–8 (1938).
7. For examples, see Kurland, *The Court of the Union or Julius Caesar Revised*, 39 NOTRE DAME LAWYER 636 (1964).
8. BLACK, A CONSTITUTIONAL FAITH xvi (1968).

He explained the reasons for this attitude:

> . . . I realize that in following this procedure in many recent cases I have reached results which many people believe to be undesirable. This has caused a new criticism to spring up that I have now changed my views. But I assure you that in attempting to follow as best I can the Constitution as it appears to me to be written, and in attempting in all cases to resist reaching a result simply because I think it is desirable, I have been following a view of our government held by me at least as long as I have been a lawyer. The view is based on my belief that the Founders wrote into our Constitution their unending fear of granting too much power to judges. Such a fear is perhaps not so prevalent today in certain intellectual circles where the judiciary is generally held in high esteem for changes which it has made in our society which these people believe to be desirable. Many of these changes I believe were constitutionally required and thus I wholeheartedly support them. But there is a tendency now among some to look to the judiciary to make all the major policy decisions of our society under the guise of determining constitutionality. The belief is that the Supreme Court will reach a faster and more desirable resolution of our problems than the legislative or executive branches of the government. To the people who have such faith in our nine justices, I say that I have known a different court from the one today. What has occurred may occur again. I would much prefer to put my faith in the people and their elected representatives to choose the proper policies for our government to follow, leaving to the courts questions of constitutional interpretation and enforcement.[9]

It is true that there are those who think that this is the language of a Justice Black who has been converted in his old age to the notions of the limited judiciary once so eloquently championed by Learned Hand and Felix Frank-

9. *Id.* at 10–11.

furter. But the fact is that this kind of language is to be found throughout Black's judicial opinions. Consider, for example, his statement on "neutrality" made even before Herbert Wechsler was read out of the liberal ranks for his appeal to "neutral principles."[10] In *Green v. United States,*[11] Mr. Justice Black asserted: "The courts were established and maintained to provide impartial tribunals of strictly disinterested arbiters to resolve charges of wrongdoing between citizen and citizen or citizen and state." The word used by the Justice to describe the proper attitude of the Court toward the problems before it was "disinterested."[12] And I would remind you that this was written in 1958.

10. See Wechsler, *Toward Neutral Principles of Constitutional Law,* 73 HARV. L. REV. 1 (1959). The damnation of Wechsler may be found, *inter alia,* in Miller & Howell, *The Myth of Neutrality in Constitutional Adjudication,* 27 U. CHI. L. REV. 661 (1960); Mueller & Schwartz, *The Principle of Neutral Principles,* 7 U.C.L.A. L. REV. 571 (1960); Rostow, *American Legal Realism and the Sense of the Profession,* 34 ROCKY MOUNT. L. REV. 123 (1962).

11. 356 U.S. 165, 200 (1958).

12. I am reminded of a bit of dialogue written by the poet laureate of Great Britain, C. Day Lewis, in one of his pseudonymous murder mysteries:

" 'Another fellow who says "disinterested" when he means "uninterested," ' he snarled. 'This debasing of the language is intolerable.'

" 'Words have changed their meanings in the past.'

" 'That's the point. The point is, there's no synonym for "disinterested." We can't afford to lose the word.'

" 'Perhaps we have lost what the word means.'

" 'Lost disinterestedness? As an ideal? I wonder.' The little man's face was suddenly sad—ravaged by a sadness Nigel had rarely seen: the blank eyes, the downturned corners of the mouth changed it into a tragic mask." BLAKE, END OF CHAPTER 50–51 (Berkley Medallion ed. 1968).

Perhaps it should be noted that WEBSTER'S DICTIONARY OF SYNONYMS (1st ed. 1951) does provide several synonyms for the word "disinterested": "Detached, aloof, unconcerned, indifferent, incurious." This may only prove that the ideal has long since been lost. The dictionary goes on, however, to afford some support to Lewis's proposition: "Disinterested now implies a lack of personal concern, not only to selfish motives or thought of advantage, but also of bias,

Even Mr. Justice Douglas, from time to time, has espoused the notion of disinterestedness as an ideal, as when he has asserted his rejection of the concept of "substantive due process." In *Flast v. Cohen*,[13] for example, with all the appearances of sincerity created by the awesome nature of a Supreme Court opinion, he suggested that the restraints of *Frothingham v. Mellon*[14] were no longer needed:

> *Frothingham,* decided in 1923, was in the heyday of substantive due process, when courts were sitting in judgment on the wisdom or reasonableness of legislation. . . . When the Court used substantive due process to determine the wisdom or reasonableness of legislation, it was indeed transforming itself into the Council of Revision which was rejected by the Constitutional Convention. . . . A contrary result in *Frothingham* in that setting might well have accentuated an ominous trend to judicial supremacy.
>
> But we no longer undertake to exercise that kind of power.

(I am told that he announced this position with a perfectly straight face.)

I do not, of course, cite these statements by the most activist of Justices to suggest that they do in fact reject the political mode and adhere to the judicial one. I cite them,

---

predilection, or prejudice. Uninterested, which now means not having the mind or feelings engaged, suggests inattentiveness, apathy, or indifference. Thus, a *disinterested* witness is one that either has no personal interest in the outcome of a trial or is able to put aside such interest and give impartial testimony; an *uninterested* witness is bored and unresponsive to attempt to elicit testimony. When a problem is up for discussion, a *disinterested* person refuses to allow any ulterior considerations to affect his judgment; an *uninterested* person maintains an attitude of indifference or refuses to participate in the discussion."

Compare the legal literature cited in note 10 *supra.*

13. 392 U.S. 83, 107 (1968).

14. 262 U.S. 447 (1923).

rather, to show that these Justices, too, think it important to wrap themselves in their judicial trappings. One can only speculate as to the reasons.

It might be that these men have deceived themselves into a belief that they really are Delphic oracles rather than Platonic Guardians, that they are transmitters of the Word and not its originators. Or, it might be that they recognize the need for maintaining the appearance of adhering to the cult of the robe in order to retain their constituency, so necessary to the survival of the institution; that they recognize the fact that their capacity to legitimize or invalidate other governmental action depends on their own legitimacy; that they recognize that their own legitimacy depends on giving the appearance of—if not adhering to—the judicial mode and not the political one. Irony there may be in the fact that, in the contest between those advocating the use of judicial power to effectuate political ends and those crying for judicial restraint, the Justices speak on the side of the latter.

At least so far as their words are concerned, if not their actions, the Justices seem to know that the issue of discretion versus restraint goes to the very heart of constitutionalism. For it is of the essence of constitutionalism that all government—not excepting the courts—is to be contained by established principles. The Justices in espousing the notion that they are the creatures of the higher law and not the creators of it are not indulging myth so much as they are confronting the paradox implicit in constitutional democracy. The paradox has been described, if not so labeled, by Charles McIlwain:

> We live under a written constitution which classifies some things under *jurisdictio,* as legal fundamentals, and thus puts them under the protection of the courts, while it leaves other matters to the free discretion of the organs of positive government it has created. The distribution of these matters between *jurisdictio* and *guber-*

naculum, made so many years ago, is of course in constant need of revision by interpretation or by amendment; and it may also be that the mode of amendment is somewhat too slow and cumbersome for the best interests of all. But the surest safeguard of a proper balance between the *jurisdictio* and the *gubernaculum*—and that even in a government *of* the people as well as *for* them—would seem to consist in some such constitution containing some such distribution. There is the problem of restriction and the problem of responsibility, and practical politics involves their interrelation. One of them is legal, and it is far the older; the other is political and in its present form it is much more recent. The people have now replaced the king in these political matters of government; but even in a popular state, such as we trust ours is, the problem of law *versus* will remains the most important of all practical problems. We must leave open the possibility of an appeal from the people drunk to the people sober, if individual minority rights are to be protected in the periods of excitement and hysteria from which we unfortunately are not immune. The long and fascinating story of the balancing of *jurisdictio* and *gubernaculum* . . . should be, if we could study it with an open mind, of some help in adjusting and maintaining today the delicate balance of will and law, the central practical problem of politics now as it has been in all past ages. The two fundamental correlative elements of constitutionalism for which all lovers of liberty must yet fight are the legal limits to arbitrary power and a complete political responsibility of government to the governed.[15]

On the other hand, we must recognize that Professor McIlwain's appeal to history is different in kind from the historical rhetoric of the disputants over the proper role of the Supreme Court in American government today. They, too,

15. MCILWAIN, CONSTITUTIONALISM: ANCIENT & MODERN 145–46 (rev. ed. 1947).

9

make an appeal to history, to show either the wisdom or the lack of it in a judiciary seeking to exercise—to use Hamilton's words—not merely "judgment," but "FORCE" and "WILL."[16] The contemners of the present Court point, even as did Mr. Justice Black, to the Court of the Nine Old Men and its immediate predecessors, to show the evils of such excesses of judicial power. The defenders of the present Court refer to the greatness of the Marshall Court and its exercise of judicial power to effectuate the political ideals of its members. But these historical analogies should be resorted to only with a recognition of the differences as well as the similarities between now and then. For we are living neither in times like those of the early days of the nation nor yet in times like those of the late nineteenth and early twentieth centuries. "No court," as the Supreme Court once announced even before it refused to turn the clock back, "can make time stand still."[17] Neither, it should be added, can any of the Court's friendly or unfriendly critics.

The Marshall Court was writing on a blank page. The restraints that the demands of precedents impose were nonexistent. The form of government but recently adopted was a unique experiment: none like it had ever before been tried. The centrifugal forces were great. It appeared that only the Court stood between the demands of the states and their people and the dissolution of the Union. Certainly the prime constitutional issue of importance was the allocation of power between the states and the nation. The contribution of the Court to the survival of one indivisible nation cannot be gainsaid. Yet, one might, as Professors Kelly and Harbison have done, describe the achievement of the Marshall Court in less than glorious terms:

> The first third of the nineteenth century, however, was to witness an increasingly successful demand for popular

16. THE FEDERALIST, No. 78, 522–23 (Cooke ed. 1961).
17. Scripps-Howard Radio, Inc. v. F.C.C., 316 U.S. 4, 9 (1942).

10

participation in government, and any party which proclaimed the incompetence of the masses was bound to
go down before the rising tide of democracy. In the
future, conservative groups and vested interests were to
use political organization as a means to influence and
control governmental policies, but they would pretend
to be concerned primarily with the welfare of the people
as a whole and would not openly espouse aristocratic
political principles. Under these circumstances the federal judiciary under the able leadership of Marshall
was to become a conservative and nationalistic bulwark
against the dominant political forces of democracy and
states' rights.[18]

In drawing the analogy to the Marshall Court, the defenders of the Warren Court are calling on it because of what
the Marshall Court has become rather than for what it was.
One expects that those who today applaud the Warren
Court's decisions would, if they lived then and were of the
same persuasion, be drawn more to Marshall's critics, to
Thomas Jefferson and Spencer Roane, than to his defenders.
For the words that have since become anathema to liberal
thought, the words "states' rights," were then shibboleths
for democracy and popular control of government. It could
certainly be argued that much that the Marshall Court did
in its most famous judgments stood opposed to rather than
in favor of the tenets of constitutionalism just quoted from
McIlwain: "the legal limits to arbitrary power and a complete political responsibility of government to the governed."

As Mr. Justice Holmes pointed out when commemorating
the centennial of Marshall's ascension to the bench, the glory
of Marshall is essentially symbolic:

> We live by symbols, and what shall be symbolized by
> any image of the sight depends upon the mind of him
> who sees it. The setting aside of this day in honor of

18. KELLY & HARBISON, THE AMERICAN CONSTITUTION 201 (3d
ed. 1963).

a great judge may stand to a Virginian for the glory of his glorious State; to a patriot for the fact that time has been on Marshall's side, and that the theory for which Hamilton argued, and he decided, and Webster spoke, and Grant fought, and Lincoln died, is now our cornerstone. To the more abstract but farther-reaching contemplation of the lawyer, it stands for the rise of a new body of jurisprudence, by which guiding principles are raised above the reach of statute and State, and judges are entrusted with a solemn and hitherto unheard-of authority and duty. To one who lives in what may seem to him a solitude of thought, this day—as it marks the triumph of a man whom some Presidents of his time bade carry out his judgments as he could—this day marks the fact that all thought is social, is on its way to action; that, to borrow the expression of a French writer, every idea tends to become first a catechism and then a code; and that according to its worth his unhelped meditation may one day mount a throne, and without armies, or even with them, may shoot across the world the electric despotism of an unresisted power. It is all a symbol, if you like, but so is the flag. The flag is but a bit of bunting to one who insists on prose. Yet, thanks to Marshall and to the men of his generation— and for this above all we celebrate him and them—its red is our lifeblood, its stars our world, its blue our heaven. It owns our land. At will it throws away our lives.[19]

Not all this Holmesian symbolism will be appealing to those who today invoke the shades of the Marshall Court as justification for what the Warren Court is doing. Patriotism is not as fashionable today as it was in Holmes's day or even in Marshall's. The most perceptive of those words of Holmes, however, referred not to symbol but to what we have come to recognize as fact: "time has been on Marshall's side." And on this point the analogy cannot yet be drawn,

19. HOLMES, COLLECTED LEGAL PAPERS 270–71 (1920).

however much we may hope that time will prove to be on the side of what the Warren Court has attempted to accomplish.

Then, too, we should be hesitant to denigrate or praise the Supreme Court of the 1920s and 1930s solely because of its decisions that came to bear the stigma of "substantive due process." For it was in these years that the Court began its incorporation of the First Amendment freedoms into the Fourteenth Amendment.[20] And this, too, as Mr. Justice Brandeis reminded us, was the application of "substantive due process."[21] It was the Hughes Court, too, that started the high court on the road toward effective determination of minimal standards of decency to which the states must adhere in their procedures for the enforcement of the criminal laws.[22] And this at a time when the executive branch of the national government had made clear the evils,[23] but when neither the national nor the state legislatures or executives were willing to confront them.

Indeed, there are many other credit items to enter on the balance sheet of the pre–New Deal Court in assaying its behavior at the very time that it was condemned by liberals for its aggressive conduct that thwarted the will of the majority.[24] The point to be made here, however, is that we

20. See Palko v. Connecticut, 302 U.S. 319, 327 (1937); *cf.* Patterson v. Colorado, 205 US. 454, 462 (1907).

21. See Whitney v. California, 274 U.S. 357, 373 (1927): "Despite arguments to the contrary which had seemed to me persuasive, it is settled that the due process clause of the Fourteenth Amendment applies to matters of substantive law as well as to matters of procedure. Thus all fundamental rights comprised within the term liberty are protected by the Federal Constitution from invasion by the States."

22. See, *e.g.,* Schaefer, *Federalism and State Criminal Procedure,* 70 HARV. L. REV. 1 (1956).

23. See NATIONAL COMMISSION ON LAW OBSERVANCE AND LAW ENFORCEMENT, REPORT ON LAWLESSNESS IN LAW ENFORCEMENT (1931).

24. See, *e.g.,* BOUDIN, GOVERNMENT BY JUDICIARY (1932).

cannot look to history alone to guide us in evaluating the proper role of the Warren Court. Again to use Mr. Justice Holmes's language:

> The past gives us our vocabulary and fixes the limits of our imagination; we cannot get away from it. There is, too, a peculiar logical pleasure in making manifest the continuity between what we are doing and what has been done before. But the present has a right to govern itself so far as it can; and it ought always to be remembered that historic continuity with the past is not a duty, it is only a necessity.[25]

Time is of the essence of the matter in several of its aspects. Mr. Justice Frankfurter pointed to the difference that time made in the work of the Court on which he sat and that which was guided by the presidency of John Marshall:

> The vast change in the scope of law between Marshall's time and ours is at bottom a reflection of the vast change in the circumstances of society. The range of business covered by Marshall's Court, though operating under a written Constitution, was in the main not very different from the concerns of the English courts, except that the latter dealt much more with property settlements. The vast enveloping present-day role of law is not the design of a statesman nor attributable to the influence of some great thinker. It is a reflection of the great technological revolution which brought in its train what a quiet writer in The Economist could call "the tornado of economic and social change of the last century." Law has been an essential accompaniment of the shift from "watchdog government"—the phrase is George Kennan's—to the service state. For government has become a service state whatever the tint of the party in power and whatever time-honored slogans it may use to enforce and promote measures that hardly vindicate

25. HOLMES, note 19 *supra*, at 139.

the slogans. Profound social changes continue to be in the making, due to movements of industrialization, urbanization, and permeating egalitarian ideas.[26]

In this regard, the Court of the Nine Old Men and its immediate predecessors, however distant from the Marshall period, were closer to it than to the present-day world. The service state, which these Courts were trying to throttle, was an infant whose character was yet to be determined. However complete the movement toward industrialization, a movement that the Court was defending, the problems of urbanization had only begun to show their ugly faces, and the "permeating egalitarian ideas" were still concerns of the future. And so, those who would damn the present Court by invoking the excesses of these early twentieth-century predecessors must also recognize the differences, the very basic changes that have occurred in American society since that time.

One might, however, see values in enhancing judicial power in contemporary society that were not readily visible in the eras that preceded the Great Depression and the Second World War. For, if Judge Learned Hand was right —and I think he was—about the nature of our modern life, any reasoned device, judicial or otherwise, that might save us from its abominations would be justified. It was in the midst of the Second World War that, in paying tribute to Mr. Justice Brandeis, Judge Hand described the contemporary scene in these dismal tones:

> As the social group grows too large for mutual contact and appraisal, life quickly begins to lose its flavor and significance. Among multitudes relations must become standardized; to standardize is to generalize, and to generalize is to ignore all those authentic features which mark, and which indeed alone create, an individual.

26. Frankfurter, *John Marshall and the Judicial Function*, in THAYER, HOLMES & FRANKFURTER, JOHN MARSHALL 152–53 (Phoenix ed. 1967).

Not only is there no compensation for our losses, but most of our positive ills have directly resulted from great size. With it has indeed come the magic of modern communication and quick transport; but out of these has come the sinister apparatus of mass suggestion and mass production. Such devices, always tending more and more to reduce us to a common model, subject us —our hard-won immunity now gone—to epidemics of hallowed catchword and formula. The herd is regaining its ancient and evil primacy; civilization is being reversed, for it has consisted of exactly the opposite process of individualization. . . .

. . . It is hard to see any answer to all this, the day has clearly gone forever of societies small enough for their members to have personal acquaintance with each other, and to find their station through appraisal of those who have any first-hand knowledge of them. Publicity is an evil substitute, and the art of publicity is a black art; but it has come to stay; every year adds to its potency and to the finality of its judgments. The hand that rules the press, the radio, the screen and the far-spread magazine, rules the country; whether we like it or not, we must learn to accept it. And yet it is the power of reiterated suggestion and consecrated platitude that at this moment has brought our entire civilization to imminent peril of destruction. The individual is helpless against it as the child is helpless against the formulas with which he is indoctrinated. Not only is it possible by these means to shape his tastes, his feelings, his desires and his hopes; but it is possible to convert him into a fanatical zealot, ready to torture and destroy and to suffer mutilation and death for an obscene faith, baseless in fact and morally monstrous.[27]

As we approach with ever increasing speed the actual and symbolic year of 1984, we are in dire need of an institution that might shield us from the fate that Orwell pre-

27. HAND, THE SPIRIT OF LIBERTY 170–73 (Dilliard ed., 2d ed. 1953).

dicted. The propriety of turning to the Court for help in times like these cannot be measured solely in terms of the uses to which it was put at earlier periods.

Indeed, if the role of the Supreme Court were to be measured solely by history, it would be the only part of American government that remained so restrained in its functions. Since the second Roosevelt's first election, the power of the executive branch of the national government has burgeoned, not only absolutely but by comparison with the other areas of governmental operation. Congress, on the other hand, although authorized to act in more and more areas, has tended to become the tool of the White House.[28] Almost no major legislation originates in Congress that has not been sponsored by the executive. Even a Congress whose majority is of a different party from the president's sits on its haunches and awaits instructions to beg or fetch, only occasionally balking until it has been thrown a bone. A recognition of this relationship between executive and legislative branches would alone justify a more vigorous Court. For, if the history of the origins of our Constitution teach us anything, it must be that one great fear of the Constitution's makers was the danger of a strong and arbitrary executive. Thus, the Court would remain true to its function of preserving the original meaning of the Constitution if it were to act more aggressively to help prevent the executive from overreaching his constitutionally limited function.

There is at least one lesson to be derived from the history of the Marshall and pre–New Deal Courts and that is that the equation cannot be drawn—as it so frequently is drawn —between "activist" and "liberal" or between "judicial restraint" and "conservative." An "activist" Court is essentially one that is out of step with the legislative or executive branches of the government. It will thus be "liberal" or "conservative" depending upon which role its prime antago-

28. See, *e.g.*, Kurland, *The Impotence of Reticence,* 1968 DUKE L.J. 619.

nist has adopted. Certainly the Marshall Court and the Court of the Nine Old Men were "activist" Courts. Their appellation in terms of "liberal" and "conservative" is a little harder to draw. Since the phrases tend to be meaningless except as pejoratives or adulation, the establishment of such identities is at best useless and at worst misleading. It was the most intellectually accomplished of the late President Kennedy's advisers—classify Richard Goodwin as "liberal" or "conservative" as you will—who recently made the relevant point in this way:

> [T]he nine justices of the Supreme Court make major political decisions, unresponsive to the democratic process, in secret meetings on Friday afternoons. Both the number and the scope of such decisions steadily mount. Liberal critics have generally approved this development, because they approve the content of the decisions, while the fundamental reshaping of an important institution seems not to trouble them. But it is a transformation which almost certainly will come back to plague us as judicial personnel and social attitudes change, and as an institution which has become more and more political develops an even greater sensitivity to transitory shifts in political temper.[29]

The time of the plague may well have arrived.

In seeking to avoid the approach of the blind men describing the elephant, one should avoid one other form of self-deception indulged both by the Warren Court's claque and by its critics. Again I turn to the words of Holmes, who constantly reminded us: "We must think things not words, or at least we must constantly translate our words into the facts for which they stand, if we are to keep to the real and the true."[30] Herein lies the primary teaching

29. Goodwin, *The Shape of American Politics*, COMMENTARY 25, 26–27 (June 1967)
30. HOLMES, note 19 *supra*, at 238.

of the realist school of jurisprudence to which both sides of the alleged controversy over the Warren Court pretend to adhere. In assaying the work of the Court, it is not enough to understand what it has said, although even that is a difficult enough task. It is necessary, too, to learn what effect its words have had. The Court may command those who are brought before it. The question remains what changes does obedience to that command bring about. One must even ask to what extent has there been obedience to that command. The Court is credited with much, it is blamed for much—usually the credit and the blame are imposed for the same purported accomplishments—but it must be conceded that in many instances it is not entitled to either the credit or the blame.[31] And it is important to those who would consider the work of the Court in more than its symbolic facet to look beyond the plethora of words that have been forthcoming from the Warren Court in its multitude of opinions. Our society has been substantially modified during the existence of the Warren Court. The Court is responsible for some of that change. It is certainly not responsible for all of it. Indeed, it is responsible for preventing much change. But it is not responsible for all our failures to adapt the law to the changing society.

I end my sermon on the need to search through the fog of controversy that covers the work of the Court, to ignore the rhetoric of the partisans, to seek reality, with still more words of Felix Frankfurter and Learned Hand. In so doing, I must acknowledge my bias. I am, indeed, at least in part what Dean Allen warned you against, a would-be epigone of Holmes, Frankfurter, and Learned Hand, if not of Adam Smith. It was Frankfurter who reminded us: "Only for those who have not the responsibility of decision can it be easy to decide the grave and complex problems they raise, espe-

---

31. See Kurland, *Equal Educational Opportunity: The Limits of Constitutional Jurisprudence Undefined,* 35 U. CHI. L. REV. 583 (1968).

cially in controversies that excite public interest."[32] And it was Learned Hand, speaking in 1935 of the difficult task that we ask our judges to perform, who said:

> And so, while it is proper that people should find fault when their judges fail, it is only reasonable that they should recognize the difficulties. Perhaps it is also fair to ask that before the judges are blamed they shall be given the credit of having tried to do their best. Let them be severely brought to book, when they go wrong, but by those who will take the trouble to understand.[33]

32. FRANKFURTER, note 26 *supra,* at 156.
33. HAND, note 27 *supra,* at 110.

2

The Congress,
the President,
and the Court

WHEN THE MAKERS of the Constitution provided for the national government, the legislature was created as the first branch,[1] the executive as the second,[2] and the judiciary as the third and, in Hamilton's terms, "the least dangerous branch."[3] It is not clear whether the framers were mindful of the biblical admonition that "many that are first shall be last; and the last shall be first."[4] What is certain is that there has been much shifting of authority and place among these branches since 1789. And, while none today believes that the Constitution was framed in the pure image of Montesquieu's concept of separation of powers, none would deny that the structure created did include the notion of each branch affording some check on the others. As Robert H. Jackson said:

> The seeds of a struggle for power were planted in the Constitution itself. That instrument set up a legislative and executive branch, each in a large degree representative of popular will. It created on the other hand an

1. For a program to restore the primacy of the legislative branch, see AMERICAN ENTERPRISE INSTITUTE, CONGRESS: THE FIRST BRANCH OF GOVERNMENT (1966).
2. The justification for executive supremacy may be found in such works as BURNS, PRESIDENTIAL GOVERNMENT (1966); KOENIG, THE CHIEF EXECUTIVE (1964).
3. See BICKEL, THE LEAST DANGEROUS BRANCH (1962).
4. Matt. 19:30.

appointive Court, whose Justices are chosen for life, and thus set up an overriding legal authority completely independent of popular will. These differently constituted institutions characteristically respond to the interests of different factions of society, as the founders foresaw they would. A struggle for power between these "equal" branches was inevitable.[5]

It is a tribute to the originators and those who have succeeded them that the adjustments among the three divisions of national government, unlike the allocation of power between nation and states, have always been peacefully effected. This is not to say that the conflicts among them have not been sharply and bitterly contested. The political storms over Supreme Court behavior have been as persistent as tropical rain.

There is obviously little merit in rehearsing the arguments about whether it was intended to grant the Supreme Court the power of judicial review over national legislation.[6] Even the question of the scope of that authority, which is still much mooted, puts undue emphasis on what has not been a central question. For the fact of the matter is—whatever the romance may be—that so far as the relations between Court and Congress are concerned, the invalidation of national legislation has proved historically to be neither so important nor so exacerbating of the differences between the two branches as law professors would make it.

A glance at the history of judicial invalidation of national legislation only buttresses the famous Holmes dictum: "I do not think the United States would come to an end if we lost our power to declare an Act of Congress void. I do think that the Union would be imperiled if we could not make that declaration as to the laws of the several States."[7] It will be

5. JACKSON, THE STRUGGLE FOR JUDICIAL SUPREMACY viii (1941).
6. See BICKEL, note 3 *supra,* at ch. 1; HAND, THE BILL OF RIGHTS (1958).
7. HOLMES, COLLECTED LEGAL PAPERS 295–96 (1920).

recalled that no federal statute was declared invalid by the Court between the famous *Marbury* case[8] in 1803 and the infamous *Dred Scott* case[9] in 1857. The Court became more temerarious after the Civil War. Even so, until the era of the Warren Court only sixty-eight such decisions were rendered. When one considers the vast increase in the scope of federal legislative activities in the period between the Civil War and 1954, the number does not seem extraordinarily high.

Moreover, an examination of these pre-Warren Court decisions negativing the use of national legislative power reveals the small stake actually involved in such actions. Some momentous decisions, such as those in *Dred Scott* and in the *Income Tax Cases,*[10] have been changed by constitutional amendments. Others, as with the *Legal Tender Cases,*[11] *Hammer v. Dagenhart,*[12] and *Adkins v. Children's Hospital,*[13] were sooner or later, specifically overruled. For the rest, most have been invalidated by time, left as derelicts on the sea of constitutional law, not worth the cost of litigation to remove them from the books. What, for example, is now left of the notion of improper delegation of legislative powers?[14]

The Warren Court has not been bashful about adding restrictions to the national legislative power. And, without the perspective of time that is afforded to view more ancient judicial judgments of doom, the recent decisions commend themselves as potentially longer lasting than similar conclu-

8. Marbury v. Madison, 1 Cranch 137 (1803).

9. Dred Scott v. Sandford, 19 How. 393 (1857).

10. Pollock v. Farmers' Loan & Trust Co., 157 U.S. 429 (1895), 158 U.S. 601 (1895).

11. Hepburn v. Griswold, 8 Wall. 603 (1870), *overruled* in Knox v. Lee, 12 Wall. 457 (1871).

12. 247 U.S. 251 (1918), *overruled* in United States v. Darby Lumber Co., 312 U.S. 100 (1941).

13. 261 U.S. 525 (1923), *overruled* in West Coast Hotel Co. v. Parrish, 300 U.S. 379 (1937).

14. See Schechter Corp. v. United States, 295 U.S. 495 (1935); Panama Refining Co. v. Ryan, 293 U.S. 388 (1935).

sions of earlier Courts. On the other hand, a catalog of these opinions does not reveal that they cut to the bone of our governmental structure. Several have utilized the Self-Crimination Clause to prevent the government from compelling individuals to reveal information that would be usable to convict them of violating the laws—state or federal.[15] Several others have severely restricted, if they have not destroyed, the use of denationalization as a sanction against criminal acts or otherwise.[16] The power of the military to try civilians—ex-servicemen or camp followers—or even to try military personnel for nonmilitary crimes has been seriously curtailed.[17] Congressional authority to inhibit travel of persons affiliated with subversive organizations has been severely limited.[18] A District of Columbia law requiring one year of residence before qualifying for relief moneys was held to be an unconstitutional restriction on travel.[19] Limitations on deliveries of mail from certain lands alien in politics were ruled invalid.[20]

With ample precedent,[21] presumption of guilt from an act that cannot logically give rise to such a presumption has been held beyond the ken of Congress.[22] Congressionally imposed disqualifications from service in a labor union

15. Albertson v. Subversive Activities Control Bd., 382 U.S. 70 (1965); Marchetti v. United States, 390 U.S. 39 (1968); Grosso v. United States, 390 U.S. 62 (1968); Haynes v. United States, 390 U.S. 85 (1968); Leary v. United States, 395 U.S. 6 (1969); United States v. Covington, 395 U.S. 57 (1969).

16. Trop v. Dulles, 356 U.S. 86 (1958); Kennedy v. Mendoza-Martinez, 372 U.S. 144 (1963); Schneider v. Rusk, 377 U.S. 163 (1964); Afroyim v. Rusk, 387 U.S. 253 (1967).

17. Toth v. Quarles, 350 U.S. 11 (1955); Kinsella v. United States, 361 U.S. 278 (1960); Graham v. Hagan, 361 U.S. 278 (1960); McElroy v. United States, 361 U.S. 281 (1960); O'Callahan v. Parker, 395 U.S. 258 (1969); *cf.* Lee v. Madigan, 358 U.S. 228 (1959).

18. Aptheker v. Secretary of State, 378 U.S. 500 (1964).

19. Shapiro v. Thompson, 394 U.S. 618 (1969).

20. Lamont v. Postmaster General, 381 U.S. 301 (1965).

21. Tot v. United States, 319 U.S. 463 (1943).

22. Leary v. United States, 395 U.S. 6 (1969).

office[23] or a defense facility,[24] because of Communist affiliations, were removed by judicial order. And the death penalty provision of the Lindbergh kidnapping law was invalidated on procedural grounds, not because the death penalty itself is yet unconstitutional.[25] The total number of national statutes held invalid by the Supreme Court in its entire history still falls far short of the century mark.

Even then, some of the cited decisions have left Congress free to provide more restrained alternatives to the excessive means that were struck down.[26] The legislature was merely admonished to use a scalpel instead of a meat-ax to remove what it regarded as a cancerous growth. Taken all in all, the Warren Court's essays in invalidating national legislation were more numerous than the average of its predecessors. And, on the whole, the opinions were neither better constructed nor more persuasive than such notorious antecedents as *Marbury, Dred Scott,* and the *Income Tax Cases.*[27] But one does not get the feeling from an examination of this catalog that these judgments represent anything like the major changes in the fabric of our constitutional system that were essayed by the Warren Court through means other than judicial review of congressional action. Certainly their effect was nothing like that of the Court's decisions on New Deal legislation,[28] or on post–Civil War Reconstruction legislation.[29]

23. United States v. Brown, 381 U.S. 437 (1965).
24. United States v. Robel, 389 U.S. 258 (1967).
25. United States v. Jackson, 390 U.S. 570 (1968).
26. See, *e.g.,* Aptheker v. United States, note 18 *supra.*
27. See, *e.g.,* Kurland, *"Equal in Origin and Equal in Title to the Legislative and Executive Branches of the Government,"* 78 HARV. L. REV. 143, 169–75 (1964).
28. See JACKSON, note 5 *supra;* BAKER, BACK TO BACK: THE DUEL BETWEEN FDR AND THE SUPREME COURT (1967); Leuchtenburg, *The Origins of Franklin D. Roosevelt's "Court-Packing" Plan,* 1966 SUPREME COURT REVIEW 347; Kurland, *A Phoenix Too Frequent,* 35 U. CHI. L. REV. 376 (1968).
29. See 2 WARREN, THE SUPREME COURT IN UNITED STATES HISTORY ch. 30 (rev. ed. 1937).

Nor did these judgments of unconstitutionality particularly arouse the ire of Congress. Certainly there were expressions of exasperation from individual senators and representatives. And, perhaps, had the cold war been at a hotter point, such "pro-Communist" decisions as *Albertson, Aptheker, Brown, Lamont,* and *Robel*[30] would have created a far greater furor among the people's representatives. But a reading of the *Congressional Record* for this period—a Herculean task, I assure you—does not suggest that the power of judicial review of national legislation was the critical issue between the first and third branches of the federal government. Nor should history have suggested a different answer.

The Reconstruction Congress was irate at the Court's treatment of its legislation aimed at assuring the conversion of the South to nonslave territory.[31] But that was the only time that Congress was sufficiently moved to do anything about it. In the *McArdle* case,[32] Congress terminated the Court's jurisdiction over pending litigation, with the Court's acquiescence. Congress has made threats of more serious inroads on the Court's power, as it did in the 1867 period and again in the 1937 period. But for the most part, strong attacks on the power of judicial review of national legislation have derived not from Capitol Hill but from the White House, as was clearly the case with the 1937 Court-packing plan.[33]

If Congress was not particularly aroused by the Court's invalidation of its legislation, it was certainly extraordinarily upset by other aspects of the Supreme Court's business during the Warren chairmanship. At the beginning there was *Brown v. Board of Education.*[34] This decision solidified the hard core of very influential congressional

30. See notes 15, 18, 20, 23, and 24 *supra.*
31. See note 29 *supra.*
32. *Ex parte* McArdle, 7 Wall. 506 (1869).
33. See note 28 *supra.*   34. 347 U.S. 483 (1954).

opposition to the Court. Thereafter, explosions about the Court's activities were irregular but numerous. An example may be derived from congressional and judicial behavior in 1957.

That year there was a series of cases that, by judicial interpretation of federal statutes or invalidation of state laws, threatened serious inhibition of the Red-baiting that continued after the McCarthy era. Moreover, these decisions represented a real threat to the scope of congressional investigatory power, a power apparently more highly cherished by congressmen than the constitutional power to legislate. In *Watkins v. United States*,[35] the conviction for contempt of Congress of a labor leader who had refused to testify about former party members was upset. In *Yates v. United States*,[36] the Court reversed the convictions of the second-string Communist party leaders without, however, impugning the validity of the Smith Act. In *Sweezy v. New Hampshire*,[37] the Court invalidated a state legislative search for "subversive persons." *Service v. Dulles*[38] placed the "loyalty-security" system under severe procedural checks. And the Court held that a state could not exclude persons from membership in its bar simply because they had prior membership in the Communist party.[39] All this supplied the gunpowder. The fuse had already been lighted by a decision of the Court attacking, as congressional leaders saw it, the holy of holies, the Federal Bureau of Investigation. In *Jencks v. United States*,[40] the Court ruled that reports to the FBI made by trial witnesses were subject to examination in court to permit impeachment of the witnesses in the event that the testimony was inconsistent with the report. It was at this point that Congress erupted. (As an aside to newly

35. 354 U.S. 178 (1957).   37. 354 U.S. 234 (1957).
36. 354 U.S. 298 (1957).   38. 354 U.S. 363 (1957).
39. Schware v. New Mexico Bd. of Examiners, 353 U.S. 232 (1957).
40. 353 U.S. 657 (1957).

converted admirers of Felix Frankfurter, it should be noted that he voted with the majority of the Court in each of these decisions.)[41]

Kenneth Keating, a representative from New York, later a senator, then a New York Court of Appeals judge, and now an ambassador of the United States, immediately alerted his colleagues in the House to the threat of the *Jencks* case, in these words:

> If this decision stands and nothing is done by the legislative branch it may well result, as Justice Clark has indicated in his minority opinion, in our investigative agencies having to close up shop. . . .
>
> I have asked the Attorney General to assist me in the preparation of legislation which can immediately be studied by the Judiciary Committee in order that we can come to grips with this serious threat to our security.[42]

It should be noted that the *Jencks* case did not rest on constitutional grounds and so was, indeed, appropriately subject to legislative review.

Action in the House, the Senate, and the Court all contributed to the anticlimax that followed. First came a series of debates over various legislative proposals to limit the effect of the *Jencks* decision.[43] The Court was assigned the devil's role in these discussions, but the statute that emerged really did more to bulwark than to limit the *Jencks* ruling.[44]

In the Senate came an attack on the Court of grosser proportions, led by the redoubtable Senator William E. Jenner of Indiana, Senator Joseph McCarthy's *dauphin*. The battle, waged over a bill introduced by Jenner, was clearly ad-

---

41. He wrote concurring opinions in *Watkins,* 354 U.S. at 216; *Sweezy,* 354 U.S. at 255; and *Schware,* 353 U.S. at 273.

42. 103 CONG. REC. 8290 (1957).

43. The story is excellently told in MURPHY, CONGRESS AND THE COURT ch. 6 (1962).

44. 71 Stat. 595 (1957), 18 U.S.C. § 3500.

dressed to the reversal of the decisions enumerated above. Under S.2646,[45] the Court would have been deprived of all jurisdiction to review cases concerning: (1) contempt of Congress; (2) the loyalty-security program; (3) state anti-subversive statutes; (4) regulation of employment and subversive activities in schools; (5) admission to the practice of law. Senator Thomas C. Hennings of Missouri successfully prevented the railroading of the bill through the Judiciary Committee before the end of the session. Full-scale hearings were conducted when the second session of the Eighty-fifth Congress convened.[46] To those interested in a study of obscenity in Dr. Johnson's definition of the word, I commend a reading of these hearings. From those outside the halls of Congress, only law school professors and, more timorously, the American Bar Association came to the defense of the Court.

While the Senate was engaged by the Jenner bill and its almost as restrictive amendment known as the Jenner-Butler bill, the House was equally concerned with evolving means for restricting the judiciary. H.R. 3 was a result of the Court's earlier invalidation, in *Pennsylvania v. Nelson*,[47] of the Pennsylvania Sedition Act on the ground that the federal law had occupied the field and preempted state action. The bill would have provided that, except in those instances where the federal legislation specifically deprived the states of power to act, the Supreme Court was not to invoke the preemption doctrine. This bill passed the House and went to the Senate which, by now, was concerned with a plethora of legislation to curb the Court and reverse some of its decisions.

The battle was a long and close one. It has been admirably detailed in separate volumes by C. Herman Pritchett

45. 85th Cong., 1st Sess. (1957).
46. Hearings on S.2646 before the Internal Security Subcommittee, Committee on the Judiciary, U.S. Senate, 85th Cong., 2d Sess., pt. 2 (1958).
47. 350 U.S. 497 (1956).

and Walter F. Murphy,[48] political scientists who demonstrate an interest in the legislative process in the constitutional field that lawyers would do well to emulate. Since my reference to this controversy is only by way of example of the congressional attitude toward the Supreme Court, I will say no more than that the Court escaped intact. But I would add that the single figure most responsible for defeat of this anti-Court legislation—whatever his motives—was the leader of the Senate Democrats, Lyndon Baines Johnson.

How much of the congressional restraint exhibited by the failure to pass any of these bills was attributable to a strategic retreat on the part of the Court itself is too difficult a question to answer. Certainly *Barenblatt v. United States*[49] and *Uphaus v. Wyman*[50] make it look as though the Court tempered its sails to the prevailing winds. The first sustained a contempt conviction of a professor who refused to tell the House Un-American Activities Committee about his own past connections with the Communist party. The second sustained New Hampshire's search for "subversive persons" by affirming the conviction of Uphaus for refusing to submit membership lists in his allegedly untrustworthy organization to the state attorney general, Louis Wyman. During the same Term, however, the Court also decided *Greene v. McElroy*,[51] *Rosenberg v. United States*,[52] and *Palermo v. United States*.[53] *Greene* imposed further procedural safeguards on the loyalty-security program; *Rosenberg* and *Palermo* gave readings to the Jencks Act in keeping with the terms of the original decision. Thus, if the Court was more reticent, it certainly was not cowed. There was no such retreat as that which the Court indulged in 1937 in the face of the Roosevelt Court-packing plan.

48. PRITCHETT, CONGRESS VERSUS THE SUPREME COURT, 1957–1960 (1961); MURPHY, note 43 *supra*.
49. 360 U.S. 109 (1959).
50. 360 U.S. 72 (1959).   52. 360 U.S. 367 (1959).
51. 360 U.S. 474 (1959).   53. 360 U.S. 343 (1959).

On the other hand, it is equally true that Congress did not become reconciled to what it regarded as the Court's errant behavior. The fragile peace between the Court and Congress has continued precariously to this date. The 1957–58 episode was but one wave of congressional attacks on the Court that advance and retreat like the tides of the sea. The possibility that high tide might again be approaching should not be discounted.

If the Red scare provides less of an irritant, Congress continues to be frenzied by the Court's opinions in the desegregation areas, as is evidenced by the recent House appropriations bill[54] that would all but cancel the effect of the Court's decisions[55] on "freedom of choice" plans as a means of meeting the constitutional requirement. Congress's rancor at the decisions in the obscenity cases[56] which prevent successful prosecution of purveyors and users of pornography was made abundantly clear by the hearings on Mr. Justice Fortas's nomination for Chief Justice of the United States, where some senators were concerned far more with obscenity than with Fortas's qualifications for office.[57] The reapportionment cases are still the cause of great dissatisfaction.[58] Even the Court's construction or reconstruction of congressional labor legislation affords an example of real

54. New York Times, 1 August 1969, p. 1.
55. See Green v. County School Bd., 391 U.S. 430 (1968); Raney v. Bd. of Educ., 391 U.S. 443 (1968); Monroe v. Bd. of Comm'rs, 391 U.S. 450 (1968).
56. See Kalven, *Metaphysics of the Law of Obscenity*, 1960 SUPREME COURT REVIEW 1; Magrath, *The Obscenity Cases: Grapes of Roth*, 1966 SUPREME COURT REVIEW 7; Krislov, *From Ginzburg to Ginsberg: The Unhurried Children's Hour in Obscenity Litigation*, 1968 SUPREME COURT REVIEW 153.
57. See Hearings on the Nomination of Abe Fortas and Homer Thornberry, before the U.S. Senate, Committee on the Judiciary, 90th Cong., 2d Sess. (1968) (2 parts).
58. Senator Dirksen's push for a constitutional amendment affords an appropriate example of the point of view of the group of which he was the leader. See 37 CONG. Q. W. REPT. 1372 (1969).

congressional anger at the Court.[59] And the many changes in the rules governing the administration of criminal justice have set the stage for another direct confrontation when the Court will be called upon to apply the terms of Title II of the Safe Streets Act,[60] as it is certain to be asked to do in light of Attorney General Mitchell's instructions to the Department of Justice to abide the congressional mandate.[61]

Certainly a part of the congressional wrath might be attributed to frustrations of Congress's own making. For the Court's interpretations of congressional legislation are subject to amendment whenever Congress is truly dissatisfied with them. But the national legislative machinery is so cumbersome and awkward[62] as to make Congress unable to deal with individual cases in which the Court has misinterpreted the legislative will.

For all this there is an optimistic interpretation such as that offered by one of the Court's more astute critics, Archibald Cox. In his recent lectures on the Supreme Court, he said:

> Although the Warren Court has expanded federal judicial power at the expense of the States, its history has been relatively free from the fundamental conflicts between the judicial and legislative branches that marred the constitutional history of the first third of the present century. The Court is not popular in Congress. There

59. See *Congressional Oversight of Administrative Agencies (National Labor Relations Board)*, Hearings before the Subcommittee on the Separation of Powers of the Committee on the Judiciary, U.S. Senate, 90th Cong., 2d Sess. (1968) (2 parts).

60. See Burt, *Miranda and Title II: A Morganatic Marriage*, 1969 SUPREME COURT REVIEW 81.

61. New York Times, 1 August 1969, p. 16.

62. See, *e.g.*, CLARK, CONGRESS THE SAPLESS BRANCH (rev. ed. 1965); DONHAM & FAHEY, CONGRESS NEEDS HELP (1966); THOMAS & LAMB, CONGRESS, POLITICS AND PRACTICE (1964); HARRIS, CONGRESSIONAL CONTROL OF ADMINISTRATION (1964); BAILEY, THE NEW CONGRESS (1966); CLARK, ed., CONGRESSIONAL REFORM (1965).

has been outspoken criticism and even efforts to nullify its decisions. Acts of Congress and an even larger number of State laws and municipal ordinances have been held unconstitutional. Still, one has the sense that the decisions do not thwart representative democracy in quite the same way as the older cases invalidating the income tax, consumer protection, price regulation, and laws on labor relations and minimum wages. Part of the explanation may be that the present Court is moving with the current whereas the Taft Court sought to reverse it, but there are three other plausible explanations:

(1) The Court's most creative role has been played either in areas which have always been the special prerogative of the judiciary, such as criminal procedure and libel, or else in areas which the legislative branch has neglected, such as school desegregation and reapportionment.

(2) The legislative measures invalidated by the Warren Court were rarely based upon careful study of social and economic needs of the community, and, except in the case of massive resistance to desegregation, were rarely supported by much long-range popular sentiment.

(3) The Court has been noticeably careful to avoid square conflicts, if it can, even in the area of the First Amendment.[63]

These reasons do not seem persuasive. Direct conflicts between the Court and legislature have abounded. The legislation that the Warren Court has reviewed and construed has been the result of at least as much or as little study of social and economic needs as that which came before the Court in earlier generations. While it is true that the areas of criminal procedure and libel, for examples, have been largely within the judicial domain, it was the domain of the state judiciaries and not of the national courts. Whether the Court is going with the tide or against it is a judgment that only history can make. I am reminded of

63. COX, THE WARREN COURT 15–16 (1968).

Mr. Justice Frankfurter's proposition: "There is no inevitability in history except as men make it."[64]

The absence of a conflict between Court and Congress that even Professor Cox would consider fundamental might be explained by another thesis. This one has been championed by Charles Black. He suggests that we have overemphasized the negative aspects and undervalued the positive role of judicial review of national legislation.[65] He tells us that we must look to the cases in which the Court has put its stamp of constitutional approval on national legislation, for this is a legitimizing of national policy that is essential to its acceptance by the people.

Certainly it is true that the Warren Court has placed its imprimatur on much of the national legislation of any importance that has been brought before it. One need mention only the cases approving the Civil Rights Act to understand the thrust of Professor Black's thesis. *Heart of Atlanta Motel v. United States*[66] and *Katzenbach v. McClung*[67] sustained the 1964 Civil Rights Act with dispatch and vigor. Without bothering much about the truth of the legislative facts on which Congress relied, the Court held that the legislative reach under the Commerce Clause was sufficient to compel the local hamburger stand and motel to surrender their dubious privilege of refusing to serve Negroes. What the Congress could not reach under the Commerce Clause—an area of necessarily small size under the 1964 Civil Rights Act cases and *Wickard v. Filburn*[68]—it was authorized by the Court to control under § 2 of the Thirteenth Amendment, § 5 of the Fourteenth Amendment, and § 2 of the Fifteenth Amendment. *Katzenbach v. Morgan*[69] and *South Carolina v. Katzenbach*[70] sustained the 1965 Voting Rights

64. FRANKFURTER, MR. JUSTICE HOLMES AND THE SUPREME COURT 44 (2d ed. 1961).
65. BLACK, THE PEOPLE AND THE COURT (1960), esp. ch. 3.
66. 379 U.S. 241 (1964).
67. 379 U.S. 294 (1964).   69. 384 U.S. 641 (1966).
68. 317 U.S. 111 (1942).   70. 383 U.S. 301 (1966).

Act, even in the face of what Professor Pritchett called "an unprecedented abridgement of the power to set voting qualifications."[71] In *Jones v. Alfred H. Mayer Co.*,[72] the Court found warrant in the Thirteenth Amendment for broad application of the long-moribund 1866 Civil Rights Act, thus making much of the Fourteenth Amendment redundant. That these were indeed exercises of the power of legitimation is underscored by the shabby opinions by which the Court reached its conclusions in each of these three cases.[73] They read more like fiat than reason, more pronouncement than explanation.

There are, however, several difficulties with Professor Black's thesis that "the most conspicuous function of judicial review may have been that of legitimizing rather than that of voiding actions of government,"[74] especially as applied to the work of the Warren Court.

First, the Court's decisions in the cases that I have cited as examples hardly came as a surprise to anyone. There was no need for "legitimation" of congressional power here. The only question that the Court watchers asked was how the Court would rationalize its conclusions, not what conclusions it would reach. To the extent that the public was prepared to see these statutes as valid exercises of lawful governmental authority, the Court added nothing to the public's confidence in its conclusion. And for those, and they remain many, who saw these particular statutes as gross incursions on individual rights, it is safe to say that their attitude has not been changed by the opinions rendered by the Court.

---

71. PRITCHETT, THE AMERICAN CONSTITUTION 756 (2d ed. 1968).

72. 392 U.S. 409 (1968).

73. See, *e.g.*, Bickel, *The Voting Rights Cases*, 1966 SUPREME COURT REVIEW 79; Casper, *Jones v. Mayer: Clio, Bemused and Confused Muse*, 1968 SUPREME COURT REVIEW 89; Henkin, *On Drawing Lines*, 82 HARV. L. REV. 63, 82–89 (1968).

74. BLACK, note 65 *supra*, at 52–53.

We may have reached the stage of political evolution when "legitimation" of congressional authority is unnecessary. There may now be consensus that there are no areas of individual behavior not subject to national governmental control except to the extent that the Court, in its discretion, may find a violation of the Bill of Rights. Those who accept this as political fact do not need the Court to legitimize it. Those who reject it see the Court as an important part of the conspiracy to subjugate individual rights and the American capitalist system. Certainly the Civil Rights Act provisions involved in these particular cases represent only expansions of rulings already promulgated by the Court. Thus, legitimacy, to the extent that it was conferred by the Court, had been conferred long before these cases were decided.

Second, the vast amount of national legislation and the small number of cases in which the Court affixes its stamp of approval suggest that legitimacy, acquired in this fashion, is certainly not a *sine qua non* of effective national legislation. In addition to the cases cited, there have been a few in which the Warren Court has exercised the power of judicial review in order to approve congressional legislation. Among these was the approval of the investigatory procedures of the Civil Rights Commission, under the Civil Rights Act of 1957,[75] procedures smelling every bit like those of some despised congressional committees that had been condemned by the Court. There was the extension of the coverage of more ancient civil rights legislation in *Price*[76] and *Guest,*[77] overruling, to a great extent at least, the *Civil Rights Cases* of 1883.[78]

Perhaps among those decisions approving legislation about which real doubts had existed, at least among "right-thinking" people, was that sustaining the registration pro-

75. Hannah v. Larche, 363 U.S. 420 (1960).
76. United States v. Price, 383 U.S. 787 (1966).
77. United States v. Guest, 383 U.S. 745 (1966).
78. 109 U.S. 3 (1883).

visions of the Subversive Activities Control Act of 1950.[79] But the Court, in *Aptheker, Albertson,* and *Robel,*[80] soon gutted the statute that it had first legitimated. Cases sustaining the Immunity Act of 1954,[81] the Revenue Act provision creating presumption of guilt from presence at the site of an illegal still,[82] the ban on distribution by a "panderer" of obscene literature through the mail,[83] and the reaffirmation of the constitutionality of the Smith Act[84] may be still more of the kind of legislation that Professor Black had in mind.[85]

A third difficulty with the legitimation theory is the Court's own unwillingness to treat its prior decisions as affording such status to legislation on which it has passed. The Warren Court's reluctance to be guided by precedent in constitutional cases is too well known to require documentation here. It is not a novel proclivity on the part of

79. Communist Party v. Subversive Activities Control Board, 367 U.S. 1 (1961).

80. See notes 15, 18, and 24 *supra.*

81. Ullmann v. United States, 350 U.S. 422 (1956); Reina v. United States, 364 U.S. 507 (1960); Piemonte v. United States, 367 U.S. 556 (1961).

82. United States v. Gainey, 380 U.S. 63 (1965).

83. Ginzburg v. United States, 383 U.S. 463 (1966); and see Roth v. United States, 354 U.S. 476 (1957).

84. Scales v. United States, 367 U.S. 203 (1961).

85. See also Alabama v. Texas, 347 U.S. 272 (1954) (Submerged Lands Act of 1953); United States v. Harriss, 347 U.S. 612 (1954) (Regulation of Lobbying Act); Galvan v. Press, 347 U.S. 522 (1954) (Internal Security Act of 1950; deportation provision); Adams v. Maryland, 347 U.S. 179 (1954) (18 U.S.C. § 3486); Berman v. Parker, 348 U.S. 26 (1954) (District of Columbia Redevelopment Act); Railway Employes' Dept. v. Hanson, 351 U.S. 225 (1956) (Railway Labor Act; union shop provision); United States v. Sharpnack, 355 U.S. 286 (1958) (Assimilative Crimes Act); FHA v. The Darlington, Inc., 358 U.S. 84 (1958) (National Housing Act); Steelworkers v. United States, 361 U.S. 39 (1959) (Labor Management Relations Act § 208); Fleming v. Nestor, 363 U.S. 603 (1960) (Social Security Act § 202 [n]); United States v. Oregon, 366 U.S. 643 (1961) (Escheat Law—38 U.S.C. § 17); United States v. O'Brien, 391 U.S. 367 (1968) (draft-card burning).

the Supreme Court. Even so, no Court has indulged the pastime so fully and frequently as the Warren Court. And, when the Court itself refuses, not as an aberration but as a rule, to treat its own decisions as the established law of the land, it becomes difficult to convince others that they should do so. The Warren Court, for example, on several occasions quickly "illegitimated" what it had first legitimated.[86] There is not much legitimacy created by decisions whose life expectancy is only until the next change of judicial personnel. Nor, it might be added, does the frequent close division of the Court in constitutional cases add to the legitimacy of the legislation in question.

Then, too, the legitimacy theory must rest either on the premise of a comprehension by the public of the Supreme Court's opinions or the premise that the public requires no more than knowledge of the conclusions reached. The first is unlikely in the light of the very poor press coverage that is available. The second is consistent with a concept of legitimation by fiat but not by reason, a matter of faith, not persuasion.

Finally, it is doubtful that there has been the historic need for the concept of legitimation in this country as there may have been in lands where such a tradition has long existed. As Professor Black said: "Since her first Revolution, France has been unable to establish an absolutely settled consensus on a genuine legitimacy."[87] He asserts that the same problem has not existed here. He concludes that this is due to the existence of the Constitution and the acceptance of the legitimation function of the Supreme Court. One need not quarrel with him about the role of the Constitution. It has been admirably shown by Hannah Arendt, however,

---

86. *E.g., compare* Lewis v. United States, 348 U.S. 419 (1955), *with* Marchetti v. United States, 390 U.S. 39 (1968), *and* Grosso v. United States, 390 U.S. 62 (1968); *compare* Perez v. Brownell, 356 U.S. 44 (1958), *with* Afroyim v. Rusk, 387 U.S. 253 (1967).

87. BLACK, note 65 *supra*, at 35.

who would seem to agree with Professor Black's thesis,[88] that the French and American revolutions created very different needs for "legitimating" the governments that followed the revolutions.[89] The European tradition was sufficiently different from the American colonial experience that the first required such an authority, while the second did not.

In any event, except by resort to the subconscious, concerning which we have little evidence except the insight of a poet, there is nothing to indicate that either Congress or the people look to the Court to legitimize national legislation. The dark side of judicial review is and has been both the popular and the political understanding. This is not to deny that charismatic values may be added to government action by Supreme Court decision. But that is dependent on the question to be resolved and the respect in which the Court is held at the time of the decision. That the Court's command of the people's respect and affection is an undulating one is attested both by history and, more recently, by the Gallup and Harris polls.

The fact is that the Court and Congress were in a great state of tension during the entire tenure of Chief Justice Warren. One may put the blame on the one or the other according to one's disposition. The tension is unlikely to erupt into a true constitutional crisis, as the relatively passive reception of the *Powell*[90] decision indicates, until such time as the president is prepared to play a role. For history reveals that despite the absence of power in the so-called nonpolitical branch, it has been in no real danger of submission except when Congress and the president join forces, or one or the other remains totally unconcerned.

88. ". . . the true seat of authority in the American Republic is the Supreme Court." ARENDT, ON REVOLUTION 201 (1963).

89. *Id.* at ch. 4, esp. p. 164.

90. Powell v. McCormack, 395 U.S. 486 (1969).

Thus, the real threat of the 1957–58 legislative attack[91] derived from the fact that the then occupant of the White House was likely to remain unconcerned about the contest, permitting Congress to have its way if it could muster enough votes to enact legislation. The 1937 crisis, on the other hand, revealed a president willing—indeed, anxious—to put the Court in its place, but a Congress that was reluctant to do so. Whether Congress would have failed the president had not the Court indulged what Thomas Reed Powell called "the switch in time that saved nine" must remain a matter of conjecture. The 1867–68 Congress could not count on aid from the first President Johnson to discipline the Court; nor could it come up with a sufficient majority to force the issue on the president. But Congress was certainly close to drastic action.

The attempt of Jefferson and his cohorts in Congress to make the impeachment process a viable political weapon against the Court narrowly failed, probably only because of the ineptitude of John Randolph, friend neither of Thomas Jefferson nor of his kin John Marshall. But the impeachment threat was real enough to evoke from Marshall a fearful concession: "I think the modern doctrine of impeachment should yield to an appellate jurisdiction in the legislature. A reversal of those legal opinions deemed unsound by the legislature would certainly better comport with the mildness of our character than a removal of the Judge who has rendered them unknowing of his fault."[92] Thus would the great Chief Justice have surrendered more than any Congress has been willing to claim in battle between legislature and Court. Randolph himself, after his defeat, asked only for a constitutional amendment to provide for judicial removal on joint address of both houses of Congress.[93] (A Senate subcommittee is today prepared to pro-

91. See text *supra,* at notes 35–53.
92. 3 BEVERIDGE, LIFE OF JOHN MARSHALL 177 (1919).
93. ANNALS, 8th Cong., 2d Sess. 1213 (1805).

vide for the removal of judges with less process than that, but its present target is only the lower federal courts.)[94]

Historically, dependence on the good will of the president has been a shaky platform for the Court to stand on. As Robert Jackson wrote when he was justifying the Roosevelt Court-packing plan:

> [The Court] has been in angry collision with most dynamic and popular Presidents in our history. Jefferson retaliated with impeachment; Jackson denied its authority; Lincoln disobeyed a writ of the Chief Justice; Theodore Roosevelt, after his Presidency, proposed a recall of judicial decisions; Wilson tried to liberalize its membership; and Franklin D. Roosevelt proposed to "reorganize" it. It is surprising that it should not only survive, but with no might except the moral force of its judgments should attain actual supremacy as a source of constitutional dogma.[95]

Generally speaking, however, the Warren Court has not been engaged in conflict with the president. Its decisions have been only mildly restrictive of executive power. In one case touching directly on the question of separation of powers the Court came down against the president, denying him the removal power in *Wiener v. United States,*[96] much as it was later to deny Congress its exclusion power in the *Powell* case. In earlier years, the presidential power of removal had been a hot political issue, even resulting in the impeachment of a president of the United States. A ruling denying Franklin Roosevelt power to remove a member of the Federal Trade Commission irked him even more than the treatment afforded New Deal legislation.[97] The *Wiener*

94. See Kurland, *The Constitution and the Tenure of Federal Judges: Some Notes from History,* 36 U. CHI. L. REV. 665 (1969).
95. JACKSON, note 5 *supra,* at ix–x.
96. 357 U.S. 349 (1958).
97. This opinion was expressed by Jackson in his private papers. In his book, Jackson put it this way: ". . . the touch of malice that

case, however, stirred little excitement in the quiescent years of the Eisenhower administration. And the president's involvment in the other cases decided by the Court and affecting the executive branch was attenuated. The Court has generally directed its fire at lesser mortals in the executive branch than the president himself. And, at the constitutional level, limitations have been rare. At the level of statutory construction, the executive has prevailed far more often than had the legislature whose legislation was reconstructed.

The State Department's control over passports affords one example of restraint of the executive. In *Kent v. Dulles*,[98] the Court avoided constitutional sanctions by finding that the statute did not authorize the secretary of state to exercise the discretion in the issuance of passports that he and Congress thought he had. And in two other cases, the Court dismissed criminal indictments for travel to Cuba without passports validated for such travel, again on statutory grounds.[99] So, too, the postmaster general found his discretion more limited than he had believed in the exclusion of allegedly obscene magazines from the mails.[100] The federal loyalty-security program was narrowed to minimal proportions by statutory construction that avoided constitutional issues.[101]

It was, of course, the Department of Justice, in its role

was thought to be in [*Humphrey's Executor v. United States*, 295 U.S. 602 (1935)] excited the most Administration resentment." JACKSON, note 5 *supra*, at 109.

98. 357 U.S. 116 (1958).

99. United States v. Laub, 385 U.S. 475 (1967); Travis v. United States, 385 U.S. 491 (1967).

100. Manual Enterprises, Inc. v. Day, 370 U.S. 478 (1962).

101. Joint Anti-Fascist Refugee Committee v. McGrath, 341 U.S. 123 (1951); Peters v. Hobby, 349 U.S. 33 (1955); Service v. Dulles, 354 U.S. 363 (1957); Taylor v. McElroy, 360 U.S. 709 (1959); Vitarelli v. Seaton, 359 U.S. 535 (1959). The *Peters* case was the one case argued before the Supreme Court by Warren Earl Burger, when he was assistant attorney general of the United States.

as prosecutor of criminal cases, that bore the brunt of the Court's expansion of the constitutional restraints on criminal procedure. Unreasonable searches and seizures,[102] the privilege against self-crimination,[103] coerced confessions,[104] right to counsel,[105] trial by jury,[106] due process in juvenile cases,[107] double jeopardy,[108] the right of confrontation,[109] among other rights protected by the first eight amendments took on new, varied, and usually more expansive meanings.

Although these cases, together with the even more frequent stringencies imposed on state criminal procedure, came to the point of a campaign issue in the presidential election of 1968, the relations between the Court and the president remained cordial. President Johnson's reference to Warren as the greatest Chief Justice of all time[110] is indicative of these warm feelings, whether or not the admiration was reciprocated.

If the Court has little direct effect on the functions of the executive branch of the national government, it is equally true that the president's powers to check the Court must be exerted by indirection. He can refuse, as Lincoln did, to obey mandates from the judiciary. He can, as Jackson did,

102. *E.g.*, Jones v. United States, 362 U.S. 257 (1960); Henry v. United States, 361 U.S. 98 (1959); Kremen v. United States, 353 U.S. 346 (1957); Wong Sun v. United States, 371 U.S. 471 (1963); Preston v. United States, 376 U.S. 364 (1964); Elkins v. United States, 364 U.S. 206 (1960); Black v. United States, 385 U.S. 26 (1966).

103. *E.g.*, Emspak v. United States, 349 U.S. 190 (1955); Curcio v. United States, 354 U.S. 118 (1957); see cases cited in note 15 *supra*.

104. *E.g.*, Mallory v. United States, 354 U.S. 449 (1957).

105. *E.g.*, United States v. Wade, 388 U.S. 218 (1967).

106. *E.g.*, United States v. Barnett, 376 U.S. 681 (1964); Cheff v. Schnackenberg, 384 U.S. 373 (1966).

107. *E.g.*, Kent v. United States, 383 U.S. 541 (1966).

108. *E.g.*, Green v. United States, 355 U.S. 184 (1957).

109. *E.g.*, Bruton v. United States, 391 U.S. 123 (1968).

110. See Kurland, *Earl Warren, the "Warren Court," and the Warren Myths,* in SEGLER, BOYER & GOODING, eds., THE WARREN COURT 162 (1968).

prevent enforcement of judicial decrees by refusing necessary aid. He can, as Roosevelt did, arouse public opinion against the Court in an effort to change its direction. He can, as Eisenhower did, simply refuse to put the moral force of his office behind the Court's judgments. Public opinion is the power by which the chief executive works his will, with the Court and the Congress, as with the people.

The most direct influence that the president exerts on the Court is by his choice of its personnel. None need accept President Nixon's hyperbole about the role of the Chief Justice in American history in order to concede that the presidential power of appointment of Supreme Court Justices is an important one. Although judicial behavior after appointment tends to be unpredictable,[111] once a president has had the opportunity to make appointments to the Supreme Court, friction between the two branches tends to diminish.

The Warren Court was a strange conglomeration of presidential choices. For some years, the Court's dominant figures have been Roosevelt appointees, of whom five served for longer or lesser periods with Warren: Justices Black, Reed, Frankfurter, Douglas, and Jackson. Black and Douglas were there when Warren arrived and were still there when he left. And, as Justice Frankfurter was wont to observe, the influence of a Justice on constitutional doctrine is often a function of longevity of service. Of the other eleven members of the Warren Court, Burton, Clark, and Minton were Truman appointees. Harlan, Brennan, Whittaker, and Stewart, like Warren, were Eisenhower appointees. Kennedy contributed White and Goldberg. Johnson appointed Fortas and Marshall. It is difficult to discover patterns in any single president's appointments, either in terms of standards for appointment or behavior of the Justices after appointment. One thing is clear, however, as Mr. Justice Frankfurter

111. See Kurland, *Wanted: A Nonpolitical Supreme Court*, 56 NATION'S BUSINESS 87 (May 1968).

pointed out in 1957: "One is entitled to say without qualification that the correlation between prior judicial experience and fitness for the functions of the Supreme Court is zero."[112]

Appointments to the Supreme Court have largely become the exclusive patronage of the president. Seldom does the Senate offer more than cursory scrutiny or token opposition. Since 1930 four Supreme Court nominations have failed to carry. In 1930, the Senate rejected the nomination of John J. Parker, a United States Court of Appeals judge with impeccable judicial credentials. In 1968, the nomination of Mr. Justice Fortas to be Chief Justice was stalled and finally withdrawn. In 1969, Clement Haynsworth was rejected, largely because he and some Republican senators fell into the trap that had been built to catch Mr. Justice Fortas. Parker was essentially faulted only because he followed Supreme Court precedents. The nominations of Fortas and Parker had each been made by a president whose political power had been sapped: Hoover's by the onset of the Great Depression and Johnson's by the Vietnam War. The rejection of Judge Harrold G. Carswell was something of an anomaly. If most of the votes could be accounted for by party loyalty or views on desegregation, some of the senators took measure of Carswell's capabilities for the high judicial post and found them seriously wanting. It is to be hoped that the Senate will find precedent here in exercising judgment about the nominee's merits. The confirmation of Judge Harry Blackmun afforded no test, for he so clearly qualified that the Senate vote in favor of his confirmation was 94 to 0.

Historically there have been two other connections between the president and the Supreme Court that should be noted. One of these showed in the Warren Court, the other did not. Some Justices of the Court, from its beginnings, have had political ambitions for offices other than

112. FRANKFURTER, OF LIFE AND LAW AND OTHER THINGS THAT MATTER 97 (Kurland ed. 1965).

the high judicial posts they held. John Jay left the Court to become governor of New York. David Davis became senator from Illinois. Arthur Goldberg departed the judicial scene to become ambassador to the United Nations after the death of Adlai Stevenson. The most common bug to infect Justices of the Court, however, and the most dangerous to the life of the institution, is the presidential bug. How many Justices have actually suffered the disease without showing any symptoms cannot be known. But there were many whose ambition for presidential power was worn on their sleeves. Only Charles Evans Hughes was ever nominated for the presidency from the Court. But a glance at a comparatively noncontroversial Court, that of Chief Justice Waite, reveals the virulence of the disease. I quote from C. Peter Magrath's excellent biography of Waite:

> During Waite's tenure a number of his associates, in addition to [David] Davis, were at least fleetingly tempted by thoughts of moving into the White House. Stephen Field twice indicated a willingness to answer the call of a higher duty, but in both 1880 and 1884 the Democratic Party failed to issue the summons. His colleague Samuel Miller, with something of a reputation as an agrarian radical, entertained mild hopes for the Republican nomination in 1880 and 1884. Unlike Field, . . . Miller did little to promote his candidacy. . . . John Marshall Harlan's name was briefly brought forward by Republicans loyal to the Negroes' interest. The flurry ended as quickly as it began when the Justice emphasized that, for him, politics and his judicial duties were "utterly irreconcilable."[113]

Chief Justice Waite agreed with Harlan: "I have for many years believed that a man cannot be both judge & politician. He need not forego his political opinions when he goes on the bench, but he must his political aspirations."[114]

113. MAGRATH, MORRISON R. WAITE: THE TRIUMPH OF CHARACTER 286–87 (1963).
114. *Id.* at 287.

So far as public information is concerned, the Warren Court was relatively free of presidential aspirants. Warren seems to have had his fling at this goal before his appointment to the bench. Douglas's hopes dissipated by the time of Truman's election, if not before. The others showed no signs of presidential fever during the Warren tenure.

On the other hand, extrajudicial roles in government for the Justices, historically a not infrequent occurrence, were again prominent in the Warren Court.[115] Essentially, the process consists of borrowing either judicial prestige or judicial brainpower by the president. Very early, the Court rejected the notion that it would act as a body in any advisory capacity to the president.[116] But individual Justices have always felt free—whatever their views about the desirability of such action—to advise or help the president, at least with some of his problems. The public commitments of the members of the Warren Court ranged from "goodwill" tours on behalf of the State Department to the chairmanship of the commission investigating the assassination of President Kennedy. Informal advice-giving, in the pattern of Frankfurter and Roosevelt,[117] continued under both Roosevelt's and Frankfurter's successors. Mr. Justice Fortas brought down the wrath of many, apparently because he gave unpopular advice to an unpopular president, which is thought to be different from giving popular advice to a popular president. And there's merit in this attitude, for in accepting both formal and informal assignments, the Justice cannot help using the prestige of his office to assist the

115. See Hearings before Committee on the Judiciary, Subcommittee on Separation of Powers, U.S. Senate, 91st Cong., 1st Sess., which were concerned with the subject of extrajudicial activities. The first set of hearings was held on 14–16 July 1969.

116. See WOLFSON & KURLAND, ROBERTSON & KIRKHAM, JURISDICTION OF THE SUPREME COURT OF THE UNITED STATES § 262 (1951).

117. See ROOSEVELT & FRANKFURTER: THEIR CORRESPONDENCE 1928–1945 (Freedman ed. 1967).

executive. The cost in judicial prestige is highest when the presidential prestige is lowest. And when the Court's claim to the support of the public is already precarious, it is dangerous to trade any prestige away.

The warm relations between Court and president in the Kennedy and Johnson administrations—Eisenhower's approach to the Court was more wary and aloof—have tempted political journalists and political scientists to discern a new and desirable rearrangement of governmental powers. Thus, Louis W. Koenig in his tract for expansion of presidential power wrote:

> The United States Supreme Court, in its civil rights rulings and its requirement of a wholesale revision of the districts of the House of Representatives, has clearly befriended the cause of the continuously strong Presidency. The Court, altogether logically, could take up the executive power clause with results equally favorable to the Presidency.[118]

Professor Koenig does not explain how the Court "could take up the executive power clause," but that is a separate problem.

Louis Heren, Washington correspondent for *The Times,* in an attempt to emulate Lord Bryce's descriptions of the American political scene for the British and American observer, reported: "To a large extent the modern Presidency has been assisted, if unwittingly, by the third branch of government, the Supreme Court."[119] Thus, did the lion lie down with the lamb. Heren also slipped, if unwittingly, into the legitimation theory of the Court's function when he wrote: "In its relationship to the modern Presidency, the Court is what the church was to a medieval monarch."[120]

118. KOENIG, note 2 *supra,* at 406.
119. HEREN, THE NEW AMERICAN COMMONWEALTH 18 (1967).
120. *Id.* at 80.

But Heren would have the Court creating legitimacy not in the actions of the legislature but in those of the president.

It was another student of the presidency, James Mac-Gregor Burns, who, in 1965, wrote:

> The Court is composed of men who respond to the same general ideas of freedom and equality as have recent Presidents. . . . The election of Barry Goldwater, and the kind of judicial appointments he would have made, would of course have disrupted the harmony between the two branches, at least if Goldwater could have put enough of his own men on the bench, but Goldwater's rejection diminishes the likelihood of a sharp presidential-judicial break in the foreseeable future. As long as we elect liberal Presidents from either of the presidential parties we can anticipate a generally liberal court.[121]

One may find paradox in the suggestion that presidential-judicial relations would be disrupted by a president who appointed a large number of his own choices to the high court. But the essential question suggested by Professor Burns's remarks is who will control the Court's role in American government now that we have, not Goldwater, but Nixon in the White House. There are three possibilities: The first is that the Court will adhere to its stated positions and the president to his. A joinder of forces between the president and Congress could then result in judicial restraint imposed from the outside rather than from within. A second possibility is that the Court may be adapted to the presidential point of view by reason of appointments that the president has and will make. Certainly the outlook of the Court has already been vastly changed by the substitution of Warren Burger for Earl Warren and Harry Blackmun for Abe Fortas. The third potentiality is that the Court will remain relatively unchanged, but the president's views will change. This is unlikely, but presidents, like Justices, have been known to be

121. BURNS, note 2 *supra*, at 316–17.

different men after assuming office from what they were while campaigning for it. In this event, too, there will be no external limits placed on the Court's behavior.

Part of the interest in Court watching is due to the continuous element of suspense that inheres in the sport. The only consolation for the moment may be found in words of Ralph Waldo Emerson uttered in 1864: "These times of ours are serious and full of calamity, but all times are essentially alike."[122]

122. *Public and Private Education,* in EMERSON, UNCOLLECTED LECTURES 14 (1932).

⁂ 3
Federalism
and the
Warren Court

ONE OF THE TENETS of American constitutionalism
has been the concept of federalism, a division of powers between the central government and those of the states. The
evidence of my one-time colleague William W. Crosskey to
the contrary notwithstanding,[1] it remains orthodox learning
that at the time of the ratification of the Constitution, the
national government was established as a government of limited, delegated powers. To make this more certain, the Bill
of Rights promulgated by the new nation contained ten
amendments, since reduced to eight or possibly nine,[2] the
ninth and tenth of which confirmed that most governmental
authority was retained by the states and by the people.

Forty years after the creation, the desirability and unique-
ness of this division of authority between nation and states
were noted and applauded by Tocqueville. He recognized
that the federal plan in the United States was different from
federal plans that had preceded it. But he did not see that this
very difference sowed the seeds of its destruction. This nation was, Tocqueville said, "[a]nother form of society . . .
in which several states are fused into one with regard to certain common interests, although they remain distinct, or only

1. See CROSSKEY, POLITICS AND THE CONSTITUTION (1953).
2. As to the revival of the Ninth Amendment, see Griswold v. Connecticut, 381 U.S. 479 (1965); Kelly, *Clio and the Court*, 1965
SUPREME COURT REVIEW 119, 149–55.

confederate with regard to all other concerns. In this case the central power acts directly upon the governed, whom it rules and judges in the same manner as a national government, but in a more limited circle."[3] Amid general praise for the new system, Tocqueville pointed out: "It is generally believed in America that the existence and permanence of the republican form of government in the New World depend upon the existence and duration of the federal system."[4]

A half-century after Tocqueville another astute foreign observer, Lord Bryce, found the constitutional scheme of federalism essentially unchanged.[5] About the same time, still another titled Englishman found in federalism a contribution toward freedom of a different kind than that suggested by Tocqueville. Lord Acton wrote:

> Of all checks on democracy, federalism has been the most efficacious and congenial. . . . The Federal system limits and restrains sovereign power by dividing it, and by assigning to Government only certain defined rights. It is the only method of curbing not only the majority but the power of the whole people, and it affords the strongest basis for a second chamber, which has been found essential security for freedom in every genuine democracy.[6]

If for nothing else, one must give Acton credit for recognizing the United States Senate as an essential ingredient of federalism; indeed, it has become probably the last important vestige of American federalism.

Even in recent years paeans to the concept of federalism as an essential ingredient of American constitutional government have been regularly issued. Two of our most respected

3. 1 Tocqueville, Democracy in America 158–59 (Bradley ed. 1945).

4. *Id.* at 163–64.

5. 1 Bryce, The American Commonwealth 318–19 (2d ed. rev. 1891).

6. Acton, History of Freedom 98 (1907).

governors—Terry Sanford of North Carolina and Nelson Rockefeller of New York—have produced books in support of the concept of federalism, books that assume the original constitutional scheme to be still viable.[7] A national commission, made permanent by Congress in 1959, is concerned with the problems of federalism, issues regular reports, and suggests ways to keep it alive.[8] Even Justices of the Supreme Court of the United States speak as if the constitutional scheme described by Tocqueville and Bryce were still effective, but they usually do so in dissenting opinions.[9]

The fact of the matter is, of course, that the areas of government in which the states are sovereign have been reduced almost to nonexistence. This is not to deny that the states are spending more and more money on more and more projects. But the independence of the states, even in the areas of their greatest activities—education, crime control, health, and welfare—is a matter of the past. And as K. C. Wheare has told us:

> What is necessary for the federal principle is not merely
> that the general government, like the regional governments,
> should operate directly upon the people, but,
> further, that each government should be limited to its
> own sphere, and within its sphere, should be independent of the other.[10]

7. SANFORD, STORM OVER THE STATES (1967); ROCKEFELLER, THE FUTURE OF FEDERALISM (1962).

8. The commission is the Advisory Commission on Intergovernmental Relations. Its original study of federalism culminated in the FINAL REPORT OF THE COMMISSION ON INTERGOVERNMENTAL RELATIONS (1955). Subsequent studies of particular areas of federal-state cooperation fill a good-sized library shelf. The Ninety-first Congress has announced continued support of this effort. See, e.g., S. 2042, H.R. 10483, H.R. 10814, H.R. 11963, 91st Cong., 1st Sess. (1969).

9. See, e.g., Roth v. United States, 354 U.S. 476, 496 (1957) (Harlan, J., dissenting); South Carolina v. Katzenbach, 383 U.S. 301, 355 (1966) (Black, J., dissenting).

10. WHEARE, FEDERAL GOVERNMENT 14 (4th ed. 1964).

Perhaps, as Governor Rockefeller has said: "The reports of the death of federalism, so authoritatively asserted in the nineteen-thirties, were . . . highly exaggerated."[11] If so, however, it is only for the reason suggested in another context by the Reverend Sydney Smith: "Death must be distinguished from dying, with which it is often confused."[12]

The practical reasons for the decline of federalism are many. As one might expect of a Marxist, Harold Laski saw the cause in peculiarly economic terms:

> Federalism, which began by seeking to maintain variety in unity, has ended succumbing to the influence of giant capitalism, which is, by its inherent nature, unfavourable to the variety which federalism seeks to maintain. . . . The central result of economic development has been to emphasize the obsolescence of the federal idea.[13]

The capitalist, so despised by Laski, would reach exactly the opposite conclusion, that the decline of federalism is a direct consequence of the development of the welfare state that imposes a uniformity and conformity inconsistent with principles of federalism.

Tocqueville's euphoria about federalism rested on the proposition that the United States was geographically protected from the need to engage in the wars that racked the European continent. The shrinking of the globe by modern transport and communications and the consequent entry of the United States as a major world power would account, in his terms, for the pressures to abandon the realities of the federal structure.[14] Tocqueville would also recognize in Learned Hand's description of contemporary American so-

11. ROCKEFELLER, note 7 *supra,* at 29.
12. PEARSON, THE SMITH OF SMITHS 271 (1934).
13. LASKI, THE AMERICAN DEMOCRACY 50 (1948).
14. TOCQUEVILLE, note 3 *supra,* at 170–71.

ciety, to which I have already referred,[15] one that was totally inconsistent with the continuance of federalism as he saw it.

If the enervation of the forces of federalism is the consequence of the societal movement away from individualism, some explain it, nonetheless, in more prosaic terms. William O. Douglas, for example, in his role as author of books rather than as Supreme Court Justice, set forth the reasons for the decline of federalism in this way:

> In America the trend has been toward the development of a strong and powerful national government. The impetus for that growth has in part been decisions of the Supreme Court from the time of Chief Justice Marshall to date. It has in part been the increased use by Congress of the great arsenal of power contained in the Constitution. Powers long neglected, *e.g.*, powers over interestate commerce, have been increasingly used by Congress since the turn of the twentieth century. The increased complexities of American life, the growth of industrialism, the disappearance of the frontier, the increase in population, the growing dependence of one part of the nation on the others—these were all powerful pressures creating the need and demand for federal regulation in fields where previously only the States had legislated. The depression of the 1930's emphasized the need for planning by central government. The advent of two World Wars made necessary the close integration of the national economy under the National Government. And the war powers of Congress and the President . . . were ample for that purpose.
>
> The federal income tax [and here is the essence of national power] which came to use as a result of the Sixteenth Amendment [in turn made necessary by an obdurate Supreme Court's battle against "communism"][16] has also given centralization a powerful push.[17]

15. See chapter 1, *supra,* at note 27.
16. See Pollock v. Farmers' Loan and Trust Co., 157 U.S. 429, 158 U.S. 601 (1895).
17. DOUGLAS, WE THE JUDGES 42–43 (1956).

To what extent the Supreme Court has caused centralization rather than acquiesced in it is a question that does not produce a ready answer. Not since Marshall's day has there been any doubt that one of the prime functions of the Supreme Court has been to act as "umpire of the federal system," to allocate or justify the assumption of power as between the nation and the states.[18] To return to Lord Bryce:

> . . . By placing Constitution above both the National and the State governments, [the Constitution] has referred the arbitrament of disputes between them to an independent body, charged with the interpretation of the Constitution, a body which is to be deemed not so much a third authority in the government as the living voice of the Constitution, the unfolder of the mind of the people whose will stands expressed in that supreme instrument.[19]

The metaphor of "umpire" between the nation and the states has remained a popular one.[20] I submit that it is a misleading one. Insofar as the metaphor implies a contest for authority between the central government and those of the states, it is not inappropriate, although the contest has long since become a most unequal one. If, however, the notion is intended to suggest that the Supreme Court has been wholly neutral in this contest, applying rules formulated by the Constitution rather than writing them, it is certainly inaccurate. At least in one respect, Jefferson's diatribe against the Court has proved to be more accurate:

> The judiciary of the United States is the subtle corps of sappers and miners constantly working under ground to undermine the foundations of our Confederated fabric. They are construing a Constitution from a co-

18. See Schmidhauser, The Supreme Court as Final Arbiter in Federal State Relations, 1789–1957 (1958).

19. Bryce, note 5 *supra,* at 348.

20. See, *e.g.,* Freund, The Supreme Court of the United States 92 (1961).

ordination of a general and special government to a general and supreme one alone. This will lay all things at their feet, and they are too well versed in English law to forget the maxim *"boni judicis est ampliare jurisdictionem."*[21]

The Court has no more achieved neutrality between the interests of state power and national power than would any umpire paid by one of two contestants. The Court is and always has been an integral part of the central government.

Because it is the branch of the national government with the least political responsibility either to the states or the electorate, connected as it is with the electoral process only through the appointive power of the president and the confirmation power of the Senate, the Court has great advantages as an instrument of national policy that are not available to either of its coordinate branches of government. Perhaps a more appropriate analogue than that of "umpire," therefore, would be that the Court has been a dam regulating the flow of power from the states to the nation. The dam cannot reverse the direction of flow. It can control only its speed, and even that is subject to the pressures that other forces might build up behind the dam. But the dam is capable of allocating the flow into one or more of the three channels of national authority: the legislative, the executive, or the judicial.

This analogy, too, fails if it suggests that it has been the Court's business, even in part, to maintain a reservoir of authority in the states. The Court's role has been exactly the opposite. It has been engaged from the beginning in a constant attrition of state power. Its efforts toward centralization began even before Marshall spent almost thirty-five years on the supreme bench in doing little else, as witness the early Court's opinions in *Ware v. Hylton*,[22] *Hylton v.*

---

21. Quoted in HUGHES, THE SUPREME COURT OF THE UNITED STATES 46 (1928).
22. 3 Dall. 199 (1796).

United States,[23] and *Chisholm v. Georgia.*[24] The first of these established the breadth and supremacy of the treaty power; the second removed limitations on the national taxing power; and the third would, but for the speedy intervention of the Eleventh Amendment, have in a large measure destroyed the immunity of the states from suit in the federal courts. The Court's primary function has been the nationalization of the federation, even if, to the extent that where it has only justified the exercise of power by Congress, it has sometimes left the timing of the exercise of that power to the legislature.

On the other hand, if it is true that the Court has given its blessing to the assumptions of power by the other branches of the national government, this acknowledgment of congressional or executive authority may have been nothing more than acts of supererogation. For history demonstrates that even when the Court has, at first, refused its approval, the power sought from the states by the nation has ultimately been secured by the central government.

In 1934, Professor Felix Frankfurter described the functions of the Supreme Court to include these august duties: "This tribunal is the ultimate organ—short of direct popular action—for adjusting the relationship of the individual to the separate states, of the individual to the United States, of the forty-eight states to one another, of the states to the union, and of the three departments of government to one another."[25] But, if one looks at the work of the Court in historical perspective, the conclusion is readily reached that, of all the important functions it purports to perform, its essential role has been to act as a centripetal force, to modify the Constitution in order to sustain the enhancement of national authority and the despoliation of state power. There have been a few aberrations in this behavior, but none that re-

23. 3 Dall. 171 (1796).
24. 2 Dall. 419 (1793).
25. FRANKFURTER, LAW AND POLITICS 21 (MacLeish & Prichard eds. 1939).

mains uncorrected. Certainly the same consistency and vigor cannot be found in the exercise of the Court's other functions.

Indeed, even with regard to Frankfurter's suggestion that the Court's readings of the Constitution are subject to the control of the people by the amendment process—a suggestion also made by Mr. Justice Black concerning the proper means for appropriate constitutional change[26]—the erosion of the principles of federalism in that process is to be noted. Faced with the question of how the Constitution would be amended, the founders decided that initiation of amendments could not be exclusively conferred on Congress, for it might then never be used to correct abuses by the national government. Nor they decided, could such a power to propose amendments be left solely with the states, for then needed restraints of state authority or expansion of national authority would never be forthcoming. In a fashion typical of the Constitutional Convention, they authorized both the states and Congress to initiate such proceedings.[27]

The fact is, however, that never have enough states combined to propose an amendment to the Constitution. And now that the possibility of such a proposal exists, the battle in Congress is for means to preclude the fruition of this possibility.[28]

The Warren Court stands in the great tradition of its predecessors in its efforts at transferring areas of governmental control from the states to the nation. Every one of its major constitutional developments falls in this category. The school desegregation cases, the criminal procedure cases, the reapportionment cases, all emphasize this single theme of restraint on state power. In this regard, at least, the Warren

26. See chapter 1, *supra,* at note 8.
27. See Kurland, *The Constitution: Article V and the Amending Process,* in 1 BOORSTIN, ed., AN AMERICAN PRIMER 130 (1966).
28. See Federal Constitutional Convention, Hearings on S. 2307 before the Subcommittee on the Separation of Powers of the Committee on the Judiciary, U.S. Senate, 90th Cong., 1st Sess. (1967).

Court is more like the Marshall Court than any of those that served between them.

Before turning to an examination of these major doctrinal changes of constitutional law, however, I should like to point out that the theme of centralization was also dominant in the other areas of the Court's work. Unlike the major cases that rest exclusively on constitutional grounds, some of these other decisions are, in theory at least,[29] subject to revision by congressional action. And yet, the trend toward centralization has become so dominant in American government that Congress has met these decisions with inaction, abandoning its power to protect the states' rights about which it is so frequently vocal.

One example of this phenomenon is to be found in the labor law cases. Here the Court has, more or less consistently, construed national legislation to be preemptive of state authority. While the cases do not afford a uniform pattern, the tendency is sufficiently clear.[30] Two particular cases suffice to make the point. The first was one of the largest federal judicial power grabs indulged by the Court. Reading § 301 of the Taft-Hartley law in a manner that was certainly hard to derive either from its words or its legislative history, in *Textile Workers Union v. Lincoln Mills*[31] and its progeny, the Court decided that judicially created federal law should thereafter provide the controlling rules for the resolution of controversies over almost all labor relations contracts.[32] Among its last gasps, the Warren Court uttered *Railroad Trainmen v. Terminal Co.*,[33] in which it ruled that, although there was no federal statutory law to control the question of

29. See chapter 2, *supra,* at note 62.
30. See Meltzer, *The Supreme Court, Congress and State Jurisdiction of Labor Relations,* 59 COLUM. L. REV. 6, 269 (1959) (2 parts); SHAPIRO, LAW AND POLITICS IN THE SUPREME COURT ch. 3 (1964).
31. 353 U.S. 448 (1957).
32. See Bickel & Wellington, *Legislative Purpose and the Judicial Process: The Lincoln Mills Case,* 71 HARV. L. REV. 1 (1957).
33. 394 U.S. 369 (1969).

secondary picketing at a railroad terminal, "the application of state law is limited by paramount federal policies of nationwide import."[34] The dissent, written by Mr. Justice Douglas and joined by Justices Black and Stewart, appropriately asserted: "Legislating interstitially is one thing; judicial insertion into our federal railway labor law of rules governing secondary boycotts is formulation of national policy in the raw. Whether it should be done and, if so, how, are matters for the Senate and the House."[35] This, mind you, from the author of the *Lincoln Mills* decision.

To a less marked degree, the Supreme Court has been using federal statutes as an excuse for absorbing corporation law into the national domain.[36] The degree is less marked than with the labor-law cases because there are fewer of them and the lower federal courts have anticipated the Supreme Court's direction. As Stanley Kaplan put it: "If the courts continue to interpret Rule 10(b) (5) with the sweep and breadth that has heretofore been accorded to it, the rule's scope may very well largely absorb into federal jurisdiction the entire development of control over fiduciaries when a purchase or sale of securities is involved."[37] Since the definition of securities is also a burgeoning one, thanks to the Court,[38] this means an ever widening sphere for federal control. The unabated trend here is clearly revealed in the few cases that the Warren Court has called up for review.[39]

Perhaps the last great judicial upheaval on behalf of the states was *Erie R.R. v. Tompkins,*[40] and its explication in

34. *Id.* at 382.
35. *Id.* at 396.
36. See Ruder, *Civil Liability under Rule 10b-5: Judicial Review of Legislative Intent?* 57 Nw. U. L. Rev. 627 (1962).
37. Kaplan, *Wolf v. Weinstein: Another Chapter on Insider Trading,* 1963 SUPREME COURT REVIEW 272, 323.
38. See Tcherepnin v. Knight, 389 U.S. 332 (1967).
39. See, *e.g.,* S.E.C. v. Capital Gains Research Bureau, Inc., 375 U.S. 180 (1963); J. I. Case Co. v. Borak, 377 U.S. 426 (1964).
40. 304 U.S. 64 (1938).

Guaranty Trust Co. v. York.[41] Purporting to rest on constitutional grounds, *Erie* required the federal courts to recognize the sovereignty of the states by applying state law to cases having no federal aspect other than congressional authority to provide an impartial tribunal to hear a contest between persons of different citizenship. As late as 1964, no less an authority than Judge Henry Friendly thought that the constitutional mandate of the *Erie* doctrine was clear, strong, and sound.[42] As I read the Warren Court's decisions, however, I find an erosion of the constitutional authorization and a destruction of the statutory basis for the *Erie* doctrine.

The rule of *Erie* and *York* has been severely restricted by decisions like *Hannah v. Plumer*[43] and *Byrd v. Blue Ridge Rural Electric Co-op., Inc.*[44] But even more important has been the elimination of the Rules of Decision Act[45] simply by treating it as if it did not exist. That statute, codified in 1948, still unrepealed by Congress, and never held invalid by the Court, provides: "The laws of the several states, except where the Constitution or treaties of the United States or Acts of Congress otherwise require or provide, shall be regarded as rules of decision in civil actions in the courts of the United States, in cases where they apply." The Supreme Court has amended the congressional statute to provide that the federal courts may—even in the absence of constitutional, treaty, or statutory command—create their own rules of decision for cases that may come before them. Thus, although Mr. Justice Brandeis told us in *Erie* that there was no "general federal common law," we are now told that there

41. 326 U.S. 99 (1945); see Kurland, *Mr. Justice Frankfurter, the Supreme Court, and the Erie Doctrine in Diversity Cases,* 67 YALE L. J. 187 (1957).

42. *In Praise of Erie—and of the New Federal Common Law,* in FRIENDLY, BENCHMARKS 155 (1967).

43. 380 U.S. 460 (1965).

44. 356 U.S. 525 (1958).   45. 28 U.S.C. § 1652.

is a federal common law which is to be as "general" as the Court wishes to make it.[46]

In a not dissimilar area, the Court has constantly construed jurisdictional statutes and the Federal Rules of Civil Procedure to expand the jurisdiction of the federal courts.[47] There have been a few exceptions, as with a 1969 case refusing to permit aggregation of claims in a diversity action in order to create the necessary jurisdictional amount.[48] Certainly that decision, logically compelled as it was, came as a surprise because it bucked the strong tide running in the other direction. At the same time, such bows to state competency as were found in the abstention doctrine have tended to disappear.[49]

One Warren Court decision and its progeny removed an entire subject from the control of the states to that of the national courts. I speak, of course, of the famous *New York Times* case.[50] The case means, as Professor Cox has stated, "that the Supreme Court rather than the State courts will have the last word upon much of the law of libel."[51] One may hail the decision, as Harry Kalven has done, as a great move toward the establishment of the essence of the First Amendment, *i.e.*, the destruction of the notion of seditious

46. See Wallis v. Pan American Petroleum Corp., 384 U.S. 63 (1966); Wheeldin v. Wheeler, 373 U.S. 647, 665–66 (1963); Kurland, *The Romero Case and Some Problems of Federal Jurisdiction,* 73 HARV. L. REV. 817, 831–33 (1966); FRIENDLY, note 42 *supra;* Note, *The Federal Common Law,* 82 HARV. L. REV. 1512 (1969).

47. See, *e.g.,* State Farm Fire & Casualty Co. v. Tashire, 386 U.S. 523 (1967); United Mine Workers v. Gibbs, 383 U.S. 715 (1966); Provident Tradesmens Bank & Trust Co. v. Patterson, 390 U.S. 102 (1968); United States v. Mississippi, 380 U.S. 128 (1965); Horton v. Liberty Mut. Ins. Co., 367 U.S. 348 (1961); Smith v. Sperling, 354 U.S. 91 (1957).

48. Snyder v. Harris, 394 U.S. 332 (1969); see also United Steelworkers of America v. R. M. Bouligny, Inc., 382 U.S. 145 (1965).

49. See Note, *Federal Question Abstention: Justice Frankfurter's Doctrine in an Activist Era,* 80 HARV. L. REV. 604 (1967).

50. New York Times Co. v. Sullivan, 376 U.S. 254 (1964).

51. COX, THE WARREN COURT 14 (1968).

libel and anything that can possibly be brought within that notion.[52] Even so, one must also recognize, as Professor Kalven has done,[53] that the result has been the nationalization of the law of defamation, if not its destruction. The ultimate effect remains to be seen. But it must be apparent that what it means is a greater protection for the defamer and a diminution of the very small protection that was available to the defamed. Whether in this age of media control of the American mind this consequence should be regarded as wholesome is far more dubious to me than to Mr. Kalven. The *New York Times* case and those that have followed it seem to excuse all defamation except that which can be proved to have been committed with malice. Malice will be very difficult to prove, since proof of gross negligence, stupidity, or avarice will not be enough.[54] The press has had few restraints imposed on its capacity to degrade individuals. As with other institutions, self-restraint has not provided enough restraint. One wonders whether the wisdom that came too late to Thomas Jefferson will not also come too late to us.[55]

Some of the classic problems of federalism also reappeared on the Warren Court dockets. To what extent does the Commerce Clause inhibit state power; to what degree does that clause authorize the national government to act? It was the Commerce Clause, it will be recalled, that afforded Marshall and his successors their prime means of serving as a centralizing force in government. As Professor Frankfurter said:

> What Marshall merely adumbrated in *Gibbons* v. *Ogden*[56] became central to our whole constitutional

52. See Kalven, *The New York Times Case: A Note on "The Central Meaning of the First Amendment,"* 1964 Supreme Court Review 191.

53. See Kalven, *The Reasonable Man and the First Amendment: Hill, Butts, and Walker,* 1967 Supreme Court Review 267.

54. See, *e.g.,* St. Amant v. Thompson, 390 U.S. 727 (1968).

55. Levy, Jefferson and Civil Liberties: the Darker Side (1963).

56. 9 Wheat. 1 (1824).

scheme: the doctrine that the commerce clause, by its own force and without national legislation, puts it into the power of the Court to place limits on state authority. . . . Marshall's use of the commerce clause greatly furthered the idea that though we are a federation of states we are also a nation, and gave momentum to the doctrine that state authority must be subject to such limitations as the Court finds it necessary to apply for the protection of the national community. It was an audacious doctrine, which, one may be sure, would hardly have been publicly avowed in support of the adoption of the Constitution. Indeed, *The Federalist* in effect denied it.[57]

The Warren Court, too, without the benefit of national legislation, decided whether a state tax did[58] or did not[59] unduly impinge on interstate commerce. And it determined whether state regulation of business activities regulated interstate commerce too much[60] or did not regulate it too much.[61] No doctrine seems derivable from these decisions

57. FRANKFURTER, THE COMMERCE CLAUSE 18–19 (1937).
58. Railway Express Agency v. Virginia, 347 U.S. 359 (1954); Michigan-Wisconsin Pipe Line Co. v. Calvert, 347 U.S. 157 (1954); West Point Grocery Co. v. Opelika, 354 U.S. 390 (1957); National Bellas Hess, Inc. v. Dep't of Revenue, 386 U.S. 753 (1967); Norfolk & Western Ry. v. Missouri Tax Comm'n, 390 U.S. 317 (1968).
59. Braniff Airways, Inc. v. Nebraska State Bd., 347 U.S. 590 (1954); Railway Express Agency v. Virginia, 358 U.S. 434 (1959); Northwestern States Cement Co. v. Minnesota, 358 U.S. 450 (1959); Scripto, Inc. v. Carson, 362 U.S. 207 (1960); Alaska v. Arctic Maid, 366 U.S. 199 (1961); State Tax Comm'n of Utah v. Pacific States Pipe Co., 372 U.S. 605 (1963); General Motors Corp. v. Washington, 377 U.S. 436 (1964).
60. Castle v. Hayes Freight Lines, Inc., 348 U.S. 61 (1954); Moore v. Mead's Fine Bread Co., 348 U.S. 115 (1954); Natural Gas Pipeline Co. v. Panoma Corp., 349 U.S. 44 (1955); City of Chicago v. Atchison, T. & S. F. Ry., 357 U.S. 77 (1958); Bibb v. Navajo Freight Lines, Inc., 359 U.S. 520 (1959); Polar Co. v. Andrews, 375 U.S. 361 (1964).
61. Collins v. American Buslines, Inc., 350 U.S. 528 (1956); Huron Cement Co. v. City of Detroit, 362 U.S. 440 (1960); Eli Lilly & Co. v. Sav-on-Drugs, Inc., 366 U.S. 276 (1961); Colorado Anti-

other than that different Justices reach different conclusions at different times about how much is too much. On the other hand, the cases dealing with the affirmative aspects of the Commerce Clause, that which authorizes the exertion of national power, were all answered in the affirmative.[62] There can be no difficulty in discovering a doctrine here.

The old judicial tool for restraining states, the Contract Clause, was also called upon in some cases before the Warren Court; but it was too ancient and enfeebled to have any bite.[63] And, shades of *McCulloch v. Maryland,*[64] the Court was repeatedly asked both: (1) whether a federal instrumentality was immune from a state tax[65] or regulation[66] and

---

Discrimination Comm'n v. Continental Air Lines, Inc., 372 U.S. 714 (1963); Head v. New Mexico Bd. of Examiners, 374 U.S. 424 (1963).

62. Maneja v. Waialua Agricultural Co., 349 U.S. 254 (1955); United States v. Green, 350 U.S. 415 (1956); Railway Employes' Dep't v. Hanson, 351 U.S. 225 (1956); California v. Taylor, 353 U.S. 553 (1957); Katzenbach v. McClung, 379 U.S. 294 (1964); Maryland v. Wirtz, 392 U.S. 183 (1968).

63. See Watson v. Employers Liability Assurance Corp., 348 U.S. 66 (1964); McGee v. International Life Ins. Co., 355 U.S. 220 (1957); El Paso v. Simmons, 379 U.S. 497 (1965); and see WRIGHT, THE CONTRACT CLAUSE OF THE CONSTITUTION (1938); Hale, *The Supreme Court and the Contract Clause,* 57 HARV. L. REV. 512, 621, 852 (1944) (3 parts).

64. 4 Wheat. 316 (1819).

65. Kern-Limerick, Inc. v. Scurlock, 347 U.S. 110 (1954); Society for Savings v. Bowers, 349 U.S. 143 (1955); Werner Machine Co. v. Director of Taxation, 350 U.S. 492 (1956); Offutt Housing Co. v. County of Sarpy, 351 U.S. 253 (1956); United States v. City of Detroit, 355 U.S. 466 (1958); United States v. Muskegon, 355 U.S. 484 (1958); City of Detroit v. Murray Corp., 355 U.S. 489 (1958); Phillips Chemical Co. v. Dumas School Dist., 361 U.S. 376 (1960); Federal Land Bank v. Bd. of County Comm'rs, 368 U.S. 146 (1961); Humble Pipe Line Co. v. Waggonner, 376 U.S. 369 (1964).

66. Franklin Nat. Bank v. New York, 347 U.S. 373 (1954); Leslie Miller, Inc. v. Arkansas, 352 U.S. 187 (1956); Public Utilities Comm'n of California v. United States, 355 U.S. 534 (1958); United States v. Georgia Public Serv. Comm'n, 371 U.S. 285 (1963); Paul v. United States, 371 U.S. 245 (1963); Florida Lime & Avocado Growers, Inc. v. Paul, 373 U.S. 132 (1963); Sperry v. Florida Bar, 373 U.S. 379 (1963).

(2) what a federal instrumentality was for purposes of this immunity. As with Marshall, the Court concluded, with few exceptions, that the states were precluded from exercising their authority except with congressional approval.

The Supremacy Clause also presented more contemporary problems concerning which the Court purported to rest on expressions of congressional policy rather than judgments purely of its own making. Using 18 U.S.C. § 3486, the Court prevented introduction at a state trial of evidence adduced at a congressional hearing.[67] It was the Supremacy Clause, said the Court, that obligated the states to comply with school desegregation orders.[68] For to some, the Civil War had not adequately settled the unreliability of the doctrine of interposition.

Some state laws to protect against subversion were void as preempted because federal laws occupied the field.[69] Others, however, were valid.[70] Federal tobacco inspection laws occupied the field to the exclusion of state laws.[71] Treasury regulations were held supreme over state succession laws where United States government bonds were concerned.[72] But the Bankruptcy Act could not discharge a debtor from his obligations under a state motor vehicle safety law.[73] In what yet may prove to be an important decision, state regulation of professional advertising on radio was held not to be precluded by the Federal Communications Act.[74] Perhaps the most strained but not unexpected application of the Supremacy Clause held that the Civil Rights Act of 1964 abated all pending sit-in convictions.[75] The Twenty-first Amendment

67. Adams v. Maryland, 347 U.S. 179 (1954).
68. Cooper v. Aaron, 358 U.S. 1 (1958); Bush v. Orleans Parish School Bd., 364 U.S. 500 (1960).
69. Pennsylvania v. Nelson, 350 U.S. 497 (1956).
70. Uphaus v. Wyman, 360 U.S. 72 (1959).
71. Campbell v. Hussey, 368 U.S. 297 (1961).
72. Free v. Bland, 369 U.S. 663 (1962).
73. Kesler v. Department of Public Safety, 369 U.S. 153 (1962).
74. Head v. New Mexico Bd. of Examiners, 374 U.S. 424 (1963).
75. Hamm v. City of Rock Hill, 379 U.S. 306 (1964).

helped to protect a state's demand for information about liquor prices against a claim that the conduct was prohibited by the Sherman and Robinson-Patman Acts.[76] But the amorphous foreign affairs power, still undiscovered in any particular place in the Constitution, prevented enforcement of a state law providing for escheat of personal property claimed by a nonresident alien whose country did not afford reciprocal rights to American citizens.[77] None of these decisions was countermanded by Congress.

All these cases reveal that the form and language of federalism are still used; that the old issues are still raised; and that the Court functions in its classic fashion, generally ruling against local interests. But these cases were not the center of attention of either the Court or its critics. They do suggest, however, what we should always keep in mind, that the Court's business—even its constitutional business, no less its statutory and administrative agency problems—far exceeds the number of cases that engage the attention of the Congress, the press, the public, and even the law reviews.

The more notorious cases must be considered against one aspect of federalism that has remained comparatively and surprisingly untouched. The retreat from *Erie* may forebode a change here, too, but it has not yet occurred. When dealing with decisions from national courts and cases concerning national legislation, the Court is equipped with three devices for disposing of the issues raised. One device is that of judicial review empowering it to declare unconstitutional the legislative, executive, administrative, or judicial actions under attack. The second is to assert its role as overseer of the administration of justice in the federal courts, which permits it to declare certain government conduct invalid without declaring it unconstitutional.[78] The third device is that of

76. Joseph E. Seagram & Sons v. Hostetter, 384 U.S. 35 (1966).

77. Zschernig v. Miller, 389 U.S. 429 (1968).

78. See McNabb v. United States, 318 U.S. 322 (1943); Mallory v. United States, 354 U.S. 449 (1957).

interpretation of statutes and rules so as to avoid constitutional questions by not effectuating the legislative or executive intent. As John C. Gray once put it:

> It has been sometimes said that the Law is composed of two parts—legislative law and judge-made law, but in truth all the Law is judge-made law. The shape in which a statute is imposed on the community as a guide for conduct is that statute as interpreted by the courts.[79]

In dealing with state courts and state statutes, however, the Supreme Court is restricted to an all-or-nothing policy.[80] Only the device of judicial review is available to it. The top of the state judicial system for purposes of its administration of justice is the state high court not the Supreme Court. So, too, is the highest court of the state the ultimate arbiter of the meaning of state legislation. The state action when brought for judgment before the Supreme Court must be pronounced valid or invalid. There is no happy medium. The time may come when the supremacy of national judicial power will be used to assert the same authority over the state courts and state legislation that is now claimed over national courts and national legislation. That time has not yet arrived.

Let me offer a hurried survey of the Court's efforts in what I have suggested as its three headline concerns. I shall not stop to examine the cases on the merits. That is for another time, another place, and—with good luck—another person. I propose to state only the obvious, in reliance on Holmes's dictum "that at this time we need education in the obvious more than investigation of the obscure."[81]

I must start, of course, where the Court started, with its most important decision, *Brown v. Board of Education.*[82]

79. GRAY, THE NATURE AND SOURCES OF THE LAW 125 (Beacon Press ed. 1960).
80. See, *e.g.,* Bell v. Maryland, 378 U.S. 226 (1964); Bouie v. City of Columbia, 378 U.S. 347 (1964); Ashton v. Kentucky, 384 U.S. 195 (1966).
81. HOLMES, COLLECTED LEGAL PAPERS 292–93 (1920).
82. 347 U.S. 483 (1954).

Not only did that decision set the tone for the entire judicial era, it was the symbol of change for the entire country in the resolution of the deepest and most provocative social problem that the country has ever faced. After *Brown,* the Court devoted a major portion of its efforts to the direct and indirect[83] removal of the restraints that states had imposed on Negroes' freedom and equality. No case troubled the Court more or caused the Court more trouble than those concerned with the Negro revolution. But the Court marched inexorably toward its proclaimed goal, without, of course, reaching it.

The *Brown* decision was followed by the famous decree for school desegregation "with all deliberate speed."[84] From then on the law was put to its severest test, a test that it has not yet passed. Delay in desegregation was forbidden[85] but was inevitable. All evasive devices were struck down.[86] But, as of today, school desegregation is still essentially a matter for the future.

Racial desegregation in higher education was, again,[87] banned.[88] The inhibition on discriminatory selection of juries

83. See KALVEN, THE NEGRO AND THE FIRST AMENDMENT (Phoenix ed. 1967). And see chapter 4, *infra.*

84. Brown v. Bd. of Educ., 349 U.S. 294, 301 (1955).

85. Cooper v. Aaron, 358 U.S. 1 (1958); Bush v. Orleans Parish School Bd., 364 U.S. 500 (1960).

86. Orleans Parish School Bd. v. Bush, 365 U.S. 569 (1961); St. Helena Parish School Bd. v. Hall, 368 U.S. 515 (1962); Goss v. Bd. of Educ., 373 U.S. 683 (1963); Griffin v. County School Bd., 377 U.S. 218 (1964); Louisiana Financial Assistance Comm'n v. Poindexter, 389 U.S. 571 (1968); Green v. County School Bd., 391 U.S. 430 (1968); Raney v. Bd. of Educ., 391 U.S. 443 (1968); Monroe v. Bd. of Comm'rs, 391 U.S. 450 (1968).

87. See McLaurin v. Oklahoma State Regents, 339 U.S. 637 (1950); Sweatt v. Painter, 339 U.S. 627 (1950); Sipuel v. Bd. of Regents, 332 U.S. 631 (1948); Missouri *ex rel.* Gaines v. Canada, 305 U.S. 337 (1938).

88. Lucy v. Adams, 350 U.S. 1 (1955); Florida *ex rel.* Hawkins v. Bd. of Control, 350 U.S. 413 (1956); *cf.* Pennsylvania v. Bd. of Directors of City Trusts, 353 U.S. 230 (1957).

was tightened.[89] After a false start,[90] the Court condemned a state law that discriminated in punishment for illegal cohabitation,[91] and then boldly invalidated a state miscegenation law.[92]

The ban on discrimination was quickly extended to all public facilities.[93] States were forbidden to compel public disclosure of membership lists of organizations engaged in behalf of the civil rights movement or to inhibit their capacities to carry the issues to the courts.[94] The problem of private and business discrimination was never adequately resolved by the Warren Court. Its desires were clear, but it was reluctant to impose the obligations of nondiscrimination on private persons engaged in private affairs. It moved slowly toward making public what had been private,[95] waiting for the legislature to provide the means for this accomplishment.[96] In the meantime, it used every excuse, real and

89. Reece v. Georgia, 350 U.S. 85 (1955); Whitus v. Georgia, 385 U.S. 545 (1967); Jones v. Georgia, 389 U.S. 24 (1967); Sims v. Georgia, 389 U.S. 404 (1967); Coleman v. Alabama, 389 U.S. 22 (1967); but cf. Swain v. Alabama, 380 U.S. 202 (1965).
90. Naim v. Naim, 350 U.S. 891 (1955).
91. McLaughlin v. Florida, 379 U.S. 184 (1964).
92. Loving v. Virginia, 388 U.S. 1 (1967).
93. Wright v. Georgia, 373 U.S. 284 (1963); Johnson v. Virginia, 373 U.S. 61 (1963); Watson v. City of Memphis, 373 U.S. 526 (1963); Lee v. Washington, 390 U.S. 333 (1968); Muir v. Louisville Park Theatrical Ass'n, 347 U.S. 971 (1954); Schiro v. Bynum, 375 U.S. 395 (1964); Mayor and City Council of Baltimore City v. Dawson, 350 U.S. 877 (1955); Holmes v. City of Atlanta, 350 U.S. 879 (1955); New Orleans Park Ass'n v. Detiege, 358 U.S. 54 (1958); State Athletic Comm'n v. Dorsey, 359 U.S. 533 (1959); Gayle v. Browder, 352 U.S. 903 (1956).
94. Bates v. City of Little Rock, 361 U.S. 516 (1960); N.A.A.C.P. v. Button, 371 US. 415 (1963); Gibson v. Florida Legislative Comm., 372 U.S. 539 (1963).
95. Burton v. Wilmington Parking Authority, 365 U.S. 715 (1961); Turner v. City of Memphis, 369 U.S. 350 (1962); Evans v. Newton, 382 U.S. 296 (1966).
96. Heart of Atlanta Motel v. United States, 379 U.S. 241 (1964); Katzenbach v. McClung, 379 U.S. 294 (1964); Hamm v. City of Rock Hill, 379 U.S. 306 (1964).

fancied, to upset convictions of protesters,[97] searching for a formula to remove the requirement of "state action" from the first section of the Fourteenth Amendment.[98] In one case, the Court in fact dispensed with that requirement in a particularly poorly reasoned opinion upsetting California's infamous "Proposition Fourteen."[99] Professors Karst and Horowitz excused the absence of reason,[100] while Professor Black offered a rationale different from and more persuasive than the Court's opinion.[101]

Every possible support was provided the executive in its attempted enforcement of the Civil Rights Acts[102] recently enacted in belated recognition by Congress of the propriety of the Court's goals. Nor did the Court snub the opportunity

97. Taylor v. Louisiana, 370 U.S. 154 (1962); Edwards v. South Carolina, 372 U.S. 229 (1963); Peterson v. City of Greenville, 373 U.S. 244 (1963); Lombard v. Louisiana, 373 U.S. 267 (1963); Gober v. City of Birmingham, 373 U.S. 374 (1963); Avent v. North Carolina, 373 U.S. 375 (1963); Shuttlesworth v. City of Birmingham, 373 U.S. 262 (1963); Bouie v. City of Columbia, 378 U.S. 347 (1964); Barr v. City of Columbia, 378 U.S. 146 (1964); Griffin v. Maryland, 378 U.S. 130 (1964); Robinson v. Florida, 378 U.S. 153 (1964); Bell v. Maryland, 378 U.S. 226 (1964); Cox v. Louisiana, 379 U.S. 536 (1965); Cox v. Louisiana, 379 U.S. 559 (1965); Brown v. Louisiana, 383 U.S. 131 (1966).

98. See Lewis, *The Sit-In Cases: Great Expectations,* 1963 SUPREME COURT REVIEW 101; Paulsen, *The Sit-In Cases of 1964: "But Answer Came There None,"* 1964 SUPREME COURT REVIEW 137; Heyman, *Civil Rights 1964 Term: Responses to Direct Action,* 1965 SUPREME COURT REVIEW 159; Kalven, *The Concept of the Public Forum: Cox v. Louisiana,* 1965 SUPREME COURT REVIEW 1; see notes 99 and 100 *infra.*

99. Reitman v. Mulkey, 387 U.S. 369 (1967); see also Hunter v. Erickson, 393 U.S. 385 (1969).

100. Karst & Horowitz, *Reitman v. Mulkey: A Telophase of Substantive Equal Protection,* 1967 SUPREME COURT REVIEW 39.

101. Black, *"State Action," Equal Protection, and California's Proposition 14,* 81 HARV. L. REV. 69 (1967).

102. United States v. Raines, 362 U.S. 17 (1960); United States v. Thomas, 362 U.S. 58 (1960); South Carolina v. Katzenbach, 383 U.S. 301 (1966); Katzenbach v. Morgan, 384 U.S. 641 (1966).

to use old civil rights statutes when they were put in motion by the government[103] or private parties.[104]

Never in the Court's history—not in Marshall's day or any other—did the Court establish its objectives and march so steadfastly toward them as did the Warren Court in its civil rights litigation. The depth of both the hatred and the admiration for the Warren Court may be largely explained by this fact.

Unlike the instances of the Warren Court's contributions to the Negro revolution and its attempts at restructuring state legislatures, the reformation of state criminal procedures has no sharp starting place. In part this is due to the fact that it inherited this movement from predecessor courts. Its remote origins are to be found somewhere in the Hughes Court period.[105] Indeed, by 1956, a perspicacious young Harvard law professor suggested that the time had come to end the Court's role as formulator of state rules of criminal practice. He proved more prescient about public reaction than about judicial behavior when he wrote:

> The recent history of the Supreme Court presents no more striking development than the dramatic expansion of federal judicial supervision over state systems of criminal law administration. . . .
>
> . . . The fundamental solution to the problem of police illegality does not lie in the indefinite expansion of rules of exclusion by the Supreme Court. We may be approaching the point where further significant broadening of the constitutional rules of exclusion by the Court will breed an attitude of resistance injurious to the development of constructive local response to these

103. United States v. Guest, 383 U.S. 745 (1966); United States v. Price, 383 U.S. 787 (1966).

104. Jones v. Alfred H. Mayer Co., 392 U.S 409 (1968); see Casper, *Jones v. Mayer: Clio, Bemused and Confused Muse,* 1968 SUPREME COURT REVIEW 89.

105. See Schaefer, *Federalism and State Criminal Procedure,* 70 HARV. L. REV. 1 (1956).

problems. This is not to deny a significant role to the Court in the stimulation of responsible local action. The Court has done much in the last two decades to engage the conscience and intelligent concern of the public in problems raised by the abuse of power which undoubtedly characterizes much American law-enforcement activity. It is clear that in many particular situations the Court has led the way to sensible local legislative action by identifying and dramatizing problems in the administration of criminal justice, problems which tend to become obscured and submerged in the welter of public issues confronting any modern legislature. The liberalizing of state rules relating to the appointment of counsel, and the modernizing of state procedures for the assertion of constitutional claims are conspicuous examples. But the Court's role, even if indispensable, is necessarily a limited one. Surely the time has come for a concentrated attack on the problems of criminal law primarily as problems of legislation and administration—and of public morality.[106]

The hostile popular reaction was to come, but not the legislative and administrative considerations, nor those of public morality.

The Court had been in the business of reviewing state criminal procedures for fairness on a retail level. It continued to do so through the early years of the Warren Court. The watershed case was probably *Mapp v. Ohio,*[107] decided in

106. Allen, *Book Review,* 69 HARV. L. REV. 1167, at 1167–69 (1956).

107. 367 U.S. 643 (1961). For the application of the *Mapp* rule by the Warren Court see: Ker v. California, 374 U.S. 23 (1963); Fahy v. Connecticut, 375 U.S. 85 (1963); Stoner v. California, 376 U.S. 483 (1964); Aguilar v. Texas, 378 U.S. 108 (1964); Stanford v. Texas, 379 U.S. 476 (1965); One 1958 Plymouth Sedan v. Pennsylvania, 380 U.S. 693 (1965); James v. Louisiana, 382 U.S. 36 (1965); Schmerber v. California, 384 U.S. 757 (1966); Cooper v. California, 386 U.S. 58 (1967); Warden v. Hayden, 387 U.S. 294 (1967); Berger v. New York, 388 U.S. 41 (1967); Bumper v. North Carolina, 391 U.S. 543 (1968); Dyke v. Taylor Implement Co., 391

1961. It was not until *Mapp* that the Court started some wholesale revisions of the rules governing state criminal procedure. And even so, both before and after *Mapp,* the case tradition substantially prevailed. But it must be conceded that after *Mapp* the controls were considerably tighter.

Throughout the Warren Court period, the question whether a confession was voluntary and admissible was largely one to be resolved in the context of the particular case.[108] So, too, until 1963, was the resolution of the issue of the obligation of the state to provide counsel for indigent defendants dependent on the circumstances of the case.[109] Before *Mapp,*

U.S. 216 (1968); Lee Art Theatre, Inc. v. Virginia, 392 U.S. 636 (1968); Mancusi v. DeForte, 392 U.S. 364 (1968); Recznik v. City of Lorain, 393 U.S. 166 (1968); Davis v. Mississippi, 394 U.S. 721 (1969).

The *Mapp* doctrine was held not to be retrospective in application. See Linkletter v. Walker, 381 U.S. 618 (1965); Angelet v. Fay, 381 U.S. 654 (1965). Lee v. Florida, 392 U.S. 378 (1968), excluding evidence obtained in violation of § 605 of the Federal Communications Act, was also held to be only prospective in its application. Kaiser v. New York, 394 U.S. 280 (1969).

108. See Leyra v. Denno, 347 U.S. 556 (1954); Fikes v. Alabama, 352 U.S. 191 (1957); Payne v. Arkansas, 356 U.S. 560 (1958); Ashdown v. Utah, 357 U.S. 426 (1958); Cicenia v. Lagay, 357 U.S. 504 (1958); Spano v. New York, 360 U.S. 315 (1959); Blackburn v. Alabama, 361 U.S. 199 (1960); Rogers v. Richmond, 365 U.S. 534 (1961); Culombe v. Connecticut, 367 U.S. 568 (1961); Reck v. Pate, 367 U.S. 433 (1961); Gallegos v. Colorado, 370 U.S. 49 (1962); Townsend v. Sain, 372 U.S. 293 (1963); Lynum v. Illinois, 372 U.S. 528 (1963); Jackson v. Denno, 378 U.S. 368 (1964); Davis v. North Carolina, 384 U.S. 737 (1966); Sims v. Georgia, 385 U.S. 538 (1967); Beecher v. Alabama, 389 U.S. 35 (1967); Pinto v. Pierce, 389 U.S. 31 (1967); Darwin v. Connecticut, 391 U.S. 346 (1968).

109. See Chandler v. Warden Fretag, 348 U.S. 3 (1954); Massey v. Moore, 348 U.S. 105 (1954); Reece v. Georgia, 350 U.S. 85 (1955); Moore v. Michigan, 355 U.S 155 (1957); Crooker v. California, 357 U.S. 433 (1958); Cash v. Culver, 358 U.S. 633 (1959); Hudson v. North Carolina, 363 U.S. 697 (1960); McNeal v. Culver, 365 U.S. 109 (1961); Ferguson v. Georgia, 365 U.S. 570 (1961); Hamilton v. Alabama, 368 U.S. 52 (1961); Chewning v. Cunningham, 368 U.S. 443 (1962); Carney v. Cochran, 369 U.S. 506 (1962).

the Warren Court had itself refused to apply the exclusionary rule to the use of illegally obtained evidence in state criminal prosecutions.[110] Until 1964 state immunity statutes were protected against claims of the privilege against self-crimination,[111] except when they were used to entrap the defendant.[112] The Court remained unreceptive to claims of double jeopardy until its very last Term when it incorporated the federal ban into the Fourteenth Amendment.[113] Loose procedures to determine the sanity of convicted felons were condoned.[114] But the right to a hearing on the issue was protected.[115]

The use of evidence of prior crimes was held not to be precluded by constitutional standards,[116] except where the prior conviction was itself tainted with unconstitutionality.[117] At first, searches and seizures without warrants by state building and health inspectors were held not improper under the Constitution,[118] but the Court reversed itself in 1967.[119] No right to counsel was found to exist for persons summoned to appear before an investigatory body analogous to a grand jury.[120]

There was one major breakthrough by the Warren Court

110. Irvine v. California, 347 U.S. 128 (1954).

111. See Regan v. New York, 349 U.S. 58 (1955); Knapp v. Schweitzer, 357 U.S. 371 (1958).

112. See Raley v. Ohio, 360 U.S. 423 (1959).

113. See Benton v. Maryland, 395 U.S. 784 (1969); *cf.* Ciucci v. Illinois, 356 U.S. 571 (1958); Hoag v. New Jersey, 356 U.S. 464 (1958); Bartkus v. Illinois, 359 U.S. 121 (1959); Cichos v. Indiana, 385 U.S. 76 (1966).

114. Caritativo v. California, 357 U.S. 549 (1958).

115. Pate v. Robinson, 383 U.S. 375 (1966); Baxstrom v. Herold, 383 U.S. 107 (1966); Westbrook v. Arizona, 384 U.S. 150 (1966).

116. Williams v. Oklahoma, 358 U.S. 576 (1959); Spencer v. Texas, 385 U.S. 554 (1967).

117. Burgett v. Texas, 389 U.S. 109 (1967).

118. Frank v. Maryland, 359 U.S. 360 (1959); and see Ohio *ex rel.* Eaton v. Price, 364 U.S. 263 (1960).

119. Camara v. Municipal Court, 387 U.S. 523 (1967); See v. City of Seattle, 387 U.S. 541 (1967).

120. Anonymous v. Baker, 360 U.S. 287 (1959).

before *Mapp* and that was its decision in *Griffin v. Illinois*[121] that the appellate processes cannot be denied a convicted defendant because he lacks the funds to purchase the necessary copies of trial records for perfecting review. The *Griffin* case was somewhat outside the general category of Supreme Court decisions concerned with state criminal procedure because it purported to rest on the Equal Protection Clause rather than the Due Process Clause.

Although it was hard to satisfy the early Warren Court that a general atmosphere of persecution precluded a fair trial,[122] and although state procedures had to be followed,[123] the states were required to provide meaningful post-conviction remedies,[124] and federal habeas corpus was available where a state had proved deficient.[125] Moreover, the Court revived the concept of substantive due process in measuring criminal statutes.[126] And it went so far as to examine a record to determine the sufficiency of the evidence to support a conviction on a minor charge.[127]

Of course, the knowing use of perjured testimony or false evidence by a state prosecutor called for reversal of a judg-

121. 351 U.S. 12 (1956). The extension of the doctrine is revealed in Eskridge v. Washington Prison Bd., 357 U.S. 214 (1958); Burns v. Ohio, 360 U.S. 252 (1959); Douglas v. Green, 363 U.S. 192 (1960); McCrary v. Indiana, 364 U.S. 277 (1960); Smith v. Bennett, 365 U.S. 709 (1961); Lane v. Brown, 372 U.S. 477 (1963); Draper v. Washington, 372 U.S. 487 (1963); Long v. District Court of Iowa, 385 U.S. 192 (1966); Gardner v. California, 393 U.S. 367 (1969); Williams v. Oklahoma City, 395 U.S. 458 (1969); *cf.* Chessman v. Teets, 354 U.S. 156 (1957).

122. United States *ex rel.* Darcy v. Handy, 351 U.S. 454 (1956).

123. Michel v. Louisiana, 350 U.S. 91 (1955).

124. Alcorta v. Texas, 355 U.S. 28 (1957); Wilde v. Wyoming, 362 U.S. 607 (1960); Sutlett v. Adams, 362 U.S. 143 (1960).

125. *E.g.,* Chessman v. Teets, 350 U.S. 3 (1955); *but see* Thomas v. Arizona, 356 U.S. 390 (1958).

126. Lambert v. California, 355 U.S. 225 (1957); Robinson v. California, 370 U.S. 660 (1962).

127. Thompson v. City of Louisville, 362 U.S. 199 (1960).

ment of conviction.[128] Indeed, the Court said that the prosecutor has a duty to make available information that would be favorable to the defense.[129] And the right to protection from adverse publicity and other improper influences on the jury was established by the Warren Court.[130]

Mapp v. Ohio, however, was of a different dimension from the cases that preceded it. As one contemporary commentator put it: "The *Mapp* case represents the Supreme Court's most ambitious effort to affect and determine the quality of state criminal justice. . . . *Mapp* intrudes farther into areas of local policy and self-determination than earlier decisions of the Court affecting state criminal procedure."[131] *Mapp* also overruled *Wolf v. Colorado,*[132] which had reflected the attitude of the Supreme Court ever since the exclusionary rule was attached to the Fourth Amendment.[133] In reversing long-established precedents, *Mapp* presaged the methods that the Court was to adopt without qualms in the years to come.

After *Mapp,* the Court's intoxication with its own power was not diminished. Like Caesar, the Court was ambitious. Like Caesar, its ambitions have been only partially requited. Unlike Caesar, the Court has not yet been assassinated. But there are some senators with a lean and hungry look.

In 1963 came *Gideon v. Wainwright,*[134] the result of at-

128. Alcorta v. Texas, 355 U.S. 28 (1957); Napue v. Illinois, 360 U.S. 264 (1959); Miller v. Pate, 386 U.S. 1 (1967).

129. Giles v. Maryland, 386 U.S. 66 (1967); *cf.* Brady v. Maryland, 373 U.S. 83 (1963).

130. Irvin v. Dowd, 366 U.S. 717 (1961); Wood v. Georgia, 370 U.S. 375 (1962); Rideau v. Louisiana, 373 U.S. 723 (1963); Turner v. Louisiana, 379 U.S. 466 (1965); Estes v. Texas, 381 U.S. 532 (1965); Sheppard v. Maxwell, 384 U.S. 333 (1966); Parker v. Gladden, 385 U.S. 363 (1966).

131. Allen, *Federalism and the Fourth Amendment: A Requiem for Wolf,* 1961 SUPREME COURT REVIEW 1, 47.

132. 338 U.S. 25 (1949).

133. See Allen, *The Wolf Case: Search and Seizure, Federalism and Civil Liberties,* 45 ILL. L. REV. 1, 11–13 (1950).

134. 372 U.S. 335 (1963).

torney Abe Fortas's successful efforts to convince the Court to do what it wanted to do. From there on it was obligatory for the states to supply counsel for the trial of all felony cases. And *Douglas v. California*[135] expanded the rule to cover appeals. It has since been extended to cover pre-trial[136] and post-trial proceedings.[137] (Perhaps it should be noted that the presence of counsel is not an unmixed blessing. It could turn a reversible error into a harmless one.)[138]

In 1964, the Court decided *Escobedo v. Illinois,*[139] requiring that a warning of the right to silence and the opportunity to consult counsel had to be given to any person on whom suspicion and investigation focused. The Fifth Amendment self-crimination privilege was also extended in its full glory during that Term to state proceedings in *Malloy v. Hogan.*[140] And immunity provisions were ruled invalid unless they conferred protection against criminal sanctions by all governments within the federal union.[141]

In 1965, the Supreme Court held that the Sixth Amendment right to confront witnesses was obligatory on the states.[142] It also decided that the failure of the defendant to

135. 372 U.S. 353 (1963). See Swenson v. Bosler, 386 U.S. 258 (1967); Anders v. California, 386 U.S. 738 (1967).
136. White v. Maryland, 373 U.S. 59 (1963).
137. Mempa v. Ray, 389 U.S. 128 (1967).
138. See, *e.g.,* Norvell v. Illinois, 373 U.S. 420 (1963).
139. 378 U.S. 478 (1964). *Escobedo* was not to be applied retroactively. Johnson v. New Jersey, 384 U.S. 719 (1966).
140. 378 U.S. 1 (1964). See Spevack v. Klein, 385 U.S. 511 (1967); Garrity v. New Jersey, 385 U.S. 493 (1967); Gardner v. Broderick, 392 U.S. 273 (1968); Uniformed Sanitation Men v. Comm'r of Sanitation, 392 U.S. 280 (1968); Campbell Painting Corp. v. Reid, 392 U.S. 286 (1968).
141. Murphy v. Waterfront Comm'n, 378 U.S. 52 (1964).
142. Pointer v. Texas, 380 U.S. 400 (1965); Douglas v. Alabama, 380 U.S. 415 (1965); Brookhart v. Janis, 384 U.S. 1 (1966); Specht v. Patterson, 386 U.S. 605 (1967); Smith v. Illinois, 390 U.S. 129 (1968); Barber v. Page, 390 U.S. 719 (1968).
This rule in Gilbert v. California, 388 U.S. 263 (1967), concerned with identification of witnesses was held retroactive. Stovall v. Denno, 388 U.S. 293 (1967). But the right established in *Barber,* to confront

take the stand may not be the subject of comment to the jury by either judge or prosecutor.[143] Thus the Court raised a federal practice resting only on statute to the level of a constitutional command to the states. The Sixth Amendment right to a speedy trial was later added to the protections afforded defendants in state criminal proceedings.[144] So, too, was the right to compel the attendance of witnesses.[145]

In 1966, the Court foreshadowed the removal of state juvenile proceedings to a place under the ever enlarging Fourteenth Amendment umbrella.[146] But not until the following year did the Court actually require the state to give a juvenile at least some of the same protections that the Fourteenth Amendment made available to adults charged with crimes.[147] It was in 1966, also, that the decision in *Miranda v. Arizona*[148] came down. I, for one, thought it a highly overrated opinion, by those who approved it no less than by those who condemned it. It held that a fourfold benediction must be said by a police officer over every person taken into custody. The policeman's target must be told that he has the right to remain silent; that if he says anything it may be used against him; that he has a right to con-

---

witness who had given testimony at a preliminary hearing to be used at trial, is to be retroactively applied. Berger v. California, 393 U.S. 314 (1969). Despite *Stovall,* however, there are some lineup procedures so inherently faulty as to require reversal even in cases occurring before *Gilbert.* Foster v. California, 394 U.S. 440 (1969).

143. Griffin v. California, 380 U.S. 609 (1965); Fontaine v. California, 390 U.S. 593 (1968). The *Griffin* rule was only prospective in operation. Tehan v. United States *ex rel.* Shott, 382 U.S. 406 (1966).

144. Klopfer v. North Carolina, 386 U.S. 213 (1967); Smith v. Hovey, 393 U.S. 374 (1969).

145. Washington v. Texas, 388 U.S. 14 (1967).

146. Kent v. United States, 383 U.S. 541 (1966).

147. *In re* Gault, 387 U.S. 1 (1967).

148. 384 U.S. 436 (1966). See Orozco v. Texas, 394 U.S. 324 (1969); Frazer v. Cupp, 394 U.S. 731 (1969).

Miranda was not to be applied retroactively. Johnson v. New Jersey, 384 U.S. 719 (1966).

sult a lawyer and have the lawyer with him while he is being interrogated; and that the state will supply a lawyer if the suspect is indigent. But it was not the substance of the statements so much as the time when they must be made that caused the furor.

The year 1967 was a quiet one on the criminal procedure front. The extension of the Sixth Amendment's right to jury trial in all cases except those concerned with "petty offenses" came in 1968.[149] But the same Term saw, what seemed to many a sacrilege, the Court's validation of police "stop-and-frisk" procedures.[150] Whether this is an omen of things to come, especially with the Warren Court converted into a Nixon Court, remains to be seen.

The final blow of importance struck by the Warren Court toward the centralization of authority over criminal procedure came in 1969 with the ruling that condemned the manner in which a state court accepted a plea of guilty.[151] Although that decision may do no more than impose an obligation on state courts to meet the requirements of the Federal Rules of Criminal Procedure in this area, it must be recognized that any severe restraints on the capacity of the courts to accept guilty pleas could result in the destruction of the entire system of criminal justice. The need to try any major fraction of the cases that are now disposed of by such pleas will put such a burden on the existing judicial machinery as to cause its breakdown. One development that was insidious rather than acute in the Warren period was the growing restriction on the allowable procedures for crimi-

149. Duncan v. Louisiana, 391 U.S. 145 (1968); Bloom v. Illinois, 391 U.S. 194 (1968); Dyke v. Taylor Implement Co., 391 U.S. 216 (1968); Witherspoon v. Illinois, 391 U.S. 510 (1968); Boulden v. Holman, 394 U.S. 478 (1969).

The right to jury trial as declared in *Duncan* was to be applied prospectively only. DeStefano v. Woods, 392 U.S. 621 (1968).

150. Terry v. Ohio, 392 U.S. 1 (1968); Sibron v. New York, 392 U.S. 40 (1968).

151. Boykin v. Alabama, 395 U.S. 238 (1969).

nal contempt,[152] a bugaboo of an earlier generation that resented government by the judiciary.[153]

In one sense, the furor that the Court has aroused over the criminal cases is difficult to comprehend. After all, the only thing that the Warren Court has done is to demand that the state criminal processes come up to the same standards that are being imposed on federal criminal processes. But then, that is what federalism is all about.

The outcry on behalf of federalism, however, seems to hide more than it reveals. Here, no more than in the case of desegregation or reapportionment, do the more rabid critics deplore the fact that the rules were made by the national government as much as they do the rules themselves. For the most part, the public and the press never knew that the Bill of Rights was not always applicable to the conduct of state government as well as national. The problem is that, in the minds of many, the Court is "coddling criminals." The fact that the rise in the crime rate is coincidental with the Court's development of higher standards of criminal procedure is read to suggest that the one is the cause of the other. This is not true of all critics of the Court, as the ably expressed doubts of some of the Warren Court's efforts by such outstanding jurists as Chief Justice Traynor, Mr. Justice Schaefer, and Judge Friendly attest.[154] But we are unfortunately caught up with the notion of a "war on crime." The metaphor is dangerous. For, as Mr. Justice Frankfurter

152. *In re* Green, 369 U.S. 689 (1962); Ungar v. Sarafite, 376 U.S. 575 (1964); United States v. Barnett, 376 U.S. 681 (1964); Holt v. Virginia, 381 U.S. 131 (1965); Bloom v. Illinois, 391 U.S. 194 (1968); Dyke v. Taylor Implement Co., 391 U.S. 216 (1968).

153. See Frankfurter & Landis, *Power of Congress over Procedure in Criminal Contempts in "Inferior" Federal Courts—a Study in Separation of Powers,* 37 HARV. L. REV. 1010 (1924).

154. See FRIENDLY, note 42 *supra,* at chs. 11 & 12; SCHAEFER, THE SUSPECT AND SOCIETY (1967); Traynor, *The Devils of Due Process in Criminal Detection, Detention, and Trial,* 33 U. CHI. L. REV. 657 (1966).

pointed out in his dissenting opinion in *On Lee v. United States*,[155] written even before Warren's trip to the 1952 Republican presidential convention:

> Loose talk about war against crime too easily infuses the administration of justice with the psychology and morals of war. It is hardly conducive to the soundest employment of the judicial process. Nor are the needs of an effective penal code seen in the truest perspective by talk about a criminal prosecution's not being a game in which the Government loses because its officers have not played according to rule. Of course criminal prosecution is more than a game. But in any event it should not be deemed a dirty game in which "the dirty business" of criminals is outwitted by "the dirty business" of law officers. The contrast between morality professed by society and immorality practiced on its behalf makes for contempt of law. Respect for law cannot be turned off and on as though it were a hot-water faucet.[156]

The problems of anti-Negro discrimination and the crudities of criminal procedure in the states were deep and dangerous cancers in our body politic. They called for drastic action. By comparison, the reapportionment problems represented nothing more than a bad case of acne, frequently embarrassing and temporarily disfiguring but not of vital importance.

With all due respect to those who raised the question and those who resolved it, reapportionment of the state and local legislatures and congressional election districts was not among the more pressing problems in post–World War II America. Reapportionment offered a nice problem of democratic theory; it also had serious practical consequences for elected officials whose districts would be changed. But, by the time of *Baker v. Carr*,[157] state legislatures had become

155. 343 U.S. 747 (1952).
156. *Id.* at 758–59.
157. 369 U.S. 186 (1962). See Neal, *Baker v. Carr: Politics in Search of Law*, 1962 SUPREME COURT REVIEW 252.

relatively irrelevant—if costly—parts of American government. Most of their tasks had been either assumed by Washington or assigned to local governments. State government was sick. But it is highly unlikely that malapportionment of its legislatures was the cause of its illness or that reapportionment would effect a cure. Again, however, once started down the road, the Court marched with the precision and determination of a toy soldier that had been wound up and pointed in a certain direction.

Baker v. Carr purported to settle nothing except the Court's willingness to hear complaints about malapportioned state legislatures. "In light of the District Court's treatment of the case, we hold today only (*a*) that the court possessed jurisdiction of the subject matter; (*b*) that a justiciable cause of action is stated upon which appellants would be entitled to appropriate relief; (*c*) because appellees raised the issue before this Court, that the appellants have standing to challenge the Tennessee apportionment statutes."[158] Members of the Court majority took umbrage at the suggestions of the dissenters that the Court had fixed on a one man–one vote formula.[159] Mr. Justice Douglas, in his concurring opinion, asserted: "Universal equality is not the test: there is room for weighting."[160]

Even academics expressed expectations that the Court would not be prepared to rest on such a "simplistic" formula, that a slogan would not be substituted for a rationale. At the time, Paul Freund wrote:

> The future will test the Court's resourcefulness in defining the rational bounds of patterns of representation without resorting to a simplistic criterion of one man, one vote—a criterion meaningful in an election for a single state-wide office or for a particular representative but question-begging in the case of a collegial body to be chosen with a view to balanced representa-

158. 369 U.S. at 197–98.
159. See *id*. at 258–59, 265.   160. *Id*. at 244–45.

tion. . . . The problem for the courts in reapportionment . . . is . . . to maintain direction while avoiding
the confounding of the rational with the doctrinaire.[161]

But in fact, the die was cast. The formula afforded a simple
rule and the Court went about its business of enforcing it.

In 1963, things were quiet on this front. The Court did
no more than declare invalid a county-unit system weighted
in favor of rural over urban counties.[162] The year of decision
was 1964. The Court left untouched the gerrymander that
created the district from which Adam Clayton Powell was
regularly reelected.[163] But the rule of one man–one vote was
enthroned during that Term[164] and applied to congressional
redistricting as well.[165] The fact that the people of a state
had chosen by referendum to have one house of a bicameral
legislature selected in a manner that varied from the Courts
mathematical formula was ruled to be an irrelevancy.[166] A
legal doctrine originated to assure majority rule was thus
held to preclude a right of the majority to establish its rule.

The Court did concede the validity of multimember districts.[167] But, as in the school desegregation cases, the Court
would brook no delay in effectuating its command.[168] Never-

161. Freund, *New Vistas in Constitutional Law*, 112 U. PA. L. REV.
631, 639 (1964).
162. Gray v. Sanders, 372 U.S. 368 (1963).
163. Wright v. Rockefeller, 376 U.S. 52 (1964).
164. Reynolds v. Sims, 377 U.S. 533 (1964); WMCA, Inc. v.
Lomenzo, 377 U.S. 633 (1964); Maryland Committee v. Tawes,
377 U.S. 656 (1964); Davis v. Mann, 377 U.S. 678 (1964); Roman
v. Sincock, 377 U.S. 695 (1964); Swann v. Adams, 385 U.S. 440
(1967); Kilgarlin v. Hill, 386 U.S. 120 (1967). See Auerbach, *The
Reapportionment Cases: One Person, One Vote—One Vote, One
Value*, 1964 SUPREME COURT REVIEW 1.
165. Wesberry v. Sanders, 376 U.S. 1 (1964); Kirkpatrick v.
Preisler, 394 U.S. 526 (1969); Wells v. Rockefeller, 394 U.S. 542
(1969).
166. Lucas v. Colorado General Assembly, 377 U.S. 713 (1964).
167. Fortson v. Dorsey, 379 U.S. 433 (1965); Burns v. Richardson,
384 U.S. 73 (1966).
168. Swan v. Adams, 383 U.S. 210 (1967).

theless, a malapportioned legislature which had been given time to correct itself could choose a governor where the electoral system had failed to produce a majority vote.[169] And some deviation from the formula was permitted in choosing school boards, at least where their functions are primarily administrative rather than legislative.[170] Otherwise, local government bodies must toe the same line.[171]

The rule was established for all legislative bodies in the United States except the Senate, whose immunity seems fairly secure. (Article V provides that the composition of the Senate is not to be changed even by constitutional amendment. But, I suppose, Article V may, despite what it says, also be subject to judicial amendment.) As stated at the 1968 Term of Court, the rule requires mathematical equivalence among voting districts with "only the limited population variances which are unavoidable despite a good faith effort to achieve absolute equality."[172]

In addition to their common attribute of depriving the states of authority over matters that were once thought to be those of peculiar state concern, the desegregation, criminal procedure, and reapportionment cases have other qualities that they share with each other and with much of the Court's constitutional business. The first of these is an egalitarian base about which I shall have something more to say later. The second universal feature is the assumption by the Court of the power that is being taken from the states. There was, however, a willingness expressed by the Court to share the burden of solving the problem of racial integration and imposition of proper standards for criminal procedure with Congress. The Court eagerly approved the new Civil Rights Acts forthcoming during the Kennedy and Johnson adminis-

169. Fortson v. Morris, 385 U.S. 231 (1966).
170. Sailors v. Bd. of Educ., 387 U.S. 105 (1967).
171. Avery v. Midland County, 390 U.S. 474 (1968).
172. Kirkpatrick v. Preisler, 394 U.S. at 531.

trations.[173] Even so, while tendering power under the enabling clauses of the Thirteenth, Fourteenth, and Fifteenth Amendments, as if it were the Court's to grant, the Court made clear its own function as final arbiter of the proper meaning of these amendments.

In no less worthy a case than *Miranda,* the Court said:

> It is impossible for us to foresee the potential alternatives for protecting the privilege which might be devised by Congress or the States in the exercise of their creative rule-making capacities. Therefore we cannot say that the Constitution necessarily requires adherence to any particular solution for the inherent compulsions of the interrogation process as it is presently conducted. Our decision in no way creates a constitutional straitjacket which will handicap sound efforts at reform, nor is it intended to have this effect. We encourage Congress and the States to continue their laudable search for increasingly effective ways of protecting the rights of the individual while promoting efficient enforcement of our criminal laws. However, unless we are shown other procedures which are at least as effective in appraising accused persons of their right of silence and in assuring a continuous opportunity to exercise it, the following safeguards must be observed.[174]

This gesture of condescension brought forth a quick response from Congress in the form of Title II of the Safe Streets and Crime Act with its potential for a confrontation between Congress and the Court.[175]

In *Katzenbach v. Morgan,* the Court announced in a footnote, a place where many of the Court's more important rulings are to be found, this caveat to Congress should it undertake legislation pursuant to the enabling clauses of the Civil War Amendments:

173. See notes 96 and 102 *supra.*
174. 384 U.S. at 467.
175. See Burt, *Miranda and Title II: A Morganatic Marriage,* 1969 SUPREME COURT REVIEW 81.

Contrary to the suggestion of the dissent . . . § 5 does
not grant Congress power to exercise discretion in the
other direction and to enact "statutes so as in effect to
dilute equal protection and due process decisions of this
Court." We emphasize that Congress' power under § 5
is limited to adopting measures to enforce the guarantees of the Amendment; § 5 grants Congress no power
to restrict, abrogate, or dilute these guarantees.[176]

In his comments on the Voting Rights Act cases, Alexander M. Bickel, with his usual acumen and realism, concluded:

The Court's other two encounters with the Voting
Rights Act of 1965 are not a little ironic. No Justices
have been more jealous guardians of the judicial prerogative, or more energetic wielders of judicial power,
than the governing majority of the present Court.
And yet *Katzenbach v. Morgan* constitutes restraint, if
not abdication, beyond the wildest dreams of the majority's usual *bête noire,* James Bradley Thayer, and in
fact beyond anything he intended to recommend. And
Harper v. Virginia Board of Elections[177] harks atten-
tively to even a timid hint from Congress. One doubts,
nevertheless, that a new trend has really been inaugu-
rated.[178]

There may yet be irony piled on irony as the "governing
majority" of which Professor Bickel spoke is changed by
reason of the transmogrification of the Warren Court into the
Nixon Court.

Another shared feature of the Court's actions in these
three areas was the absence of novelty in the governing principles that the Court announced, but startling originality in
their application. The decline and fall of the "separate but

176. 384 U.S. at 651 n. 10.
177. 383 U.S. 663 (1966).
178. Bickel, *The Voting Rights Cases,* 1966 SUPREME COURT
REVIEW 79, 101–02.

88

equal doctrine" was begun long before *Brown v. Board of Education*. Professor Cox may have been correct when he suggested that: "*Plessy v. Ferguson*[179] was still authoritative when *Brown v. Board of Education* came before the Court,"[180] if by "authoritative" he meant unreversed. But so, too, was Mr. Justice Clark when commenting on Cox's proposition. He said that *Plessy* was moribund before *Brown* was born.[181] *Plessy* had been bleeding from the wounds imposed by the earlier desegregation cases in the field of higher education;[182] by *Morgan v. Virginia*,[183] holding segregation an undue burden on interstate commerce; and by *Shelley v. Kraemer*,[184] the truly revolutionary opinion of the Vinson Court holding the enforcement of racial restrictive covenants unconstitutional. By the time *Brown* was accepted for decision the question was not whether *Plessy* would control but what new rationale would be offered in its place.[185] The fact is that *Plessy* may have been stillborn, for it never developed beyond a fictional excuse for discrimination. The states adhered to the "separate" part of the doctrine but never took notice of the "equal" proposition. It was the vast and rapid expansion of the areas of application of the new principle of equality—not its originality—that was the contribution of the Warren Court.

So, too, the one man–one vote principle was not original. Whether one traces it back to the Levellers or the Benthamites or the Jacksonian democrats, the proposition has a long history. The novelty again derived from the newfound willingness of the Court to impose it. Mr. Justice Frankfurter was clearly correct when he said of the concept:

179. 163 U.S. 537 (1896).
180. Cox, note 51 *supra,* at 25.
181. Clark, *Book Review,* 36 U. CHI. L. REV. 239, 240–41 (1968).
182. See note 88 *supra.*
183. 328 U.S. 373 (1946).
184. 334 U.S. 1 (1948).
185. See Kurland, *The Chief Justice and the School Desegregation Cases,* 27 U. CHI. L. REV. 170 (1959).

> It was not the English system, it was not the colonial
> system, it was not the system chosen for the national
> government by the Constitution, it was not the system
> exclusively or even predominantly practiced by the
> States at the time of adoption of the Fourteenth Amend-
> ment, it is not predominantly practiced by the States
> today.[186]

If it was not "predominantly practiced," neither was it un-
known. Again, it was the rigidity with which the Court first
applied and then extended the rule to its logical extreme that
made for the noteworthiness of the decisions.

The same may be said of the principles behind the criminal procedure cases. A reader of Judge Thomas McIntyre
Cooley's 1868 classic work would find acceptance there for
the substance of the rules that the Warren Court has imposed
on the states.[187] But the application of the principles and
especially the broad reliance on the exclusionary rule as the
essential method for controlling prosecutorial behavior are
what the Warren Court has added to American constitutional jurisprudence. The Court acknowledged this distinction between novelty of rule and novelty of application in its
opinion in the *Miranda* case: "We start here, as we did in
Escobedo, with the premise that our holding is not an inno-
vation in our jurisprudence, but is an application of principles long recognized and applied in other settings."[188]

Still another factor that is a constant among the Court's
decisions on these three subjects was the need to reject or
overrule earlier decisions in order to attain the desired results. This was most egregious in the criminal procedure
cases where precedents both hoary and young were felled
with the precision of modern lumberjacks cutting through a
forest. The list of opinions destroyed by the Warren Court
reads like a table of contents from an old constitutional law

186. 369 U.S. at 301.
187. See Cooley, Constitutional Limitations ch. 10 (1868).
188. 384 U.S. at 442.

casebook. The willingness to disregard stare decisis, as already suggested,[189] has a worthy pedigree. But the volume and speed of the Warren Court as it engaged in this enterprise have never been witnessed before. One can only think that the Warren Court was taking its guidance from a quotation used by Mr. Justice Sam Ervin, Jr., of the North Carolina Supreme Court: "There is no virtue in sinning against light or persisting in palpable error, for nothing is settled until it is settled right."[190] On the other hand, it was early in the Supreme Court's history that Mr. Justice Baldwin said: "There is no more certainty that a last opinion is more correct than the first."[191]

Still one more common characteristic of the three lines of cases is the inability to supply an adequate rationale for the conclusions reached. One need not accept all of Professor Wechsler's thesis to recognize that he thoroughly faulted the Court's opinion in *Brown*.[192] Indeed, one can be among the ardent admirers of the Court and still concede the defects of its opinion-writing. Thus, in concluding their laudatory essay on the Court's work in *Reitman v. Mulkey*,[193] Professors Karst and Horowitz wrote: "Granting the lack of 'comprehensive completeness of candor' for which we all yearn, granting the reshaping of precedent, granting the essential disingenuousness in the 'deference' to the California Court— granting all that, the vital fact is that in holding Proposition 14 unconstitutional the Court made one of its most significant contributions to date to the principle of substantive equal protection."[194]

So, too, with the reapportionment cases. Finding an adequate constitutional base on which to rest the Court's con-

189. See chapter 2, at notes 85–86.
190. State v. Ballance, 229 N.C. 764, 767 (1949).
191. Livingston's Executrix v. Story, 11 Pet. 351, 400 (1837).
192. See Wechsler, *Toward Neutral Principles of Constitutional Law*, 73 HARV. L. REV. 1 (1959).
193. Note 99 *supra.*
194. Karst & Horowitz, note 100 *supra,* at 80.

clusions has eluded not only the Court but some of the Court's best friends. Carl Auerbach, for example, after defending the reapportionment decisions, said:

> It is strange that the Court should conclude that the consent of the governed can be given no weight in the process of decision. If the Equal Protection Clause compels this conclusion, the Court might have sought some greater flexibility by resting its decision on the Guarantee Clause.
>
> It is unfortunate, then, that the Court agreed in *Baker v. Carr* that "any reliance" on the Guarantee Clause in apportionment controversies "would be futile." For it never adequately answered Mr. Justice Frankfurter's argument that the equal protection claim it held to be justiciable was "in effect, a Guarantee Clause claim masquerading under a different label." In fact, the Court was being asked "to establish an appropriate frame of government . . . for all the States of the Union."[195]

The fact was, said Professor Auerbach, that the Guarantee Clause presented its own difficulties.

Except as an exercise in arithmetic, we still have no justification[196] for what Professor Freund has called the "simplistic" nature of the Court's efforts here.[197] We are left, in fact, with a reading given the cases by Mr. Justice Fortas and the comment thereon by Professor Cox. Mr. Justice Fortas wrote:

> Their meaning and thrust are perhaps deeper than the mechanics of the tally. They are, one may hope, not merely much ado about form. They represent, one has been led to believe, an acknowledgment that the Republican form of government guaranteed by the Con-

195. Auerbach, note 164 *supra,* at 85.
196. See Kurland, *"Equal in Origin and Equal in Title to the Legislative and Executive Branches of the Government,"* 78 HARV. L. REV. 143, 149–57 (1964).
197. See text *supra,* at note 161.

> stitution read in the light of the General Welfare Clause, the guaranties of equal protection of the laws and the privileges and immunities of citizens of the United States, requires something more than adherence to form.[198]

That sentence is hard to parse as a matter of grammar, no less as a matter of constitutional law. Cox's more friendly comment was: "Few judicial opinions, even in dissent, claim for the Supreme Court as expansive and free wheeling a role. . . . To expand [the] vague declaration [of a republican form of government] still further 'in light of the General Welfare Clause' is to ignore all constitutional charts and sail whatever course the judge thinks will be in the public weal."[199] Whenever you get such a potpourri of constitutional provisions as suggested here by Mr. Justice Fortas, in *Bell v. Maryland*[200] by Mr. Justice Douglas, and in *Griswold v. Connecticut*[201] by several of the Justices, the feeling must grow that the answer was not found in the Constitution at all.

Nor, it must be conceded, have the criminal procedure cases been provided with opinions that persuade. Mr. Justice Brandeis once said in another context, speaking of a judge: "He may advise; he may persuade; but he may not command or coerce. He does coerce when without convincing the judgment he overcomes the will by the weight of his authority."[202] If Brandeis was right, the Court has essentially been engaging in the business of coercion rather than persuasion.

Fresh from his success in rewriting the *New York Times* case,[203] my colleague Professor Kalven suggested that per-

198. Fortson v. Morris, 385 U.S. 231, 249 (1966).
199. Cox, note 51 *supra,* at 133.
200. 378 U.S. 226, 242 (1964).
201. 381 U.S. 479 (1965).
202. Horning v. District of Columbia, 254 U.S. 135, 139 (1920).
203. *Compare* New York Times v. Sullivan, note 50 *supra, with* Kalven, note 52 *supra,* and Brennan, *The Supreme Court and the Meiklejohn Interpretation of the First Amendment,* 79 HARV. L. REV. 1 (1965).

haps the Court should announce only its judgments and leave their justification to its very willing and able group of admiring law professors. This is ancient wisdom. Lord Mansfield told new judges to state their judgments and withhold their reasons, since their judgments were probably right and their reasons probably wrong. Although it is likely to be regarded as an act of treason by my fellow law professors who make their livings by taking apart Supreme Court opinions, I quote Shakespeare's *Merchant of Venice:* "His reasons are as two grains of wheat hid in two bushels of chaff; you shall seek all day ere you find them, and when you have them they are not worth the search."[204]

Let me turn to the last similarity among the three lines of cases. Each of them is defended for a reason that the Court does not offer: that each concerned a long-endured problem of serious national proportions to which no other branch of government, state or national, was prepared to seek a solution. While this is asserted most often in the case of reapportionment, it remains equally true of segregation and criminal procedure. Whether this is an adequate reason to justify Supreme Court intervention is a matter of much debate. One may choose James Bradley Thayer's thesis that judicial action in this form removes responsibility from those who alone should and can bear it.[205] On the other hand, one may speak as did the abolitionist Theodore Parker. "When someone assured him that God in his own good time would end slavery, Parker remarked, 'The trouble is God isn't in any hurry and I am.' "[206]

Finally, about these three sets of decisions, I would look at one more defense of them. There is no doubt in my mind that the Court has assumed a moral position in these mat-

204. Act I, sc. 1, line 115.

205. See Thayer, *The Origin and Scope of the American Doctrine of Constitutional Law,* 7 HARV. L. REV. 129 (1893); THAYER, HOLMES, & FRANKFURTER, JOHN MARSHALL 82–88 (1967).

206. BINKLEY, THE MAN IN THE WHITE HOUSE 131 (rev. ed. 1964).

ters that it would behoove others to emulate. If the Court could convince the people of the rightness of its ways, it would not have to impose them. And, since it cannot impose them, it would do well to be convincing. What then of the Supreme Court's role as "the schoolmaster of the Republic"?[207] According to the number one sociologist in the country, Dr. Gallup, the Court itself has reached a new nadir in the esteem of the people;[208] the people think that the Court has contributed to the crime wave;[209] they believe that integration has proceeded too rapidly;[210] but they are accepting of the one man–one vote principle.[211] How good a teaching job has the Court done?

The essence of the problem of federalism, despite the Court's behavior and the centralization of power that has already occurred, is still with us, even if it is beginning to appear in a form that cannot be given the label of "states' rights." Demands are growing for a return of authority and power to local units where they are subject to more direct control by the people affected. The demand is not, however, for the return of the power to the state governments, nor even to those of the cities, but to the people. The problem is not confined to this country, as the report of the Redcliffe-Maud Commission in Great Britain, for example, clearly shows.[212] That commission has recommended sweeping reforms of local government in that country. Mr. Derek Senior's extended dissent is based on the failure of the report to make local government local enough.

There can be little doubt that the movement away from centralization is significant when the White House acknowl-

207. See Lerner, *The Supreme Court as Republican Schoolmaster,* 1967 SUPREME COURT REVIEW 127.
208. See New York Times, 15 June 1969, § 1, p. 43.
209. *Ibid.*
210. See New York Times, 17 August 1969, § 1, p. 42.
211. See New York Times, 10 August 1969, § 1, p. 80.
212. FINAL REPORT OF THE ROYAL COMMISSION ON LOCAL GOVERNMENT IN ENGLAND (Lord Redcliffe-Maud, chairman) (1969).

edges its existence. Mr. Nixon, a little short on his knowledge of history, recently said: "After a third of a century of power flowing from the people and the states to Washington, it is time for a new federalism in which power, funds and responsibility will flow from Washington to the states and to the people."[213] At the same time that he made this announcement, he also announced that the national government would assume control and responsibility for all welfare programs in the country.[214] Essentially, the president's suggested method for returning power is by a retransfer of tax moneys to the states and local governments, a scheme that Walter Heller and others urged some time ago.[215] There are more sophisticated suggestions to the same end.[216]

Federalism is dead and the Supreme Court has made its contribution to its demise. Yet, as government becomes involved in more and more of the life of the individual, there is a natural demand that the government be responsive to the varying needs and interests of the people whose lives it has invaded, by invitation or otherwise. Some form of local control of local governmental power must be developed. But this is a task beyond the capacity of a court, even the Supreme Court of the United States. It cannot be done by mandating one man–one vote principles for local governmental bodies. The power and function of these bodies are still determined elsewhere. The Court can condone the surrender of governmental power to local groups, but it cannot compel it. It cannot establish the sovereignty of urban government and its subdivisions. It is to the other branches of government that one must look for the reestablishment of "societies small enough for their members to have personal acquaintance with each other"; where the "herd" cannot as-

213. See New York Times, 9 August 1969, p. 10.

214. See New York Times, 9 August 1969, pp. 1, 10.

215. See, *e.g.*, HELLER, NEW DIMENSIONS OF POLITICAL ECONOMY ch. 3 (1966).

216. See LOWI, THE END OF LIBERALISM (1969).

sert "its ancient and evil primacy." Here lies the difficulty in accepting the rationale that the defaults of the legislature and the executive can be resolved by appeal to the courts. We cannot confront each problem with the proposition that the Court should solve it. With all the good will in the world, it is still deficient in "force" and "will."

The possibility that the Supreme Court will play a role in this reversal of the flow of government authority is small. It may have made its contribution to the new federalism by helping centralize all power so that it may now be redistributed. In any event, it is clear that when Mr. Justice Holmes justified national judicial review of state action on the ground that "one in my place sees how often a local policy prevails with those who are not trained to national views,"[217] he was speaking of a different era. When he said in that same speech that "Judges are apt to be naïf, simple-minded men, and they need something of Mephistopheles,"[218] he was clearly referring to an earlier time. For today, one in Holmes's old place would probably see how often a national policy prevails with those who are not trained to local views. Certainly he would not find our Justices naive or simple-minded men, but rather full of the devil.

217. Howe, ed., The Occasional Speeches of Justice Oliver Wendell Holmes 172 (1962).
218. *Ibid.*

4
Egalitarianism and the Warren Court

THE WARREN COURT'S commitment to the centralization of governmental authority was merely the development of a theme that originated with the creation of the Supreme Court and has been reiterated consistently throughout its history. Certainly it moved farther and faster than any Court that came before it. If we are to discover an element of leadership in the Warren Court, it must be elsewhere. As for federalism, certainly Holmes's remark in a letter to Pollock is peculiarly appropriate to the Warren Court: "They talk about our leading the procession—we only *follow it, ahead*. . . . If we turn down a side street it doesn't."[1]

To the extent that the Warren Court has opened new frontiers, it has been in the development of the concept of equality as a constitutional standard. The motif on the façade of the Supreme Court building reads: "Equal Justice under Law." If earlier Courts emphasized the words "Law" or "Justice," the Warren Court has accentuated the word "Equal."

As late as 1966, an English philosopher, John Wilson,

---

1. 1 HOLMES-POLLOCK LETTERS 124 (Howe ed. 1942). In the same letter, Holmes wrote: "Brooks [Adams] at present is in a great stir and thinks a world crisis is at hand, for us among others, and that our Court may have a last word as to who shall be the master in the great battle between the many and the few. I think this notion is exaggerated and half cracked." The letter is dated 25 May, 1906.

could say that the word "equality," unlike the words "freedom," "liberty," and "justice," was not a "value word" but only a descriptive one. He was not denigrating the term or the concept.[2] He was saying that "when people talk about equality in a political or moral context what they really mean to talk about is some closely evaluative concept such as impartiality or justice."[3] What may have been true in England in 1966 was only partially true in the United States. While the word "equality" may still be used here to invoke other notions, it has now developed—to use another word that became popular at the same time—charisma. Equality is the banner behind which there have been, both literally and figuratively, many marchers. In constitutional terms, "equality" has become the first freedom. It is a goal—a value—in itself that, to many, needs little or no justification.

The difficulty, of course, is that, even if it is self-justifying, the concept is not self-defining. A century ago, Sir James Fitzjames Stephen wrote that "equality is a word so wide and vague as to be by itself almost unmeaning."[4] A plethora of recent literature on the subject confirms both Stephen's dictum and the widespread interest that has developed in the subject.[5] These writings make it abundantly clear that there is vast disagreement about its connotations. If it is "value-free," it nevertheless arouses much excitement among both its proponents and its opponents. Indeed, the time has come

2. WILSON, EQUALITY 17–18 (1966). ". . . 'equality' is primarily at least, a descriptive and not an evaluative term. It may be more reasonable to suppose that equality is the corner-stone of a building whose more obvious features are made up of other political concepts: that the notion of equality, just because it is descriptive, is the essential point of departure of the road to liberalism." *Id.* at 18.

3. *Id.* at 19.

4. STEPHEN, LIBERTY, EQUALITY, AND FRATERNITY 201 (1873).

5. See, *e.g.,* NOMOS IX: EQUALITY (Pennock & Chapman eds. 1967); WILSON, note 2 *supra;* TENBROEK, EQUAL UNDER LAW (Collier ed. 1965); LAKOFF, EQUALITY IN POLITICAL PHILOSOPHY (1964); GRIMES, EQUALITY IN AMERICA (1964); HARRIS, THE QUEST FOR EQUALITY (1960).

when to speak out against "equality" is to invite the same reaction as once was evoked by condemning prohibition.

For my purposes, I prefer to accept the suggestion made
by Chief Judge Cardozo almost fifty years ago, when a different demand for equality was filling the air—a demand for
equality of bargaining power to combat the constitutional
concept of freedom of contract. He said then: "The same
fluid and dynamic conception which underlies the modern
notion of liberty, as secured to the individual by constitutional immunity, must also underlie the cognate notion of
equality."[6] For like the Due Process Clause, the Equal Protection Clause, which must bear most of the burden for
translating the various notions of equality into constitutional
sanctions, must be recognized as "fluid and dynamic." Certainly such a reading leads to a broad judicial authority.
At the same time, it might be noted that the background
for Cardozo's statement was provided by *Coppage v. Kansas*,[7]
a knowledge of which might give rise to some arguments for
judicial restraint.

There are those, including some who have served on the
Warren Court, who have found justification for the contemporary egalitarianism in the origins of the Constitution. For
the most part, this attitude has been based on what Alfred
Kelly has appropriately termed "law office" history.[8] It was
just such history, history that asks too much justification
from the past, that Mr. Justice Goldberg was relying on in
both his 1964 Madison lecture[9] and his 1964 opinion in *Bell*

6. CARDOZO, THE NATURE OF THE JUDICIAL PROCESS 81–82 (1921).
7. 236 U.S. 1 (1915).
8. Kelly, *Clio and the Court: An Illicit Love Affair*, 1965 SUPREME
COURT REVIEW 119.
9. Goldberg, *Equality and Governmental Action*, 39 N.Y.U. L.
REV. 205 (1964). The April dateline on this issue of the review
is reminiscent of T. S. Eliot's lines: "April is the cruellest month . . .
mixing Memory and desire." *The Waste Land,* in ELIOT, COMPLETE
POEMS AND PLAYS 37 (1958).

v. Maryland,[10] which read very much alike. He asserted that "equality and liberty were the 'twin themes' of the American Revolution."[11] Liberty and equality may well have been themes struck by some of the revolutionaries, but certainly not liberty or equality as their present advocates conceive them. Goldberg conceded that equality was not mentioned in the Constitution. But this was due, he told us, to the fact that the founders "naturally assumed [equality] was encompassed within the concept of liberty whose blessings they heralded in the preamble to the Constitution and later specifically guaranteed in the due process clause of the fifth amendment."[12] The character of his argument was best revealed when he invoked Magna Carta as providing one of the traditions of equality on which the American Revolution rested. Magna Carta may have become a noble myth.[13] But the notion that King John and the barons were concerned about their equality with the people would be difficult to justify.[14]

Certainly there is evidence that some goals of equality were considered at Philadelphia in 1787. And, as Goldberg noted, some are in fact stated in the Constitution. He found solace, for example, in the Privileges and Immunities Clause of Article IV, which equated citizens of one state with citizens of the other states. But as for who were citizens, the Constitution was silent. And the privileges and immunities provided, to the extent they were defined, would seem trivial compared with the egalitarian aspirations of today.[15] He referred also to the guarantee of a republican form of govern-

10. 378 U.S. 226, 286 (1964). The lecture was delivered on 11 February, 1964; the opinion came down on 22 June, 1964.

11. Goldberg, note 9 *supra,* at 205.

12. *Id.* at 207.

13. See THORNE, DUNHAM, KURLAND, & JENNINGS, THE GREAT CHARTER 48–74 (1965).

14. The arguments about and the ambiguities of Magna Carta have recently been canvassed in HOLT, MAGNA CARTA (1965).

15. See Corfield v. Coryell, 6 Fed. Case 546 (No. 3,230) (C.C.E.D. Pa. 1823).

ment also contained in Article IV. But he did not talk about the limited franchise then available in most jurisdictions or the structure of the upper houses of the state legislatures or the elitist character of the United States Senate.

One can find forms of equality everywhere, if that is what one is looking for. At the convention itself, Benjamin Franklin suggested that the pressure for a monarchy was based on the desire for equality. He said, "[T]here is a natural inclination in mankind to Kingly Government. It sometimes relieves them of Aristocratic domination. They had rather have one tyrant than five hundred. It gives more of the appearance of equality among Citizens, and that they like."[16] The distinction between equality and the appearance of equality is an important one, as we have come to know.

The abolition of titles of nobility and the provision for apportionment of direct taxes in Article I, § 9 are also egalitarian in their direction. So, too, was the abolition of bills of attainder and the ban on a religious test for office. Indeed, the Necessary and Proper Clause might even be so construed, as well as the Supremacy Clause, insofar as they contribute to natural uniformity of applicable rules of law.

The sticking point always comes with the recognition that the Constitution also dealt with slavery. Mr. Justice Goldberg disposed of it this way: "In sum, then, the Constitution of the new nation, while heralding liberty, in effect declared all men to be free and equal—except black men, who were to be neither free nor equal. This inconsistency reflected a fundamental departure from the American creed, a departure which it took a civil war to set right."[17] Which was the creed and which the aberration is easier for Goldberg to be sure of than for many historians, professional as well as amateur. Nor did the Civil War set it right.

The facts seem to indicate that, at the time of the Revo-

16. 1 Farrand, The Records of the Federal Convention of 1787 83 (1966 ed.)
17. Goldberg, note 9 *supra,* at 208.

102

lution, however much one man was the equal of the other, it was not thought to be the role of government to effect that equality. It was expected that government would treat one man as it would another. But that is still a far cry from the meaning of equality confronted by the Warren Court.

A description of the Revolutionary scene more fitted to the facts and less to the wish may be found in John P. Roche's remarks:

> If one were to have the temerity to translate this portion of The Declaration [of Independence] into operational political theory, a different proposition would emerge—the proposition which, I submit, is basic to an understanding of the development of equality in America over the past three centuries. It would run roughly as follows—*all those who have been admitted to membership in the political community are equal.* In other words, men achieve equality as a function of membership in the body politic—and this membership is not an inherent right, but a privilege which the majority accords on its own terms.
>
> The myth of the libertarian past dies hard, but if we are going to grasp historical reality, we must once and for all lay to rest the notion that our forefathers built a pluralistic society around the principles of liberty and equality.[18]

The phrase in the Declaration of Independence, that "all men are created equal," to which Professor Roche refers, is the keystone on which the myth was built by the Justices of the Warren Court, both on and off the bench.[19] The phrase took hold, so far as I know, only once in the early history of our country, in the 1783 Massachusetts case of *Quock Walker v. Nathaniel Jennings,*[20] an opinion that did not see

18. Roche, *Equality in America: The Expansion of a Concept,* 43 N.C. L. REV. 249, 251–52 (1965).
19. See notes 9 and 10 *supra.*
20. See COMMAGER, ed., DOCUMENTS OF AMERICAN HISTORY 110 (8th ed. 1968).

the light of day until 1874. The Declaration asserted the
equal rights of all men "to life, liberty, and the pursuit of
happiness." It is doubtful that it encompassed any more. In
any event this happy phrase saw no consequence in the Constitution.[21]

It is far easier to accept the proposition that the founders
contemplated an open society than that they anticipated a
classless one. Charles Pinckney certainly spoke for an open
society at the convention when he said:

> The people of the U. States are perhaps the most sin-
> gular of any we are acquainted with. Among them are
> fewer distinctions of fortune & less of rank, than among
> the inhabitants of any other nation. Every freeman has
> a right to the same protection & security; and a very
> moderate share of property entitles them to the posses-
> sion of all the honors and privileges the public can
> bestow: hence arises a greater equality, than is to be
> found among the people of any other country, and an
> equality which is more likely to continue—I say this
> equality is likely to continue, because in a new Coun-
> try, possessing immense tracts of uncultivated lands,
> where every temptation is offered to emigration &
> where industry must be rewarded with competency,
> there will be few poor, and few dependent—Every
> member of the Society almost, will enjoy an equal
> power of arriving at the supreme offices & consequently
> of directing the strength & sentiments of the whole Com-
> munity. None will be excluded by birth, & few by for-
> tune, from voting for proper persons to fill the offices
> of Government—the whole community will enjoy in
> the fullest sense that kind of political liberty which
> consists in the power the members of the State reserve
> to themselves, of arriving at the public offices, or at
> least, of having votes in the nomination of those who
> fill them.[22]

21. See BECKER, THE DECLARATION OF INDEPENDENCE 234 (1942
ed.).
22. 1 FARRAND, note 16 *supra*, at 398.

This was the attitude of one whom Hans Morgenthau has labeled an outstanding egalitarian of his time.[23] There is some evidence of the same attitude in the expressed views of Alexander Hamilton, who can hardly be characterized in the same way. For example, as Clinton Rossiter has pointed out:

> Article II, section 1 of [Hamilton's] draft constitution placed the vote for members of the House in "the free male citizens and inhabitants of the several States comprehended in the Union, all of whom, of the age of twenty-one years and upwards shall be entitled to an equal vote." Other articles set a modest property qualification for voters in senatorial and presidential elections,[24] and this may be an accurate measure of how far Hamilton was prepared to go in making popular government truly popular. While he welcomed some political democracy in his ideal polity, he certainly did not want it to take command.[25]

If the Court's egalitarian bent cannot find specific justification in the language or history of the Constitution as originally framed, it is almost as bereft of assistance from the history and purpose of the Equal Protection Clause of the Fourteenth Amendment, the place where the doctrine of equality specifically entered constitutional language. Again, however, the Warren Court preferred to indulge its liking for rewriting history. At the outset, in *Brown v. Board of Education*,[26] the unanimous Court took solace in the ambiguity of the amendment's history. Since then, however, a divided Court has purported to resolve contemporary problems by

23. See MORGENTHAU, THE PURPOSE OF AMERICAN POLITICS 11–18 (1960).

24. Pinckney proposed a property requirement for officeholders of not less than $50,000 for legislators and judges and $100,000 for the executive. 2 FARRAND, note 16 *supra*, at 248. This may have been foresighted, but it was hardly egalitarian.

25. ROSSITER, ALEXANDER HAMILTON AND THE CONSTITUTION 158–59 (1964).

26. 347 U.S. 483, 489 (1954). See Bickel, *The Original Understanding and the Segregation Decision*, 69 HARV. L. REV. 1 (1955).

finding words here and there in congressional debates and reports, or in polemical writings of that time and this.[27]

There are few things in the history of the Equal Protection Clause of the Fourteenth Amendment that are clear. One is that it was aimed at the destruction of the Black Codes of the South. A second is that it, along with other provisions of the amendment, was intended to protect the terms of the 1866 Civil Rights Act against judicial invalidation and legislative repeal. How far beyond legislative and administrative discrimination openly based on race the amendment was intended to go cannot be told from the language or spirit of the times. Nor is it clear from the legislative history what the scope of the 1866 Act was intended to be.[28] But, as Dean Allen has told us in his summary of the role of the Fourteenth Amendment: "[T]he great moral imperatives of due process and equal protection could not be confined to their historical understandings when applied to the emerging issues of modern American life. There is evidence that those who drafted Section 1 intended that the meanings of these phrases should evolve and expand with the passage of time and change of circumstances."[29]

The legislative history and language of the Fourteenth Amendment's Equal Protection Clause have afforded little support to the Court's resolution of specific problems that have come before it. Not much more solace could be gained

27. See, *e.g.*, Lewis, *The Sit-in Cases: Great Expectations*, 1963 SUPREME COURT REVIEW 101; Paulsen, *The Sit-In Cases of 1964: "But Answer Came There None,"* 1964 SUPREME COURT REVIEW 137; Van Alstyne, *The Fourteenth Amendment, the "Right" to Vote, and the Understanding of the Thirty-ninth Congress*, 1965 SUPREME COURT REVIEW 33; Kelly, note 8 *supra*, at 142–49; Karst & Horowitz, *Reitman v. Mulkey: A Telophase of Substantive Equal Protection*, 1967 SUPREME COURT REVIEW 39. The relevant cases and the vast literature on the subject may pretty well be garnered from the footnotes in the above-cited articles.

28. See Casper, *Jones v. Mayer: Clio, Bemused and Confused Muse*, 1968 SUPREME COURT REVIEW 89.

29. Allen, *The Constitution: The Civil War Amendments: XIII–XV*, in 1 BOORSTIN, AN AMERICAN PRIMER 165 (1966).

from that kind of history in which the Court is supposed to be expert: earlier decisions construing the clause. The prime limitation of the application of the clause to bar only action by the states was early established[30] and was not yet rejected by the time of Warren's accession to the bench, although it may have been seriously undermined by *Shelley v. Kraemer*.[31] On the other hand, the Equal Protection Clause had been expanded in a direction uncalled for by either its history or its language. In the *Slaughter-House Cases*,[32] with a prescience that the *New Yorker* usually takes note of under the rubric "The Clouded Crystal Ball," the Court expressed doubt that "any action of a State not directed by way of discrimination against the negroes as a class, or on account of their race, will ever be held to come within the purview of this provision." It would have been better had this focus been maintained. As it turned out, Negroes were only incidentally afforded the benefits of the clause.

In part this was because the judicial process is not self-starting. Except in criminal cases, it takes an interested person with adequate resources to initiate and carry on judicial proceedings to protect his rights. Unlike the Chinese in California, Negroes as a class could not secure their rights judicially before they had the resources to support litigation or legislation, and they could not get the resources before they secured their rights. But the early cases hardly indicate a certainty of much success even had they the opportunity to utilize the courts freely.

The nadir of protection for Negroes came in 1883, with the invalidation of congressional legislation in the *Civil*

30. See, *e.g.,* Virginia v. Rives, 100 U.S. 313, 318 (1880); *Ex parte* Virginia, 100 U.S. 339 (1800); Civil Rights Cases, 109 U.S. 3 (1883). For the strongest argument advanced on behalf of the abolition of the restriction, at least in race relations cases, see Black, *"State Action," Equal Protection, and California's Proposition 14,* 81 HARV. L. REV. 69 (1967).
31. 334 U.S. 1, 22 (1948).   32. 16 Wall. 36, 81 (1873).

Rights Cases.[33] Thereafter, although moving with all the deliberate speed of a glacier, the Court proceeded in the right direction. From the beginning, the Court, with the support of Congress, was prepared to confer on Negroes the dubious privilege of serving on juries.[34] Zoning laws providing for segregation of neighborhoods were invalidated in 1917.[35] And racially restricted covenants became unenforceable in 1948, thanks to *Shelley v. Kraemer.*[36]

On the other hand, the Court borrowed from Massachusetts[37] the "separate but equal" doctrine and applied it to transportation facilities[38] and education,[39] whence it had come. But the doctrine had been—if I may use the word—disintegrating in both these areas long before the Warren Court.[40] The use of the Equal Protection Clause to protect Negro political rights was essentially abortive,[41] until the white-primary cases came along.[42] In sum, until 1954, the

33. 109 U.S. 3 (1883).
34. See, *e.g.,* Virginia v. Rives, 100 U.S. 313 (1880); Pierre v. Louisiana, 306 U.S. 354 (1939); Smith v. Texas, 311 U.S. 128 (1940); Hill v. Texas, 316 U.S. 400 (1942); Patton v. Mississippi, 332 U.S. 463 (1947); Cassell v. Texas, 339 U.S. 282 (1950); Avery v. Georgia, 345 U.S. 559 (1953).
35. Buchanan v. Warley, 245 U.S. 60 (1917).
36. 334 U.S. 1 (1948); see also Hurd v. Hodge, 334 U.S. 24 (1948); Barrows v. Jackson, 346 U.S. 249 (1953).
37. Roberts v. City of Boston, 59 Mass. 198, 209 (1849); see also People *ex rel.* King v. Gallagher, 93 N.Y. 438 (1883).
38. Plessy v. Ferguson, 163 U.S. 537 (1896).
39. Cumming v. Richmond County Bd. of Educ., 175 U.S 528 (1899); Gong Lum v. Rice, 275 U.S. 78 (1927).
40. See Missouri *ex rel.* Gaines v. Canada, 305 U.S. 337 (1938); Sipuel v. Bd. of Regents, 332 U.S. 631 (1948); Sweatt v. Painter, 339 U.S. 629 (1950); McLaurin v. Oklahoma State Regents, 339 U.S. 637 (1950); *cf.* Morgan v. Virginia, 328 U.S. 373 (1946); Henderson v. United States, 339 U.S. 816 (1950).
41. Pope v. Williams, 193 U.S. 621 (1904); Giles v. Harris, 189 U.S. 475 (1903); Williams v. Mississippi, 170 U.S. 213 (1898). But see Guinn v. United States, 238 U.S. 347 (1915) (grandfather clause invalidated).
42. Nixon v. Herndon, 273 U.S. 536 (1927); Nixon v. Condon, 286 U.S. 73 (1932); *cf.* United States v. Classic, 313 US. 299 (1941); Smith v. Allwright, 321 U.S. 649 (1944).

Equal Protection Clause had not been effectively used by the Court for the protection of Negro rights, but the climate had changed and a recognition of this function was beginning to be acknowledged.

Nor did other minorities fare much better under the Equal Protection Clause. The Chinese in California did successfully evoke the classic decision of *Yick Wo v. Hopkins:*

> Though the law itself be fair on its face and impartial in its appearance, yet, if it is applied and administered by public authority with an evil eye and an unequal hand, so as practically to make unjust and illegal discrimination between persons in similar circumstances, material to their rights, the denial of equal justice is . . . within the prohibition of the Constitution.[43]

This left the Court with powerful doctrine for restraint of state power but did not say on whose behalf it should be used. It was not used to protect other racial minorities, as is evidenced by the Japanese exclusion cases.[44] Nor to protect women[45] or aliens.[46] But, at least as for the Japanese and aliens, the trend in the other direction had started before 1954.[47] (The argument that the Equal Protection Clause is not applicable to the national government is effectively answered by *Hurd v. Hodge*[48] and *Bolling v. Sharpe.*)[49]

To the extent that it performed any function, the Equal

43. 118 U.S. 356, 373–74 (1886).

44. Hirabayashi v. United States, 320 U.S. 81 (1943); Korematsu v. United States, 323 U.S. 214 (1944). See Rostow, *The Japanese American Cases—a Disaster,* in THE SOVEREIGN PREROGATIVE 193 (1962).

45. See, *e.g.,* Goessaert v. Cleary, 335 U.S. 464 (1948).

46. See Ohio *ex rel.* Clarke v. Deckenbach, 274 U.S. 392 (1927); Patsone v. Pennsylvania, 232 U.S. 138 (1914); Heim v. McCall, 239 U.S. 175 (1915); Crane v. New York, 239 U.S. 195 (1915); Terrace v. Thompson, 263 U.S. 197 (1923).

47. See *Ex parte* Endo, 323 U.S. 283 (1944); Takahashi v. Fish & Game Comm'n, 334 U.S. 410 (1948); Oyama v. California, 332 U.S. 633 (1948).

48. 334 U.S. 24 (1948).   49. 347 U.S. 497 (1954).

Protection Clause was a supplementary device for protecting business activities against state exercises of police[50] and taxing[51] powers. With the ipse dixit that corporations were "persons" protected by the Equal Protection Clause,[52] Chief Justice White made them the primary beneficiaries of that provision. But essentially the clause was only a tail to the due process kite, as was implicit in Justice Holmes's remark in *Buck v. Bell*[53] that the Equal Protection Clause was the "usual last resort of constitutional arguments." With the decline of substantive due process in the economic realm,[54] went the fall of the Equal Protection Clause in the same area.

It is clear that prior to the Warren Court, the Equal Protection Clause was not a strong element in the Supreme Court's arsenal. The egalitarian movement was not yet a part of the American *Zeitgeist*. But equality was beginning to cast its shadow. Its entrance on the scene at center stage was heralded by *Brown v. Board of Education*.

It was appropriate that the resurrection of the Equal Protection Clause should be the result of the Negro revolution of the 1950s and 1960s. Indeed, in a way, Chief Justice Warren was wrong when he suggested in *Brown* that the Court could not turn back the clock. For the Court was doing exactly that. It was returning to a recognition of the

50. See, *e.g.*, Hartford Co. v. Harrison, 301 U.S. 459 (1937); Smith v. Cahoon, 283 U.S. 553 (1931); Mayflower Farms v. Ten Eyck, 297 U.S. 266 (1936).

51. See, *e.g.*, Stewart Dry Goods Co. v. Lewis, 294 U.S. 550 (1935); Valentine v. Great A. & P. Tea Co., 299 U.S. 32 (1936); Liggett Co. v. Lee, 288 U.S. 517 (1933); Quaker City Cab Co. v. Pennsylvania, 277 U.S. 389 (1928); Southern Ry. Co. v. Greene, 216 U.S. 400 (1910); Concordia Ins. Co. v. Illinois, 292 U.S. 535 (1934); Royster Guano Co. v. Virginia, 253 U.S. 412 (1920).

52. Santa Clara County v. Southern Pac. R.R., 118 U.S. 394 (1886). See Connecticut General Ins. Co. v. Johnson, 303 U.S. 77, 85 (1938) (Black, J., dissenting); Wheeling Steel Corp. v. Glander, 337 U.S. 562, 576 (1949) (Douglas, J., dissenting).

53. 274 U.S. 200, 208 (1927).

54. See McCloskey, *Economic Due Process and the Supreme Court: An Exhumation and Reburial*, 1962 SUPREME COURT REVIEW 34.

central purpose of the Equal Protection Clause, to protect Negroes from discrimination at the hands of legislative, administrative, and judicial bodies controlled by white majorities. It was a return to the understanding of the *Slaughter-House Cases* concerning the use for which the clause was framed. What could not be done was to treat the problems as a Court might have treated them earlier, under different circumstances, in an essentially different society.

Certainly the central problem of equality in this country has always been the Negro's right of access to American society. This was recognized early by Alexis de Tocqueville and too late by Gunnar Myrdal. The resolution of the American dilemma had been postponed until it could be postponed no longer. If other governmental bodies did not see this, at least by 1954 the Supreme Court's eyes were open.

In 1835, Tocqueville anticipated the problem with which the country is now faced: "If ever America undergoes great revolutions, they will be brought about by the presence of the black race on the soil of the United States; that is to say, they will owe their origins, not to the equality but to the inequality of condition."[55] Earlier in his epochal work he had written:

> As long as the Negro remains a slave, he may be kept in a condition not far removed from that of the brutes; but with his liberty he cannot but acquire a degree of instruction that will enable him to appreciate his misfortunes and to discern a remedy for them. Moreover, there exists a singular principle of relative justice which is firmly implanted in the human heart. Men are much more forcibly struck by those inequalities which exist within the same class than by those which may be noted between different classes. One can understand slavery, but how allow several millions of citizens to exist under a load of eternal infamy and hereditary wretchedness? . . .

55. 2 TOCQUEVILLE, DEMOCRACY IN AMERICA 256 (Bradley ed. 1945).

As soon as it is admitted that the whites and the emancipated blacks are placed upon the same territory in the situation of two foreign communities, it will be readily understood that there are but two chances for the future: the Negroes and the whites must either wholly part or wholly mingle. . . . I do not believe that the white and black races will ever live in any country upon an equal footing. But I believe the difficulty to be still greater in the United States than elsewhere.[56]

Tocqueville's doleful prediction was shared, as he told us, by Thomas Jefferson, who had written:

Nothing is more clearly written in the book of destiny than the emancipation of the blacks; and it is equally certain, that the two races will never live in a state of equal freedom under the same government, so insurmountable are the barriers which nature, habit, and opinion have established between them.[57]

It is not hard to understand why the problem was not faced before. What is more difficult to comprehend is why it had to be faced in 1954. The answer is probably contained in Tocqueville's statement. Despite emancipation, it was not until the migration to the cities that the Negroes came face to face with the awful realities of discrimination, for the migration brought them close to but not into the community that the Fourteenth Amendment intended that they share. Why was the central question then posed in terms of public education? Essentially, I suppose, because this was one of the last realms of state competence, and one, as the Supreme Court told us in the last Term of the Warren Court, basic to many of the other disqualifications that are imposed on Negroes.[58]

I shall deal with the Court's desegregation cases in some

56. 1 *id.* at 373.
57. 1 *id.* at 373 n. 46.
58. See Gaston County v. United States, 395 U.S. 285 (1969). (Literacy test for voting invalid because of educational deprivation.)

detail, for these are at the heart of its contributions toward contemporary egalitarianism. At the core of this new constitutional jurisprudence are the school desegregation cases. Then come cases that do not involve education. The third layer is provided by the cases concerned with national legislation dealing with this intractable problem. These cases demonstrate, I think, that rapid movement toward equality of the races is not attainable through the judicial process. The Court has moved faster than society is prepared to go. This is not to denigrate the Court's efforts. The goal is certainly closer than it would have been—the situation is less explosive than it might have been—without its efforts. We are, after all, dealing with problems of a social revolution, and that is not the usual grist for the judicial mill.

Brown v. Board of Education opened a Pandora's box that was about to release its contents without judicial prying. What the ensuing years were to reveal was essentially that the Court, by itself, is incapable of effecting fundamental changes in society. That is not to say that it cannot spark explosions. The special problems of school integration have remained largely unchanged, with small exceptions like Berkeley, California, and Washington, D.C. And this despite the fact that the other branches of the national government have joined the attempt to bring about the change.

When counsel for the state of South Carolina told the Supreme Court that it would take sixty to ninety years to bring public opinion around to acquiescence in school desegregation, it sounded like forensic hyperbole. Today it has all the appearance of stark reality.

The immediate result of the *Brown* decree was to shift the battle from the heights of the Supreme Court to the foxholes of the district courts.[59] In 1958, the issue was back in the Supreme Court under highly explosive conditions. *Cooper v. Aaron*[60] arose out of a conflict between good and evil in the

59. See PELTASON, FIFTY-EIGHT LONELY MEN (1961).
60. 358 U.S. 1 (1958).

city of Little Rock, Arkansas. After the *Brown* decision, Little Rock's school board prepared a plan for gradual integration of its school system, although Arkansas had not been a party to the *Brown* litigation and was not subject to the *Brown* decree. The plan called for the integration of the upper grades at the outset and annual additions of immediately lower grades until the entire program was covered. Some Negro citizens of Little Rock complained in a suit in the district court that the plan was too gradual and sought a decree ordering an increased pace. The trial court declined this relief and approved the plan and it was affirmed by the court of appeals. At the state level, however, a razorback governor, with the unlikely name of Orval Faubus, led an insurrection against the Supreme Court's decision. In 1956, the Arkansas constitution was amended to call for resistance to *Brown*. Legislation was enacted by which, it was hoped, desegregation would be prevented. But the city of Little Rock, cognizant of the meaning of the federal Constitution's Supremacy Clause, proceeded with its plan.

The day before the first Negroes were to enter a theretofore white high school in Little Rock, Faubus sent national guard troops to prevent it. What had been peaceful became chaotic. The district court ordered the integration to proceed. The national guard prevented it. The trial court then entered an injunction against interference with desegregation by Faubus and his troops. The national guard was withdrawn, but it was too late. The mob had been aroused. Only the arrival of federal troops permitted the Negro students to enter the high school. Little Rock had become an armed camp. Law and order had disappeared. On petition of the school board, the trial court granted permission to postpone the effectuation of the plan for two and one-half years.[61]

The court of appeals, however, reversed the trial court's

61. *Ibid.*

judgment. And the Supreme Court affirmed the judgment of the court of appeals. Its opinion was issued with the name of every Justice of the Court listed among its authors:

> The constitutional rights of respondents are not to be sacrificed or yielded to the violence and disorder which have followed upon the actions of the Governor and the Legislature. As this Court said some 41 years ago in a unanimous opinion in a case involving another aspect of racial segregation: "It is urged that this proposed segregation will promote the public peace by preventing race conflicts. Desirable as this is, and important as is the preservation of the public peace, this aim cannot be accomplished by laws or ordinances which deny rights created or protected by the Federal Constitution." *Buchanan* v. *Worley,* 245 U.S. 60, 81. Thus law and order are not here to be preserved by depriving the Negro children of their constitutional rights. The record before us clearly establishes that the growth of the Board's difficulties to a magnitude beyond its unaided power to control is the product of state action. Those difficulties, as counsel for the Board forthrightly conceded on oral argument in this Court, can also be brought under control by state action. . . .
>
> Article VI of the Constitution makes the Constitution the "supreme Law of the Land." In 1803, Chief Justice Marshall, speaking for a unanimous Court, referring to the Constitution as "the fundamental and paramount law of the nation," declared in the notable case of *Marbury* v. *Madison,* 1 Cranch 137, 177, that "It is emphatically the province and duty of the judicial department to say what the law is." This decision declared the basic principle that the federal judiciary is supreme in the exposition of the law of the Constitution, and that principle has ever since been respected by this Court and the Country as a permanent and indispensable feature of our constitutional system. It follows that the interpretation of the Fourteenth Amendment enunciated by this Court in the *Brown* case is the

supreme law of the land, and Art. VI of the Constitution makes it of binding effect on the States "anything in the Constitution or Laws of any State to the Contrary notwithstanding." Every state legislator and executive and judicial officer is solemnly committed by oath taken pursuant to Art. VI, cl. 3, "to support this Constitution." Chief Justice Taney speaking for a unanimous Court in 1859, said that this requirement reflected the framers' "anxiety to preserve it [the Constitution] in full force, in all its powers, and to guard against resistance to or evasion of its authority on the part of a State. . . ." *Ableman* v. *Booth,* 21 How. 506, 524.

No state legislator or executive or judicial officer can war against the Constitution without violating his undertaking to support it. Chief Justice Marshall spoke for a unanimous Court in saying that: "If the legislatures of the several States may, at will, annul the judgments of the courts of the United States, and destroy the rights acquired under those judgments, the constitution itself becomes a solemn mockery. . . ." *United States* v. *Peters,* 5 Cranch 115, 136. A Governor who asserts a power to nullify a federal court order is similarly restrained. If he had such power, said Chief Justice Hughes, in 1932, also for a unanimous Court, "it is manifest that the fiat of a state Governor, and not the Constitution of the United States, would be the supreme law of the land; that restrictions of the Federal Constitution upon the exercise of state power would be but impotent phrases. . . ." *Sterling* v. *Constantin,* 287 U.S. 378, 397–398.[62]

The Court here was being carried away with its own sense of righteousness if, by the preceding paragraphs, it meant that a decision of the Supreme Court was supreme law in the way that a legislative act of Congress was supreme law. The judgment in *Brown* was not binding on the state of Arkansas, which was not a party thereto. It was, however,

62. *Id.* at 18–19.

binding precedent on any court before which the same question should arise in a case to which the state of Arkansas was a party. And that court would have to choose the declaration of principle by the Supreme Court rather than the announced law of the state, whether the case arose in the federal or in the state courts. Here Arkansas was a party to the litigation in the United States District Court in Little Rock. And while Arkansas had the right to appeal the case in order to secure a reversal of position by the Supreme Court, it had no right to flout the order of the lower federal court. The "supreme law of the land" was not the *Brown* decision but the order of the trial court issued in the course of that court's duty to follow *Brown*. This and this alone is the meaning of *Peters,* of *Ableman,* and of *Sterling,* the cases that the Court quoted and relied upon.

The Court ended its opinion in recognition of the problems of federalism that were involved in *Brown*. But it was steadfast in adherence to its earlier position:

> It is, of course, quite true that the responsibility for public education is primarily the concern of the States, but it is equally true that such responsibilities, like all other state activity, must be exercised consistently with federal constitutional requirements as they apply to state action. The Constitution created a government dedicated to equal justice under law. The Fourteenth Amendment embodied and emphasized that ideal. State support of segregated schools through any arrangement, management, funds, or property, cannot be squared with the Amendment's command that no State shall deny to any person within its jurisdiction the equal protection of the laws. The right of a student not to be segregated on racial grounds in schools so maintained is indeed so fundamental and pervasive that it is embraced in the concept of due process of law. *Bolling* v. *Sharpe,* 347 U.S. 497. The basic decision in *Brown* was unanimously reached by the Court only after the case had been briefed and twice argued and the issues had been

117

given the most serious consideration. Since the first *Brown* opinion three new Justices have come to the Court. They are at one with the Justices still on the Court who participated in that basic decision as to its correctness, and that decision is now unanimously re-affirmed. The principles announced in that decision and the obedience of the States to them, according to the command of the Constitution, are indispensable for the protection of the freedoms guaranteed by our fundamental charter for all of us. Our constitutional ideal of equal justice under law is thus made a living truth.[63]

The state of Louisiana actually sought to invoke the antebellum doctrine of interposition to avoid the Supreme Court school desegregation efforts. The Louisiana legislature had passed three statutes. The first provided for segregation of all public schools and the withholding of funds from any integrated school. The second authorized the governor to close all public schools if any was integrated. The third provided for the takeover by the governor of any school board under a desegregation order. In a suit to enjoin enforcement of these statutes, a three-judge district court held them invalid. The Supreme Court affirmed this action without opinion.[64] Pending disposition of the case in the Supreme Court, the state sought a stay of the injunction. In denying the stay, the Court rendered a per curiam opinion giving short shrift to the ancient arguments. The ghosts of the Hartford Convention and the Kentucky and Virginia Resolutions were exorcised quickly if not finally.[65]

So far as the hard-core opposition to desegregation was concerned, however, repeated decisions of the Supreme Court were of little avail. What Arkansas and Louisiana had failed to accomplish, Virginia tried to achieve. In a case involving one of the school districts involved in the original

63. *Id.* at 19–20.
64. Orleans Parish School Bd. v. Bush, 365 U.S. 569 (1961).
65. Bush v. Orleans Parish School Bd., 364 U.S. 500 (1960).

Brown decision, the Court was called on to review the closing of the public schools in Prince Edward County, Virginia.[66] In addition to closing the schools of the county, financial assistance was afforded to students attending private segregated schools. The Court held it unconstitutional for one county in the state to close its public schools while other public schools remained open. Unanimous in rejecting the tactic as unconstitutional, the Court was divided as to the appropriate remedy. In an opinion by Mr. Justice Black, the Court said:

> [T]he record in the present case could not be clearer that Prince Edward's public schools were closed and private schools operated in their place with state and county assistance, for one reason, and one reason only: to ensure, through measures taken by the county and the State, that white and colored children in Prince Edward County would not, under any circumstances, go to the same school. Whatever nonracial grounds might support a State's allowing a county to abandon public schools, the object must be a constitutional one, and grounds of race and opposition to desegregation do not qualify as constitutional.[67]

Justices Clark and Harlan disagreed "with the holding that the federal courts are empowered to order the reopening of the public schools in Prince Edward County."[68] They apparently were of the view that the state retained the option under the Equal Protection Clause to open the Prince Edward County schools or close all the rest to assure equality of treatment.

In *Griffin,* the Court also indicated that its patience was at an end: "The time for mere 'deliberate speed' has run out,

66. Griffin v. County Bd. of Prince Edward County, 377 U.S. 218 (1964); see also Louisiana Financial Assistance Comm'n v. Poindexter, 389 U.S. 571 (1968); St. Helena Parish School Bd. v. Hall, 368 U.S. 515 (1962).

67. 377 U.S. at 231.   68. *Id.* at 234.

and that phrase can no longer justify denying these Prince Edward County school children their constitutional rights to an education equal to that afforded by the public schools in other parts of Virginia."[69] This attitude was confirmed when the Court refused to stay the Fifth Circuit's order to all the southern states within its domain to desegregate by the autumn of 1967.[70] In the autumn of 1969, the order was still not effected, but the government was hopeful.[71]

The last of the major school desegregation cases was decided in 1968.[72] At issue were so-called freedom-of-choice and freedom-of-transfer programs, allowing parents to choose the school they wanted their children to attend or permitting parents to transfer their children from a school not of their choice. These programs were the last resorts of the states to avoid desegregation. They certainly had not worked to accomplish desegregation.[73] The Court equivocated.

Mr. Justice Brennan, in *Green v. County School Board,* wrote the opinion for a Court that was again unanimous. He

69. *Ibid.*

70. Caddo Parish School Bd. v. United States, 386 U.S. 1001 (1967).

71. On 25 August, 1969, the New York Times trumpeted: "U.S. Officials See Pupil Integration Doubling in the South," p. 1, col. 1. On 26 August, 1969, in a less ebullient tone, the front page of the New York Times reported a break between the federal government and the NAACP Legal Defense Fund "because of the Nixon Administration's decision last week to throw its weight behind a slowdown in desegregation in Mississippi and, by implication, throughout the South." P. 1, col. 7.

72. Green v. County School Bd., 391 U.S. 430 (1968); Raney v. Bd. of Educ., 391 U.S. 443 (1968); Monroe v. Bd. of Comm'rs, 391 U.S. 450 (1968). In October 1969 the Court handed down what West's Supreme Court reporter emblazoned "The Immediate Desegregation Case," banning immediately dual school systems in Mississippi. Alexander v. Holmes County Bd. of Educ., 90 Sup. Ct. 29, 396 U.S. 1218 (1969). But the practical effect was not salutary. See New York Times, 6 January, 1970, p. 1.

73. See UNITED STATES COMMISSION ON CIVIL RIGHTS, SOUTHERN SCHOOL DESEGREGATION 1966–67 45–69 (1967).

suggested that the measure of the validity of a "free choice"
system was the extent to which it eliminated a "dual system"
of schools within the jurisdiction:

> It is incumbent upon the school board to establish
> that its proposed plan promises meaningful and imme-
> diate progress toward disestablishing state-imposed seg-
> regation. It is incumbent upon the district court to
> weigh that claim in light of the facts at hand and in
> light of any alternatives which may be shown as feas-
> ible and more promising in their effectiveness. Where
> the court finds the board to be acting in good faith and
> the proposed plan to have real prospects for dismantling
> the state-imposed dual system "at the earliest practical
> date," then the plan may be said to provide effective
> relief. . . .
> We do not hold that "freedom of choice" can have
> no place in such a plan. We do not hold that a "free-
> dom-of-choice" plan might of itself be unconstitutional,
> although that argument has been urged upon us. Rather,
> all we decide today is that in desegregating a dual sys-
> tem a plan utilizing "freedom of choice" is not an end
> in itself.[74]

Brennan went on to detail the failures of the particular
plan that was the subject of review in the *Green* case to meet
the Court's standards:

> The New Kent School Board's "freedom-of-choice"
> plan cannot be accepted as a sufficient step to "effec-
> tuate a transition" to a unitary system. In three years
> of operation not a single white child has chosen to at-
> tend Watkins school and although 115 Negro children
> enrolled in New Kent school in 1967 (up from 35 in
> 1965 and 111 in 1966) 85% of the Negro children in
> the system still attend the all-Negro Watkins school.
> In other words, the school system remains a dual sys-
> tem. . . . The Board must be required to formulate a
> new plan and, in light of other courses which appear

74. 391 U.S. at 439–40.

open to the Board, such as zoning, fashion steps which promise realistically to convert promptly to a system without a "white" school and a "Negro" school, but just schools.[75]

The Court went on to hold in the *Raney* and *Monroe* cases that the respective "freedom-of-choice" and "freedom-of-transfer" plans did not effectively change the "dual" systems into unitary systems. They were, therefore, invalid. The district court was ordered to retain jurisdiction to assure that desegregation took place forthwith.[76]

The Court's commitment to "disestablishmentarianism" has been, from the beginning, confined to the problems arising in states where school segregation was compelled by law before the *Brown* decisions. It has said nothing about so-called de facto segregation in non-southern communities. This problem is under vigorous attack by way of legislation.[77] Sooner or later the Court will have to pass on problems arising under this legislation and its administration by the Department of Health, Education, and Welfare.[78] Meanwhile the Court seems inclined to leave the burden of attaining desegregation to the legislative and executive branches of the national government.[79]

Although the Court has long been engaged in the transfer of power from the states to the national government, never before had it used the Equal Protection Clause so fundamentally. Never before had the knife gone so deeply into the fabric of society as in the school desegregation cases. Surgical excision of a cancer is a tricky thing. It is not clear that the prognosis is favorable.

75. *Id.* at 441–42.
76. 391 U.S. at 449.
77. Title VI, Civil Rights Act of 1964, 42 U.S.C. § 2000d (1964).
78. See, *e.g.,* United States Office for Civil Rights, HEW, Policies on Elementary and Secondary School Compliance with Title VI of the Civil Rights Act of 1964, 33 FED. REG. 4955 (1968).
79. See, *e.g.,* Bell v. School City, 342 F.2d 209 (7th Cir. 1963), *cert. den.* 377 U.S. 924 (1964). But see note 72 *supra.*

Equality as a judicial mandate is not readily accomplished. The Court's own efforts have brought about little change. Prior to the passage of the 1964 Civil Rights Act, desegregation had been minimal. Since the Civil Rights Act, the change has been better but still not good. Clearly the legislature, with its power over the purse, has more effective instruments in its hands for bringing about the change. On the other hand, Congress is far less committed to the metamorphosis than the Court has been. Whether any action at the national or state levels would have been forthcoming had not the Court taken the first step, no one will ever be able to say. Certainly Congress was not ready to act when the Court acted. The question also remains for some whether the desegregation rule was a better first step than an attempt at enforcement of the separate-but-equal doctrine. Most "right-thinking" people believe that it was. There are reasonable men, blacks as well as whites, who are of the view that the conditions of the Negro in America would have improved faster if concentration had been placed on the improvement of Negro education in the black schools; that such education would soon result in integration, not only in the schools but throughout American life. On the other hand, the advice that Learned Hand gave to the president of Harvard University way back in 1922 still sounds persuasive even in a different context:

> I cannot agree, that a limitation based upon race will in the end work out any good purpose. If the Jew does not mix well with the Christian, it is no answer to segregate him. Most of the qualities which the Christian dislikes in him are, I believe, the direct result of that very policy in the past. Both Christian and Jew are here; they must in some way learn to live on tolerable terms, and disabilities have never proved tolerable. It seems hardly necessary to argue that they intensify on both sides the very feelings which they are designed to relieve on one. If after acquaintance, the two races are

irretrievably alien, which I believe unproven, we are, it is true, in a bad case, but even so not as bad as if we separate them on race lines. Along that path lie only bitterness and distraction.[80]

The problems of segregation obviously extended far beyond the public schools. The rationale of the *Brown* case was limited to the field of education. But the Court was soon faced with a series of problems not resoluble in terms of the arguments made in *Brown*. In most of these cases—all of the early ones—the Court took the easy way out. It struck down state-imposed segregation by means of per curiam orders which failed to explain how the carefully contained *Brown* opinion opened like an umbrella to bring these other matters under its shelter. Some friends of the Court complained about this evasion of responsibility.[81] Others, more result-oriented, and pleased with the result, criticized the critics.[82]

Whatever the propriety of the means, the Court made it clear through a series of unexplained decisions that the separate-but-equal notion was, indeed, dead. The state could not impose segregation in public auditoriums,[83] on public beaches,[84] on municipal golf courses,[85] on state-sponsored athletic events,[86] in buses,[87] or even in jails.[88] The requirement of nonsegregated courtrooms was a fortiori.[89] The

80. HAND, THE SPIRIT OF LIBERTY 21 (Dilliard ed. 2d ed. 1953).

81. See, *e.g.*, WECHSLER, PRINCIPLES, POLITICS, AND FUNDAMENTAL LAW 3 (1961).

82. See, *e.g.*, ROSTOW, note 44 *supra*, at 3 *et seq.*

83. Muir v. Louisville Park Theatrical Ass'n, 347 U.S. 971 (1954); Schiro v. Bynum, 375 U.S. 395 (1964).

84. Mayor & City Council of Baltimore v. Dawson, 350 U.S. 877 (1955).

85. Holmes v. City of Atlanta, 350 U.S. 879 (1955); New Orleans Park Ass'n v. Detiege, 358 U.S. 54 (1958).

86. State Athletic Comm'n v. Dorsey, 359 U.S. 533 (1959).

87. Gayle v. Browder, 352 U.S. 903 (1956), *overruling* Plessy v. Ferguson, 163 U.S. 537 (1896).

88. Lee v. Washington, 390 U.S. 333 (1968).

89. Johnson v. Virginia, 373 U.S. 61 (1963).

failure to desegregate public parks by 1963 finally evoked a full-dress opinion by Mr. Justice Goldberg for a unanimous Court, but it was directed only to the issue of the inordinate delay.[90] By then the Court could properly rely on the fact that everyone knew or should have known that the result reached in *Brown*—if not its reasoning—governed the right of access to publicly owned and controlled facilities.[91]

The Court, however, was quickly moved into a new and even more difficult series of problems. Like the bans of the Bill of Rights which are directed to actions of the national government and not to those of its citizens, so the limitations of the Equal Protection Clause of the Fourteenth Amendment are directed, by its terms, to the actions of states and not to those of the residents thereof. This created hard issues for the Court in its attempts to solve the racial problems of the country. For the essence of racial discrimination was social not political. No laws were required to effectuate segregation; it would exist without them. Jim Crow was not the creature of state governments; state governments were the creatures of Jim Crow. Litigation that resulted only in a ban on state activity—even when the decrees were effective—could only reach the surface of the problem. The Court found itself pushed further and further to deal with the acts of individuals as though they were the subjects of the limitations of the Fourteenth Amendment. It made for the hardest kind of opinion writing, for it meant writing about one thing while acting on another.

Just as in the school desegregation cases the Warren Court had been given a leg up by its predecessor, so, too, in the area of state action, earlier Courts had started moving down the path in the direction that the Warren Court wanted to take. By the time of the Warren Court, it could be said that state action included not only activities carried out by government officials pursuant to legislative mandate but also

90. Watson v. Memphis, 373 U.S. 526 (1963).
91. See *id.* at 530 n. 2.

actions of officials even in contravention of state law,[92] actions of private citizens carrying out state functions,[93] and actions by state courts enforcing private agreements.[94] But these cases, like those to be decided by the Warren Court, afforded no clear rationale for the concept of state action.

In the 1956 Term, the Court was faced with the question whether a private school whose trustees were the Board of Directors of City Trusts, an official municipal agency, would be required to desegregate.[95] The segregation had resulted not from any decision of the board of directors but because of the terms of the trust establishing the school. The Court held that, although no discretion was exercised by the state to exclude Negroes, the state could not properly be the means for effecting such discrimination. Later, however, when the school was removed from the control of the official agency—by action of the probate court—the Pennsylvania Supreme Court held that desegregation was no longer required, and the Supreme Court refused to review that decision.[96]

Then, in 1961, came *Burton v. Wilmington Parking Authority*.[97] A private restaurant in a municipally owned and operated parking facility built on land condemned by the state and financed by tax-exempt bonds refused service to a Negro. He brought suit in the state courts seeking a declaratory judgment of his right to service. The Delaware Supreme Court rejected his claim,[98] on the ground that the restaurant

92. See, *e.g.*, Screws v. United States, 325 U.S. 91 (1945).

93. See, *e.g.*, Smith v. Allwright, 321 U.S. 649 (1944); Marsh v. Alabama, 326 U.S. 501 (1946).

94. Shelley v. Kraemer, 334 U.S. 1 (1948).

95. Pennsylvania v. Bd. of Directors of City Trusts, 353 U.S. 230 (1957).

96. Pennsylvania v. Bd. of Directors of City Trusts, 357 U.S. 570 (1958). Ultimately the school was desegregated by a reinterpretation of the will by the Court of Appeals for the Third Circuit. Pennsylvania v. Brown, 392 F.2d 120 (3d Cir. 1968). *Cf.* Sweet Briar Institute v. Button, 387 U.S. 432 (1967).

97. 365 U.S. 715 (1961).   98. 157 A.2d 894 (Del. 1960).

was acting in a "purely private capacity." The Supreme Court of the United States reversed that decision and, in a rather murky opinion, held the discrimination unconstitutional. Without isolating the factors that transmuted the action of the restaurateur into state action, Mr. Justice Clark, for a badly divided Court, held that the whole ball of wax amounted to state action.[99]

Mr. Justice Stewart would have chosen a different basis for the same result:

> In upholding Eagle's right to deny service to the appellant solely because of his race, the Supreme Court of Delaware relied upon a statute of the State which permits the proprietor of a restaurant to refuse to serve "persons whose reception or entertainment by him would be offensive to the major part of his customers. . . ." There is no suggestion in the record that appellant as an individual was such a person. The highest court of Delaware has thus construed this legislative enactment as authorizing discriminatory classification based exclusively on color. Such a law seems to me clearly violative of the Fourteenth Amendment.[100]

Both the Court's opinion and Stewart's opinion are pregnant with possibilities for broad expansion of the state-action doctrine. But the language of the majority made it unlikely that this case would spawn anything but further litigation. In the following Term of the Court, however, a case was disposed of on the authority of *Burton,* although the only analogous factors revealed were (1) the restaurant was leased from the Memphis municipal airport, and (2) there was a state law condoning, indeed requiring, segregation within the restaurant. In *Turner v. Memphis,*[101] the appellant had not been refused service but had been offered segregated service. The result was, appropriately, the same. What was surprising was that the divided *Burton* court had turned into

99. 365 U.S. at 725–26.
100. *Id*. at 726–27.   101. 369 U.S. 350 (1962).

a unanimous Court in disposing of the *Turner* case. This could be explained by the fact that the restaurant was already under compulsion to desegregate rather than that it was located within a municipal facility.

The increasingly active nature of the Negro revolution brought the Court more difficult problems in a series of "sit-in" cases in the 1962 Term. Negroes who "sat in" at lunch counters and restaurants that refused to serve them and ordered them to leave had been convicted of criminal trespass under state laws. Here the restaurants were not located in state buildings or on state property. On the other hand, while the earlier cases had involved relief sought by the persons discriminated against, in these cases it was the discriminating party who invoked the law that resulted in these criminal convictions.

In *Peterson v. City of Greenville,*[102] the ten Negro defendants had refused to leave a lunch counter at an S. H. Kress store after service was refused them and the manager ordered them to go. The manager called the police, who arrested the defendants for criminal trespass, of which they were convicted. The manager said that he had ordered them to leave because they were Negroes. No other objection to their presence was offered.

An ordinance of Greenville made it illegal to serve "white persons and colored persons in the same room [except] where separate facilities are furnished." The Supreme Court opinion, written by Chief Justice Warren for all members of the Court except Mr. Justice Harlan, rested entirely on the unconstitutionality of the ordinance as the ground for upsetting the convictions. The Court conceded that the Fourteenth Amendment did not inhibit private conduct. But this action, Warren said, could not be considered private conduct:

> It cannot be denied that here in the City of Greenville,
> an agency of the State, has provided by its ordinance

102. 373 U.S. 244 (1963).

that the decision as to whether a restaurant facility is to be operated on a desegregated basis is to be reserved to it. When the State has commanded the result, it has saved to itself the power to determine that result and thereby "to a significant extent" has become "involved" in it, and, in fact, has removed the decision from the sphere of private choice. It has thus effectively determined that a person owning, managing or controlling an eating place is left with no choice of his own but must segregate his white and Negro patrons. The Kress management, in deciding to exclude Negroes, did precisely what the city law required.[103]

The decision in *Lombard v. Louisiana*,[104] decided the same day, was more difficult to reach. Here the defendants were convicted under the state "criminal mischief" statute for refusing to leave a lunch counter after being requested to do so. The Court managed to discover what it considered an equivalent of the ordinance in *Peterson* in proclamations issued by the mayor and chief of police to the effect that they would not condone sit-ins and would enforce the law against those who engaged in the practice:

A State, or a city, may act as authoritatively through its executive as through its legislative body. . . . As we interpret the New Orleans city officials' statements, they here determined that the city would not permit Negroes to seek desegregated service in restaurants. Consequently, the city must be treated exactly as if it had an ordinance prohibiting such conduct.[105]

Mr. Justice Douglas, who joined Warren's opinion for the Court, was prepared to expand the state-action doctrine considerably further. He would find that any use of the state's judiciary to enforce private discrimination—at least in a place of public accommodation—was a violation of the Fourteenth Amendment. Moreover, he would rule that:

103. *Id.* at 247–48.
104. 373 U.S. 267 (1963).   105. *Id.* at 273.

"[t]his restaurant is . . . an instrumentality of the State since the State charges it with duties to the public and supervises its performance. The State's interest in an activity with regard to its restaurants extends far beyond any mere income-producing licensing requirement."[106]

Mr. Justice Harlan's separate opinion set forth the basis for his concern and for his unwillingness to join the opinions offered by the majority of the Court:

> Underlying the cases involving an alleged denial of equal protection by ostensibly private action is a clash of competing constitutional claims of a high order: liberty and equality. Freedom of the individual to choose his associates or his neighbors, to use and dispose of his property as he sees fit, to be irrational, arbitrary, capricious, even unjust in his personal relations are things all entitled to a large measure of protection from governmental interference. This liberty would be overridden, in the name of equality, if the strictures of the Amendment were applied to governmental and private action without distinction. Also inherent in the concept of state action are values of federalism, a recognition that there are areas of private rights upon which federal power should not lay a heavy hand and which should properly be left to the more precise instruments of local authority.[107]

Harlan did not disagree, hardly anyone could, with the rationale of the Court in these cases, which was simply that state action encompassed action taken by individuals under the compulsion of state law. His concern came over the question whether there was such compulsion here. He agreed that there was in *Peterson* but not in *Lombard*.

The issue appeared on the Court's doorstep again in the 1963 Term. Phrased as narrowly as possible, the issue was "whether the Fourteenth Amendment provides the Negro with a self-executing federal right to equal treatment

106. *Id.* at 282–83. 107. *Id.* at 250.

by the proprietors of private establishments catering to all the public except Negroes."[108] Again the Court managed to evade the troublesome question. A series of cases was disposed of on one ground or another that found state action elsewhere than in the judicial enforcement of the trespass laws. In *Robinson v. Florida*,[109] the Court found that health regulations caused burdens to desegregated restaurants that, in effect, compelled the proprietors to exclude Negroes. The evidence in the case that the health regulations had anything to do with the segregation was no more than fanciful. In another case, the Court reversed the convictions on the equally ephemeral grounds that the defendants did not have adequate notice that they were breaking the law.[110] In still a third case, the Supreme Court found the evidence insufficient to support the conviction, despite the state court decisions to the contrary.[111] In one other decision, the Court pinned the responsibility for the exclusion on the state because the amusement park employee who issued the eviction notice was a deputy sheriff.[112] The opinions in these cases were not convincing of anything except the Court's patent desire to avoid deciding the troublesome question. Any broadening of the state-action concept to include the actions of restaurant and amusement park proprietors would, as Harlan had suggested, impinge on individual freedom of association. On the other hand, to permit the conviction of these peaceful demonstrators to stand would cause the Court's collective gorge to rise.

The principal case on this issue during the 1963 Term, *Bell v. Maryland*,[113] looked like a four-square confrontation. But that expectation underestimated the Court's capacity for evasion. In *Bell*, twelve Negro students had

108. Lewis, note 27 *supra*, at 101.
109. 378 U.S. 153 (1964).
110. Bouie v. City of Columbia, 378 U.S. 347 (1964).
111. Barr v. City of Columbia, 378 U.S. 146 (1964).
112. Griffin v. Maryland, 378 U.S. 130 (1964).
113. 378 U.S. 226 (1964).

been convicted under the state's criminal trespass laws for engaging in a restaurant sit-in. They unsuccessfully challenged their convictions on both due process and equal protection grounds through the courts of Maryland. Mr. Justice Brennan, writing for the Court, did not "reach the questions that have been argued under the Equal Protection and Due Process Clauses of the Fourteenth Amendment."[114] Avoidance of the questions was based on the fact that subsequent to the time the convictions were affirmed by the Maryland Court of Appeals, both a city ordinance and a state statute had been passed making it illegal to discriminate against Negroes in restaurants in the city and state. It took some very fancy construction to read Maryland law as providing that a conviction affirmed by the highest state court was subject to attack on the ground that it was inconsistent with a subsequently enacted public accommodations law. The Court did not itself undertake to rewrite Maryland law. It sent the case back to the Maryland courts with a blueprint for so doing. The majority in support of the opinion included six members of the Court: the Chief Justice and Justices Douglas, Clark, Brennan, Stewart, and Goldberg. Nevertheless, six members of the Court spoke out on the substantive constitutional issues.

Douglas, as he had earlier, was prepared to go as far as was necessary to inhibit discrimination in places of public accommodation. The more so because this important issue was not being faced by the legislative branch:

> We have in this case a question that is basic to our way of life and fundamental in our constitutional scheme. No question preoccupies the country more than this one; it is plainly justiciable; it presses for a decision one way or another; we should resolve it. The people should know that when filibusters occupy other forums, when oppressions are great, when the clash of authority between the individual and the State is severe, they can

114. *Id.* at 228.

still get justice in the courts. When we default, as we do today, the prestige of law in the life of the Nation is weakened.[115]

The demands of justice were equally clear to Douglas. He would utilize the Equal Protection Clause to put "all restaurants . . . on an equal footing,"[116] by making the state compel them all to serve Negroes. What the state of Maryland did by legislative action, Douglas was prepared to have the Court do by constitutional compulsion. There was no conflict, he asserted, between the right of the Negro to service and the personal preference of the restaurant owner not to serve him. Many, if not most, restaurants were owned by corporations. "Here, as in most of the sit-in cases before us, the refusal of service did not reflect 'personal prejudices' but business reasons. . . . The truth is, I think, that the corporate interest is in making money, not in protecting 'personal prejudices.' "[117] But even if the choice were between the personal prejudices of the storekeeper and the right of the Negro to service, the answer should be the same. President Johnson's State of the Union message on 8 January, 1964 put the "constitutional right": "Surely they [Negroes and whites] can work and eat and travel side by side in their own country."[118] These are, for Douglas, federally created rights of citizenship that must be enforced. "Seldom have modern cases . . . so exalted property in suppression of individual rights."[119] "Apartheid"—the word is revived from earlier use—is barred by the common law and must not "be given constitutional sanction in the restaurant field."[120] There was, for Douglas, no problem about the existence of state action. Convictions for trespass clearly fall within the ban of *Shelley v. Kraemer*: "Why should we refuse to let state courts enforce *apartheid* in residential areas of our cities but let state courts enforce *apartheid*

115. *Id.* at 244–45.   117. *Ibid.*   119. *Id.* at 253.
116. *Id.* at 246.   118. *Id.* at 247.   120. *Id.* at 254.

in restaurants? If a court decree is state action in one case, it is in the other. Property rights, so heavily underscored, are equally involved in each case."[121] To reject this theory, the Justice suggested, was to enhance the power of corporate management to a greater degree than ever before: *"Affirmance would make corporate management the arbiter of one of the deepest conflicts in our society."*[122] Most corporations are already suffering the results of absentee management. Where "the corporation is little more than a veil for a man and wife or brother and brother . . . disregarding the corporate entity often is the instrument for achieving a just result. But the relegation of a Negro customer to second-class citizenship is not just. Nor is fastening *apartheid* on America a worthy occasion for tearing aside the corporate veil."[123]

Mr. Justice Goldberg, always a joiner, joined this opinion of Douglas's as well as that of Brennan. He proceeded, also, to write one of his own, in which he was joined by Douglas and the Chief Justice. Goldberg found the answer no less in the aura of the Constitution than in its words and its history. His novel argument was that the *Civil Rights Cases,*[124] should be read as sustaining the conclusion that he and Douglas offered. For there Mr. Justice Bradley had premised the Court's position on the assumption that "[i]nnkeepers and public carriers, by the laws of all the States, so far as we are aware, are bound to the extent of their facilities, to furnish proper accommodations to all unobjectionable persons who in good faith apply for them."[125] Where this is untrue, as with regard to restaurants in most states, Goldberg obviously believed that the *Civil Rights Cases* should be stood on their heads. In any event, he told us, the first Justice Harlan was right and Bradley was wrong.

There can be no recognized conflict, Goldberg continued,

121. *Id.* at 259.
122. *Id.* at 264. (Emphasis in original.)   124. 109 U.S. 3 (1883).
123. *Id.* at 271.   125. *Id.* at 25.

between the rights of Negroes to enjoy public accommodations and the rights of the owners to exclude them. There are no rights of the owners to exclude them. The Constitution commands that the state compel the owner to serve the Negro; it certainly cannot aid the owner in his refusal to do so by permitting him to invoke the state trespass laws. Indeed, Goldberg implied, if the owner resorts to self-help to remove the unwanted visitors from the premises, it is he and not the patron who should be subjected to the sanction of the laws.

The constitutional right of privacy, which he was later to embrace with such vigor, was nowhere to be found in this opinion by Goldberg:

> [Certainly there are] rights pertaining to privacy and private association . . . themselves constitutionally protected liberties.
>
> We deal here, however, with a claim of equal access to public accommodations. This is not a claim which significantly impinges upon personal associational interests; nor is it a claim infringing upon the control of private property not dedicated to public use. A judicial ruling on this claim inevitably involves the liberties and freedom both of the restaurant proprietor and of the Negro citizen. . . . The history and purposes of the Fourteenth Amendment indicate, however, that the Amendment resolves this apparent conflict of liberties in favor of the Negro's right to equal accommodations. . . . The broad acceptance of the public in this and in other restaurants clearly demonstrated that the proprietor's interest in private or unrestricted association is slight.[126]

It came as a surprise to many that it was Mr. Justice Black who picked up the gauntlet thrown down by Douglas, Goldberg, and Warren. Black was joined by Harlan and White. For the senior Justice there was no state action here.

126. 378 U.S. at 313–14.

Shelley v. Kraemer was inapposite. In that case, the Court properly held that "state enforcement of the covenants had the effect of denying to the parties their federally guaranteed right to own, occupy, enjoy, and use their property without regard to race or color. . . . When an owner of property is willing to sell and a would-be purchaser is willing to buy, then the Civil Rights Act of 1866 . . . prohibits a State, whether through its legislature, executive, or judiciary, from preventing the sale on the grounds of the race or color of one of the parties."[127] That was an interesting interpretation of *Shelley,* but certainly not the classic one. Nor a persuasive one. But neither was the construction given by Douglas to that same case a convincing one. The Court, Mr. Justice Black went on, was not Congress. Each had its own role to play:

> This Court has done much in carrying out its solemn duty to protect people from unlawful discrimination. And it will, of course, continue to carry out this duty in the future as it has in the past. But the Fourteenth Amendment of itself does not compel either a black man or a white man running his own private business to trade with anyone else against his will. . . . The case before us does not involve the power of the Congress to pass a law compelling privately owned businesses to refrain from discrimination on the basis of race and to trade with all if they trade with any. We express no views as to the power of Congress, acting under one or another provision of the Constitution, to prevent racial discrimination in the operation of privately owned businesses, nor upon any particular form of legislation to that end.[128]

And so came to an end—with a majority of the Warren Court never deciding the question on the merits—the judicial phase of the right to equal treatment in places of

127. *Id.* at 330–31. 128. *Id.* at 342–43.

public accommodation. The Civil Rights Act of 1964 became law and, for a while, took the spotlight.

The Civil Rights Act of 1964 did not solve the problem of state action but only amended it a bit. Working only with the Fourteenth Amendment, the question put to the Court was whether it could impose a rule of nondiscrimination on individuals solely because of the language and purpose of § 1 of that amendment. With the new statute, the question became whether Congress could impose such a rule of nondiscrimination. Two major differences were patent. Congress was not limited to the Fourteenth Amendment in seeking to eliminate discrimination. Congressional authorization under the Fourteenth Amendment came by way of § 5 as well as by reason of § 1. Whether § 5 authorized action that § 1 did not was a question yet to be answered by the Court.

It was with inordinate haste that the Civil Rights Act was tested in the Supreme Court. Seldom is a statute authoritatively validated by the Court in the same year that it is enacted into law. But that was the case with the Civil Rights Act.

Section 201 (a) of the law provides:

> (a) All persons shall be entitled to the full and equal enjoyment of the goods, services, facilities, privileges, advantages, and accommodations of any place of public accommodation, as defined in this section, without discrimination or segregation on the ground of race, color, religion, or national origin.[129]

The test cases involved a restaurant and a motel. Restaurants and motels were declared by the statute to be public accommodations within the meaning of the statute if their operations "affect commerce" or if they are supported by "State action." Motels affected commerce by definition. Restaurants affected commerce if they served or offered to

129. 42 U.S.C. § 2000a (1964).

serve food to interstate travelers or if "a substantial portion of the food" served had "moved in interstate commerce."

In *Heart of Atlanta Motel, Inc. v. United States*,[130] the Court upheld the validity of the statute as applied to a motel because of the "overwhelming evidence" presented to Congress that racial discrimination in motels had an adverse effect on interstate commerce.[131] Some may find the evidence less than overwhelming, made up in some measure by federal executive officials at the command of their superiors. But it does not take overwhelming evidence to justify congressional findings of fact.[132] And so the Court rested on the Commerce Clause rather than the Fourteenth Amendment to justify the federal rule of nondiscrimination in places of public accommodation.

Katzenbach v. McClung,[133] involved a restaurant: Ollie's Barbecue. Again the evidence was far from overwhelming that "a substantial portion of the food" served at Ollie's Barbecue came from interstate commerce. Or, if it did, that it was of such magnitude as to affect interstate commerce. But the Court dispensed with this necessity by invoking the principles of *Wickard v. Filburn*.[134] Ollie's interstate purchases might be insignificant, but all barbecue stands together consumed enough food through interstate commerce to have a serious effect. Again there were findings of fact by Congress, dubious but desirable, that restaurants that discriminated sold less food than would nondiscriminatory restaurants, because interstate travel by Negroes was inhibited by discriminatory action, which cut off part of the potential market. Since people tend to eat, if they can afford it, wherever they happen to be, it is not quite clear how interstate commerce would be enhanced by this com-

130. 379 U.S. 241 (1964).

131. *Id.* at 253.

132. *Cf.* the findings of legislative fact in Dennis v. United States, 341 U.S. 494 (1951).

133. 379 U.S. 294 (1964).   134. 317 U.S. 111 (1942).

pelled nondiscrimination. To the extent that they ate at Ollie's they would be forsaking some other seller of the same kind of goods. But there's no arguing by the Court with Congress where Congress has reached conclusions that the Court admires.

That the objective of the statute was not really the enhancement of interstate commerce, the Court readily acknowledged:

> In framing Title II of this Act Congress was also dealing with what it considered a moral problem. But that fact does not detract from the overwhelming evidence of the disruptive effect that racial discrimination has had on commercial intercourse. It was this burden which empowered Congress to enact appropriate legislation, and, given this basis for the exercise of its power, Congress was not restricted by the fact that the particular obstruction to interstate commerce with which it was dealing was also deemed a moral and social wrong.[135]

In any event, congressional motive is not a proper subject for judicial scrutiny.[136]

The reach of the Commerce Clause was not extended by these cases. The reach of Congress had been equated with its grasp by the Supreme Court a score of years earlier. Nor was there any judicial precedents strongly in the way of its conclusion. The *Civil Rights Cases*[137] declaring unconstitutional the 1875 statute attempting to impose integration on places of public accommodation had rested exclusively on lack of power under the Fourteenth Amendment. Congress had not sought then to rest on the Commerce Clause, which had not yet taken on its expansive new meaning,

135. 379 U.S. at 257.
136. See Alfange, *Free Speech and Symbolic Conduct: The Draft-Card Burning Case*, 1968 SUPREME COURT REVIEW 1.
137. 109 U.S. 3 (1883).

nor had the Court examined the authority that might come from that clause.

The opinions in *McClung* and *Heart of Atlanta Motel* were not persuasive, for the same reason that the earlier cases in the series were not persuasive. The result was good, but the Court was not facing the real issues, as the authors of the separate opinions made clear.

Mr. Justice Douglas "would prefer to rest on the assertion of legislative power contained in § 5 of the Fourteenth Amendment."[138] He believed:

> A decision based on the Fourteenth Amendment would have a more settling effect, making unnecessary litigation over whether a particular restaurant or inn is within the commerce definitions of the Act or whether a particular customer is an interstate traveler. Under my construction, the Act would apply to all customers in all the enumerated places of public accommodation. And that construction would put an end to all obstructionist tactics and finally close one door on a bitter chapter in American history.[139]

It is doubtful that reliance on the Fourteenth Amendment would have been more effective than reliance on the Commerce Clause. The requirements for inclusion in the Commerce Clause were so easily met as to be mere paper demands. What Douglas was anxious to do was to reassert the proposition that any judicial enforcement of discriminatory acts qualified for state action under the rule in *Shelley v. Kraemer*. His position had not changed since his opinion in *Bell v. Maryland*.

Nor had that of Mr. Justice Goldberg, who also wrote a separate opinion reasserting his notions of state action as he had stated them in *Bell v. Maryland*. There were no dissenting opinions or votes. The congressional power was unanimously sustained, but there was still no rationale for the state-action concept. And the rationale remained

138. 379 U.S. at 280.   139. *Ibid.*

important, for the statute by no means sought to put an end to all discrimination based on race or color.

The Court was still not yet off the hook. There was a plethora of cases of convictions under state trespass statutes that had been decided prior to the enactment of the 1964 act. Some of them were on their way to the Supreme Court—indeed, some had arrived—before the legislation was enacted. If the Court were compelled to decide these without resort to the Civil Rights Act, it might yet have to answer the thorny problem that it had so long evaded. *Hamm v. City of Rock Hill*[140] raised just those issues.

The Civil Rights Act provided in § 201(a)-2, that "no person shall . . . punish or attempt to punish any person for exercising or attempting to exercise any right or privilege secured by section 201." Clearly convictions resulting from such acts committed after the passage of the statute would not be sustained. What about the cases resulting in judgments prior to the passage of the act?

Mr. Justice Clark, writing for the majority, asserted that if these cases had arisen in the federal courts prior to the passage of the statute, they would abate by reason of the statute. He relied for this conclusion on common-law doctrine. He believed that cases arising in state courts should be decided no differently. His strongest argument for this position was that it avoided the need to decide a constitutional question.

Mr. Justice Black dissented:

> The Civil Rights Act of 1964, validly, I think, made it unlawful for certain restaurants thereafter to refuse to serve food to colored people because of their color. The Court now interprets the Act as a command making it unlawful for the States to prosecute and convict "sit-in" demonstrators who had violated valid state trespass laws prior to passage of the federal Act. The idea that Congress has the power to accomplish such a result

140. 379 U.S. 306 (1964).

has no precedent, so far as I know, in the nearly 200 years that Congress has been in existence. . . . The judge-made "common law rule" of construction on which the Court relies has been applied heretofore only where there was a repeal of one statute by another— not, as my Brother HARLAN points out, where as here a later law passed by Congress places certain restrictions on the operation of the still valid law of a State. But even if the old common-law rule of construction taken alone would otherwise have abated these convictions, Congress nearly a century ago passed a "saving" statute . . . to keep courts from imputing to it an intent to abate cases retroactively, unless such an intent was expressly stated in the law it passed.[141]

There was, he said, nothing in the legislative history to impute to Congress an intention to abate these convictions. Justices Harlan, Stewart, and White, wrote opinions in agreement with these conclusions. And so, by a single vote, the definition of state action was once again evaded.

The Court began a revival and reinvigoration of Reconstruction era laws in the 1965 Term. If it could not find the tools to protect and secure Negro equality in the Fourteenth Amendment itself, the Court would find it in the exercise of legislative power by Congress. If it could not find it in new congressional legislation, it would find it in old legislation. So far as the reduction of state authority and enhancement of national power were concerned, it made no difference which branch of the national government was the instrument of change. But reliance by the Court on congressional authority left with the legislature the penultimate authority to change the legislation on which the Court was relying. This was subject, of course, to the ultimate power of statutory interpretation and judicial review.

Two cases came to the Court that arose out of the attempted application of Reconstruction era laws to two

141. *Id.* at 318–19.

lynchings in the South, one of three white civil rights workers in Mississippi, the other of a Negro civil rights leader in
Georgia. Both cases came to the Court by direct appeal under the Criminal Appeals Act, with the consequence that the
Court was perfectly free to speculate about the facts and
was not confined to proof on the record. The relevant statutory provisions are found in §§ 241 and 242 of Title 18,
which read as follows:

> [§ 241] If two or more persons conspire to injure,
> oppress, threaten, or intimidate any citizen in the free
> exercise or enjoyment of any right or privilege secured
> to him by the Constitution or laws of the United States,
> or because of his having so exercised the same; or
>
> If two or more persons go in disguise on the high-
> way, or on the premises of another, with intent to pre-
> vent or hinder his free exercise or enjoyment of any
> right or privilege so secured—
>
> They shall be fined not more than $5,000 or impris-
> oned not more than ten years or both.
>
> [§ 242] Whoever, under color of any law, statute, or-
> dinance, or custom, willfully subjects any inhabitant of
> any State, Territory, or District to the deprivation of
> any rights, privileges, or immunities secured or pro-
> tected by the Constitution or laws of the United States,
> or to different punishments, pains, or penalties, on ac-
> count of such inhabitant being an alien, or by reason of
> his color, or race, than are prescribed for the punish-
> ment of citizens, shall be fined not more than $1,000,
> or imprisoned not more than one year, or both.

These sections are a potpourri of post–Civil War acts now
codified in Title 18.

United States v. Price[142] was concerned with the constitutional validity of an indictment under § 242 of three police
officials and fifteen private citizens for conspiring to interfere and interfering with the rights of the deceased to due

142. 383 U.S. 787 (1966).

143

process of law by murdering them. The trial court had dismissed the § 242 count of the indictment concerning the individual defendants on the ground that they were not acting under color of law. The Supreme Court reversed this judgment in an opinion by Mr. Justice Fortas speaking for a unanimous Court:

> In the present case, according to the indictment, the brutal joint adventure was made possible by state detention and calculated release of the prisoners by an officer of the State. This action, clearly attributable to the State, was part of the monstrous design described by the indictment. State officers participated in every phase of the alleged venture: the release from jail, the interception, assault and murder. It was a joint activity from start to finish. Those who took advantage of participation by state officers in accomplishment of the foul purpose alleged must suffer the consequences of that participation. In effect, if the allegations are true, they were participants in official lawlessness, acting in willful concert with state officers and hence under color of law.[143]

The trial court had also dismissed the § 241 counts concerning all parties on the ground that "due process of law" was not one of the rights or privileges secured to an individual by the Constitution within the meaning of the statute. Once again, the Court reversed, this time having to overcome the barrier of an earlier opinion, with which the Court dealt in a forthright manner:

> The argument, however, of Mr. Justice Frankfurter's opinion in *Williams I* [*United States v. Williams,* 341 U.S. 70 (1951)], upon which the District Court rests its decision, cuts beneath this. It does not deny that the accused conduct is within the scope of the Fourteenth Amendment, but it contends that in enacting § 241, the Congress intended to include only the rights and privileges conferred on the citizen by reason of the "sub-

143. *Id.* at 795.

stantive" powers of the Federal Government—that is, by reason of federal power operating directly upon the citizen and not merely by means of prohibitions of state action. . . . We do not agree.

The language of § 241 is plain and unlimited. . . . [I]ts language embraces *all* of the rights and privileges secured to citizens by *all* of the Constitution and *all* of the laws of the United States. There is no indication in the language that the sweep of the section is confined to rights that are conferred or "flow from" the Federal Government, as distinguished from those secured or confirmed or guaranteed by the Constitution.[144]

Despite the plain meaning of the words, this was the first time that the section had been so broadly construed. And here the Court, while expanding its jurisdiction, was essentially placing a tool within the hands of the federal executive. For prosecutorial discretion, which had made a dead letter of these sections for so many years, would still be determinative of the use to which they would be put.

The Court was fully conversant with the problem of federalism inherent in the case. It denied new incursions on the state domain but nevertheless justified them:

The present application of the statutes at issue does not raise fundamental questions of federal-state relationships. We are here concerned with allegations which squarely and indisputably involve state action in direct violation of the mandate of the Fourteenth Amendment —that no State shall deprive any person of life or liberty without due process of law. This is a direct, traditional concern of the Federal Government. It is in an area in which the federal interest has existed for at least a century, and in which federal participation has intensified as part of a renewed emphasis upon civil rights. . . . In any event, the problem, being statutory and not constitutional, is ultimately, as it was in the beginning, susceptible of congressional disposition.[145]

144. *Id.* at 800–01.   145. *Id.* at 806–07.

United States v. Guest[146] was a more controversial case. But it established, even if by indirection, the expansive powers of Congress under § 5 of the Fourteenth Amendment to affect individual action unrelated to state action required by § 1. In *Guest* the victim had been murdered while traveling between states. The defendants were charged with conspiracy to effect the killing in violation of § 241. One of those violations was the deprivation of the victim's rights to equal protection of the laws as guaranteed by the Fourteenth Amendment. The Court, per Mr. Justice Stewart, ruled that the rights protected by the Equal Protection Clause, no less than those assured by the Due Process Clause, were encompassed by the statute. The problem here, however, was that there were no state officials implicated in the conspiracy. The issue was to find state action sufficient to meet the requirements of the Fourteenth Amendment. The Court asserted that state action was necessary if there were to be any violation of the Equal Protection Clause:

> It is a commonplace that rights under the Equal Protection Clause itself arise only when there has been involvement of the State or of one acting under the color of its authority. The Equal Protection Clause "does not . . . add any thing to the rights which one citizen has under the Constitution against another." . . . As MR. JUSTICE DOUGLAS more recently put it, "The Fourteenth Amendment protects the individual against *state action,* not against wrongs done by *individuals.*" . . . This has been the view of the Court from the beginning. . . . It remains the Court's view today.[147]

The Court was capable, however, of finding the necessary element of state action even here:

> This case, however, requires no determination of the threshold level that state action must attain in order to create rights under the Equal Protection Clause. This

146. 383 U.S. 745 (1966).   147. *Id.* at 755.

is so because, contrary to the argument of the litigants, the indictment in fact contains an express allegation of state involvement sufficient at least to require the denial of a motion to dismiss. One of the means of accomplishing the object of the conspiracy, according to the indictment, was "By causing the arrest of Negroes by means of false reports that such Negroes had committed criminal acts." . . . The allegation of the extent of official involvement in the present case is not clear. It may charge no more than co-operative private and state action similar to that involved in *Bell*, but it may go considerably further. For example, the allegation is broad enough to cover a charge of active connivance by agents of the State in the making of the "false reports," or other conduct amounting to official discrimination clearly sufficient to constitute denial of rights protected by the Equal Protection Clause. Although it is possible that a bill of particulars, or the proof if the case goes to trial, would disclose no co-operative action of that kind by officials of the State, the allegation is enough to prevent dismissal of this branch of the indictment.[148]

Another count of the indictment accused the defendants of interfering with the deceased's "right to travel." The trial court's dismissal of this count was also upset. The right to travel, said the Court, was a federally created right, derivable from the Constitution.[149]

The only limitation on the invocation of § 241 as a means for punishing individual action in restraint of federal rights was a requirement that there must be proof of "specific intent to interfere with the federal right."[150]

Mr. Justice Harlan, who concurred in part and dissented in part, was alone. He objected to the creation of the right to travel as a federally created right separate and apart from the freedom from state interference with interstate commerce. And he reminded the Court that it was construing a criminal statute:

148. *Id.* at 756–57.   149. *Id.* at 757, 759.   150. *Id.* at 760.

Although the Court has ostensibly only "discovered" this private right in the Constitution and then applied § 241 mechanically to punish those who conspire to threaten it, it should be recognized that what the Court has in effect done is to use this all-encompassing criminal statute to fashion federal common-law crimes, forbidden to the federal judiciary since the 1812 decision in *United States* v. *Hudson,* 7 Cranch 32. My Brother DOUGLAS, dissenting in *United States* v. *Classic* [313 U.S. 299 (1941)], noted well the dangers of the indiscriminate application of § 241: "It is not enough for us to find in the vague penumbra of a statute some offense about which Congress could have legislated, and then to particularize it as a crime because it is highly offensive." 313 U.S., at 331–32.

I do not gainsay that the immunities and commerce provisions of the Constitution leave the way open for the finding of this "private" constitutional right, since they do not speak solely in terms of governmental action. Nevertheless, I think it wrong to sustain a criminal indictment on such an uncertain ground. To do so subjects § 241 to serious challenge on the score of vagueness and serves in effect to place this Court in the position of making criminal law under the name of constitutional interpretation. It is difficult to subdue misgivings about the potentialities of this decision.[151]

The Warren Court, in particular, had been most stringent in imposing on the states and the Congress a duty to cross their *t*'s and dot their *i*'s, or to find the statute struck down for vagueness. The fact that the Court was prepared to sustain a criminal statute so broadly construed as this one clearly suggests the absence of an objective test for vagueness.[152]

151. *Id.* at 773–74.
152. *Cf., e.g.,* Whitehill v. Elkins, 389 U.S. 54 (1967) (loyalty oath); Keyishian v. Bd. of Regents, 385 U.S. 589 (1967) (loyalty oath); Elfbrandt v. Russell, 384 U.S. 11 (1966); Baggett v. Bullitt, 377 U.S. 360 (1964) (loyalty oath); Cramp v. Bd. of Instruction, 368 U.S. 278 (1961) (loyalty oath); United States v. Robel, 389 U.S. 258 (1967) (freedom of association); N.A.A.C.P. v. Button,

The *Guest* case was important as establishing a power in the federal courts, not in the national legislature alone, to make federal crimes out of what had largely been infringements of state law. But it was also important because six members of the Court, in concurring opinions, established the scope of § 5 of the Fourteenth Amendment as reaching beyond the limitation of state action. Mr. Justice Clark, speaking also for Justices Black and Fortas said: "[I]t is, I believe, both appropriate and necessary under the circumstances here to say that there now can be no doubt that the specific language of § 5 empowers the Congress to enact laws punishing all conspiracies—with or without state action—that interfere with Fourteenth Amendment rights."[153]

The left wing of the Court—Brennan, Warren, and Douglas—reiterated the proposition that § 5 authorized Congress to act without the restraints of the state-action requirement. They had no need to conjure up the existence of state action in this case as did Stewart. For them § 5 was to the Fourteenth Amendment what the Necessary and Proper Clause is to Article I.[154]

Thus was the license issued to Congress. Whether Congress needed the authority was another question. Between the power over commerce and the power over the purse, it had tools at its command that would not have the Achilles' heel of requiring a jury from the vicinage to find defendants guilty.

Nor was this the Warren Court's last word on the subject of state action. That bête noire raised its ugly head again in

---

371 U.S. 415 (1963) (freedom of association); Shelton v. Tucker, 364 U.S. 479 (1960) (freedom of association); Cox v. Louisiana, 379 U.S. 536 (1965) (civil rights demonstration); Edwards v. South Carolina, 372 U.S. 229 (1963) (civil rights demonstration). A keen analysis of the partisan use of the void-for-vagueness doctrine may be found in Amsterdam, *The Void-for-Vagueness Doctrine in the Supreme Court*, 109 U. PA. L. REV. 67, 75–85, 98–115 (1960).

153. 383 U.S. at 762.

154. *Id.* at 782–84.

the 1966 Term. *Reitman v. Mulkey*[155] further compounded the confusion. California had adopted by referendum a constitutional provision that, in effect, banned all open housing legislation, state and local, within that state.[156] The state legislature had itself passed two such statutes that were purportedly killed by the constitutional change. Suit was brought in the state courts challenging the validity of the adoption of Proposition 14—the constitutional amendment —as invalid under the Fourteenth Amendment. The Supreme Court of California held that Proposition 14 violated the Fourteenth Amendment, but did not really say why.[157] The Supreme Court of the United States affirmed that judgment in *Reitman v. Mulkey,* but did not really say why. As two staunch supporters of the Supreme Court and the conclusion that it reached said:

> [T]he Court in *Reitman v. Mulkey* settled for an opinion that utterly failed to justify its decision. The principal alternatives available to the Court—assuming a decision to affirm the California court—were to affirm without opinion, to tackle the issue of substantive equal protection head on, or to temporize, avoiding the unavoidable by fudging. It is not shocking that the Court chose the last path.[158]

By "substantive equal protection," they obviously mean an imposition of the Court's values under the label of equal protection, just as an earlier Court engaged in the same process under the title of substantive due process. It is a dangerous game, but there are few who deny the Court's engagement in it. The search for a rationale must nevertheless continue, either to afford guidance for future decisions or to save the Court from self-destruction. The only articulated reasoning in support of *Reitman* that sounds at all

155. 387 U.S. 369 (1967).
156. Calif. Const. art. I, § 26.
157. 64 Cal.2d 529 (1966).
158. Karst & Horowitz, note 27 *supra,* at 76.

persuasive was provided by Professor Black, whose personal inclinations are to junk the whole state-action concept as an unnecessary barrier to the elimination of racial discrimination. He offered an explanation consistent with the precedents and far more convincing than anything the high courts of California or the United States produced:

> The decision in *Reitman v. Mulkey* is apt to be widely misunderstood, because both those who like it, and those who do not, are powerfully impelled to see it as holding more than it did—the former because a broad reading could open the way to attack on many more difficult situations in the field of housing and elsewhere, and the latter because a broad holding is easier, in the present state of professional thought, to assail and discredit. The broader holding would have rested on the ground that the repeal of the fair housing law was itself a state action which denied equal protection. Further, since the distinction between states which up to now have, and those which up to now have not, enacted fair housing laws would seem to be unacceptable as a criterion of state obligation, it ought to follow that all states have a duty to enact fair housing laws, and that if they do not the discrimination thus made possible is to be seen as sanctioned by their omission, and hence as infected with a forbidden state complicity that calls down the ban of the fourteenth amendment. State "neutrality," the holders of this view would insist, is not possible—or, if possible, is not a sufficient fulfillment of the "equal protection" obligation. . . .
>
> The rule which I would propose, then, as a basis for the *Reitman* decision, is that where a racial group is in a political duel with those who would explicitly discriminate against it as a racial group, and where the regulatory action the racial group wants is of full and undoubted federal constitutionality, the state may not place in the way of the racial minority's attaining its political goal any barriers which, within the state's political system taken as a whole, are especially difficult

151

of surmounting, by comparison with those barriers that normally stand in the way of those who wish to use political processes to get what they want.[159]

In effect, a state requirement that a majority of all the state's voters must approve before the state or one of its subdivisions can provide open housing legislation makes up the state action that deprives the Negro of equal protection of the laws. Most other pressure groups do not have to meet that additional requirement on the state level, no less on the local level. Proposition 14 does smack of changing the rules in the middle of the game, which none would regard as affording equal protection.

Let none be bemused by the notion that Professor Black's suggestion would afford a precedent of narrow limits. Its consequences, if not so great as placing an affirmative burden on the state to provide open housing, for example, would be felt in the destruction of many state constitutional provisions now on the books. For, as Professor Black noted in the first paragraph quoted above, to draw a line between states that act now to establish barriers to political efforts by Negroes to secure their rights and those that acted to the same end some time ago would be difficult to justify.

The capstone of this shaky edifice was *Jones v. Alfred H. Mayer Co.*,[160] which may have the effect of the last straw on the camel's back. It did not provide the long-sought rationale for state action. But it may have made it irrelevant. The plaintiffs, a Negro man and his white wife, sought an injunction and damages against the refusal of the defendant to sell them a house in a development solely on the ground of the would-be buyer's race. The Court held that plaintiffs were entitled to the relief sought, pursuant to a long-dormant 1866 statute. It held further that the statute itself was a proper exercise of congressional power under the Thirteenth

159. Black, note 30 *supra*, at 73, 82. Cf. Hunter v. Erickson, 393 U.S. 385 (1969).
160. 392 U.S. 409 (1968).

Amendment which, of course, is not entailed with a state-action clause. The potentialities of the combination of holdings are great.

The 1866 statute, as set out in the United States Code, provides:

> All citizens of the United States shall have the same right, in every State and Territory, as is enjoyed by white citizens thereof to inherit, purchase, lease, sell, hold and convey real and personal property.[161]

Given the historical background of the 1866 legislation, one might readily conclude that the statute removed the legal disabilities that had theretofore been imposed on Negroes in all parts of the country, but especially in the South. From it, however, the Court derived an obligation on the part of an individual seller not to discriminate against putative purchasers by reason of their race. The means for achieving this worthy goal were dubious logic and abominable historicism, all carefully examined and found wanting by Professor Gerhard Casper.[162]

Perhaps the important thing to be pointed out here is not the poor credentials that the opinion carries, so much as its potential utilization to make unnecessary much of the recent civil rights legislation or any additional congressional action in this sphere. It should be noted that in terms of additional remedies, the contemporary legislation could prove important. For it calls into play the forces of the national government to vindicate the rights granted, whereas the 1866 statute would depend on self-help by the injured party. On the other hand, the new legislation is always of narrower scope than the broadly drawn Reconstruction model as interpreted by the Supreme Court.

Louis Henkin has explained the *Jones v. Mayer* potential this way:

161. 42 U.S.C. § 1982 (1964).   162. Casper, note 28 *supra*.

Indeed, does not the Court's reading render superfluous the Civil Rights Act of 1964? Title II of that Act provides that certain places of public accommodation may not discriminate on the basis of race in selling goods and services; the Court's construction of section 1982, when applied to personal property, renders the title (and its limitations) superfluous. Moreover, by the Court's technique of construction, the right "to make and enforce contracts" guaranteed by the 1866 Act should prevent a restaurant or hotel management from refusing on the grounds of race to "make a contract" for service with a Negro. Indeed, that construction should prevent any employer from refusing "to make a contract" of employment with a Negro; and the fair employment provisions of the 1964 Act likewise become superfluous, as does the entire struggle, since the days of the New Deal, to enact fair employment legislation.

One should also mention the Fair Housing title of the Civil Rights Act of 1968. The majority of the Court rightly says that it is broader in coverage and in remedy than the 1866 statute as now interpreted. [This clearly overlooks the exemptions contained in the 1968 Act that are not to be found in the 1866 statute.] But Congress had made a substantial contribution towards open housing, and one may properly ask why the Court could not resist the temptation to find in the earlier act what, by a fair reading, no Congress ever put there.

The Court failed to distinguish between what meaning words will carry and what they will not, between interpretation and perversion, between the judicial function and that of Congress. And for the majority to assert that it is " 'not at liberty to seek ingenious analytical instruments' . . . to carve from § 1982 an exception for private conduct" is surely disingenuous, and borders on *chutzpah*.[163]

163. Henkin, *On Drawing Lines,* 82 HARV. L. REV. 63, 85–86 (1968).

And so, the result of this long series of decisions is that Congress is empowered, under the Commerce Clause, the Thirteenth Amendment, the Fourteenth Amendment, and, as will be seen, the Fifteenth Amendment, to legislate against discrimination public or private. That this is desirable ought not be doubted. That it is legitimate is not so easily established. To be specially noted, however, is the weaponry that the Court has placed at its own disposal. Not only are there the clear mandates of the recent civil rights legislation. In addition, there are the even broader authorizations to be garnered from the revivified Reconstruction legislation: not only the 1866 statute relied on in *Jones v. Mayer;* not only the criminal sanctions justified in *Guest* and *Price;* but, presumably, also the Civil Rights Act of 1875,[164] erroneously invalidated in the *Civil Rights Cases;* the 1870 statute,[165] erroneously invalidated in *United States v. Reese,*[166] *Hodges v. United States,*[167] and *James v. Bowman;*[168] and the 1871 statute,[169] erroneously invalidated in *United States v. Harris.*[170]

I have detailed these cases at some length because, to my mind, they represent the very heart of the Warren Court's effort. It is on these cases that its claim on history will ultimately depend. Even before most of them were decided—indeed, just two years after *Brown*—Mr. Justice Douglas coolly announced their success in one of his extracurricular efforts. In 1956, he wrote of American Negroes:

> Their right to equality of treatment has at last been realized. No minority in any country has progressed so far in the same length of time as the American Negro. Today he sits in our legislatures, on our school boards,

164. 18 Stat. 336, §§ 1 and 2 (1875).
165. 16 Stat. 140, §§ 3 and 4 (1870); 16 Stat. 144 (1870); 16 Stat. 141, § 4 (1870).
166. 92 U.S. 214 (1876).
167. 203 U.S. 1 (1906).   169. 17 Stat. 13, § 2 (1871).
168. 190 U.S. 127 (1903).   170. 106 U.S. 629 (1883).

on many of the administrative agencies, and on our courts. He is present in every profession and calling; he is an honored member of the American community.[171]

If medals were awarded for optimism, the good Justice would have earned his at that time.

It is true that once segregation had been found to be violative of the Equal Protection Clause, the cases in which a state or local government openly distinguished among its residents on the basis of race presented little difficulty for decision. Insidious discrimination by governments created only problems of ascertaining the facts. Both kinds of cases could be settled by adoption of the first Justice Harlan's famous but simple credo: "Our Constitution is color-blind, and neither knows nor tolerates classes among citizens."[172] It is of the essence of the Equal Protection Clause that certain classifications made by government are invalid. It should indeed be simple to establish the rule that any classification based on race or color is invalid. The Warren Court has never accepted this proposition. Mr. Justice White, in *McLaughlin v. Florida*,[173] striking down a criminal statute against cohabitation that imposed higher penalties on Negro or mixed couples than on white couples, stated the limits of the Court's rule:

> [W]e deal here with a classification based upon the race of the participants, which must be viewed in light of the historical fact that the central purpose of the Fourteenth Amendment was to eliminate racial discrimination emanating from official sources in the States. This strong policy renders racial classification "constitutionally suspect, "*Bolling* v. *Sharpe,* 347 U.S. 497, 499; and subject to the "most rigid scrutiny," *Korematsu* v. *United States,* 323 U.S. 214, 216; and "in most cir-

171. DOUGLAS, WE THE JUDGES 19 (1956).
172. Plessy v. Ferguson, 163 U.S. 537, 559 (1896).
173. 379 U.S. 184 (1964).

cumstances irrelevant" to any constitutionally acceptable legislative purpose, *Hirabayashi* v. *United States,*
320 U.S. 81, 100.[174]

The reference to the Japanese exclusion cases served only to
underline the difference between the presumption and an
inflexible rule.

There were three sets of hard problems presented to the
Court by the Negro revolution cases, two of which the Court
confronted and a third which it avoided. The first was the
extent to which the Court, by reason of the Equal Protection
Clause alone, would inhibit individual acts of discrimination.
Certainly the extension of the state-action concept was only
the other side of this coin. This was a hard problem because,
like it or not, it is here that the principle of equality comes
into conflict with the principle of individual freedom, freedom to do even those acts that we most sincerely deplore.
The second question was the degree to which Congress was
empowered, under § 5 of the Fourteenth Amendment or by
other constitutional provisions, to compel individuals to behave in a nondiscriminatory manner. That is, how far
would the Court allow Congress to go in choosing between
equality on the one hand and freedom to discriminate on
the other. The Court had no difficulty whatsoever in deciding
that Congress could ban discrimination in areas that it was
reluctant to take under its own control. The third problem—
the unresolved one—was to what extent a governmental
body was free to indulge in "reverse discrimination," that is,
to classify by race for the purpose of giving greater benefits
to, or imposing lesser burdens on, a minority than a majority.
This is probably the problem that will have to be faced by
the Warren Court's successor as the nation tries to avoid
the doleful prophecies of Tocqueville and Jefferson.[175]

174. *Id.* at 191–92.
175. See text *supra,* at notes 55–57. I am again reminded of Mr.
Justice Holmes's words: "Our system of morality is a body of im-
perfect social generalizations expressed in terms of emotion. To

A look at the essence of the Equal Protection Clause and its means of fulfillment may help to clarify the problems, if not the solutions. Its purpose was to prevent majorities from imposing on minorities by way of laws that provided different rules for the one than for the other. If a majority is compelled to treat a minority exactly as it treats itself, adequate protection to minority interests would be assured by the self-interest of the majority. Mr. Justice Jackson stated this in characteristically direct fashion in *Railway Express Agency v. New York:*

> I regard it as a salutary doctrine that cities, states and the Federal Government must exercise their powers so as not to discriminate between their inhabitants except upon some reasonable differentiation fairly related to the object of regulation. This equality is not merely abstract justice. The framers of the Constitution knew, and we should not forget today, that there is no more effective practical guaranty against arbitrary and unreasonable government than to require that the principles of law which officials would impose on a minority must be imposed generally. Conversely, nothing opens the door to arbitrary action so effectively as to allow those officials to pick and choose only a few to whom they will apply legislation and thus to escape the political retribution that might be visited upon them if larger numbers were affected. Courts can take no better measure to assure that laws will be just than to require that they be equal in operation.[176]

Once the rule is recognized as one created for the protection of minorities, the role of the legislature with regard to the "benevolent quota" may become clearer, if we are also

---

get at its truth, it is useful to omit the emotion and ask ourselves what those generalizations are and how far they are confirmed by fact accurately ascertained." HOLMES, COLLECTED LEGAL PAPERS 306 (1920).

176. 336 U.S. 106, 112–13 (1949).

prepared to accede to the proposition that the legislature is the voice of the majority. The rule of equality commanded by the Equal Protection Clause is binding on the courts. But, as with almost every other constitutional right, it should be treated as waivable by knowing affirmative action. Enactment of legislation favoring a minority may be treated as such a waiver by the majority of its right to equal treatment. There is no right to compel such waiver. And the discretion to withdraw it by means of later legislation imposing a rule of equality remains with the legislature so long as the Constitution does not restrain it. The Court is the voice of the Constitution; it is not the voice of the majority. Whether § 5 authorizes this waiver or some other provision of the Constitution authorizing the legislation must be found is not a pressing question now that the national legislature's power is plenary, except insofar as it may violate the provisions of the Bill of Rights or other specific restraints of the Constitution. Local legislatures may by their actions also waive the protection of equality.

If this analysis is correct, there should be little problem with the open question of legislative power to invoke "inverse discrimination." The thesis will not, however, support judicial or administrative use of "inverse discrimination," since neither the judiciary nor the executive branch is entitled to speak for the people, unless it be the president himself, and the Necessary and Proper Clause makes me doubt that authority. Nor can the legislature waive the right of the minority to equal treatment, for by definition the legislature can enact legislation only as representatives of the majority. There remain problems, of course, but they are the kind of problems that the Court must always face in applying the Equal Protection Clause. How do you define a majority? When is a quota beneficent?

This thesis, I submit, has been tested hundreds of times a year by the passage of private bills affording special treatment, usually, to a minority of one.

Paul A. Freund has reached the same conclusion about "beneficent quotas," by a different route:

> Suppose . . . that the question of preference is raised without evasion. To characterize a preference as compensatory is hardly a satisfying answer to all the complexities. . . .
>
> But the concept of compensation does suggest some possible differentiations or gradations in the problem of preference. Where the government itself was responsible for discrimination in the past, there is a better case for its reverse preference now. So, too, where the preference is, so to speak, transitional, by way of preparing the members of the group to be treated as individuals. And it is the easier to justify a preference the less positive harm to others; easier to justify additional attention in schooling than a competitive preference in the job market. Moreover there is an ethical sense in which discrimination in favor of a minority is not to be equated with a discrimination against it. . . . If this is a sound moral judgment, it is relevant to the judgment of the law as well, for equal protection of the law is at bottom the embodiment of a moral standard.[177]

The essential difficulty about inroads on individual freedoms is not resolved, however, by appeal to the purpose or morality of the Equal Protection Clause. Here the problem essentially will have to be resolved under other provisions of the Constitution. Thus far, the Court has treated it too cavalierly. If Congress has authority to act by § 5 of the Fourteenth Amendment or otherwise, it may still do so only within the confines of stated constitutional limitations. Clearly it cannot do so by infringing an individual's right to freedom of speech or a jury trial or to due process of law, with all the ambiguities that involves, or to rights offered by the

177. Freund, *The Civil Rights Movement and the Frontiers of Law,* in THE NEGRO AMERICAN 366–67 (Parsons & Clark eds. 1966).

"penumbra" of the Bill of Rights.[178] Here it is the Court that will have to do the weighing. And let no one say that the Court's discretion is not invoked when two constitutional rights come into conflict. It might be asked that the Court do the weighing publicly and state the reasons for its choice rationally, however difficult such a task might be. The invocation of absolutes is hardly responsive.

Like the cases concerned with the Negro revolution, the reapportionment cases[179] rested on the Equal Protection Clause. Unlike the Negro cases, the reapportionment cases were concerned with form more than with substance. They represent a sterile concept of equality for the sake of equality. Given the premise of one man–one vote, one vote–one value, the Court needed nothing more for its decision than the principle of *reductio ad absurdum*. There is an element of "Catch-22" in the opinions in these cases. The Court has repeatedly said that justifiable deviations from the arithmetical formula will be tolerated but has yet to accept any justification proffered.

Yet these cases must be chalked up as a judicial success inasmuch as compliance has readily occurred and the public is quiescent if not acquiescent. If there were goals to be achieved aside from the aesthetic one of every electoral district containing the same number of voters as every other district, more doubts about the Court's accomplishments might be expressed. If the Court's objective was the revival of state legislatures, it has failed; state legislatures remain moribund. If its objective was the transfer of power from

178. *"Griswold* v. *Connecticut* [381 U.S. 479] (1965) saw the Court in a most creative mood. It wanted to argue with a legislature, but it had no specific constitutional provisions on which to base its judgment. And so it created a constitutional foundation for its position, just as it had done with substantive due process three-quarters of a century earlier." PRITCHETT, THE AMERICAN CONSTITUTION 686 (2d ed. 1968).

179. See Dixon, *The Warren Court Crusade for the Holy Grail of "One Man–One Vote,"* 1969 SUPREME COURT REVIEW 219.

rural to urban voters, it has failed; the beneficiaries of the transfer have been the reactionary suburbs. If its objective was to secure more meaningful representation, it has failed for the simple reason that arithmetic has no sense of community.

The Equal Protection Clause has not been a powerful weapon of the Warren Court in the other major field of its effort, the reform of criminal procedure. Aside from the jury selection cases, in which the Court has upset the selection process in every case it accepted for review,[180] the clause was utilized only to support the doctrine of *Griffin v. Illinois* seeking to assure equality between poor and rich in the conduct of appeals,[181] including access to appellate counsel.[182] At the substantive level, the Equal Protection Clause was the reason for holding Virginia's miscegenation law invalid.[183] But attacks on habitual criminal statutes imposing higher punishments on recidivists,[184] on the imposition of a higher sentence on retrial than at the original trial,[185] and on the award of a new trial on the issue of punishment but not on the question of guilt[186] were all rebuffed despite claims of violation of the Equal Protection Clause.

180. Hernandez v. Texas, 347 U.S. 475 (1954) (Mexicans); Eubanks v. Louisiana, 356 U.S. 584 (1958); Arnold v. North Carolina, 376 U.S. 773 (1964); Whitus v. Georgia, 385 U.S. 545 (1967); Coleman v. Alabama, 389 U.S. 22 (1967); Sims v. Georgia, 389 U.S. 404 (1967).

181. Griffin v. Illinois, 351 U.S. 12 (1956); Douglas v. Green, 363 U.S. 192 (1960); McCrary v. Indiana, 364 U.S. 277 (1960); Smith v. Bennett, 365 U.S. 708 (1961); Lane v. Brown, 372 U.S. 477 (1963); Draper v. Washington, 372 U.S 487 (1963); Norvell v. Illinois, 373 U.S. 420 (1963); Long v. District Court of Iowa, 385 U.S. 192 (1966); Roberts v. La Vallee, 389 U.S. 40 (1967); Williams v. Oklahoma City, 395 U.S. 458 (1969).

182. Douglas v. California, 372 U.S. 353 (1963); Anders v. California, 386 U.S. 738 (1967).

183. Loving v. Virginia, 388 U.S. 1 (1967).

184. Oyler v. Boles, 368 U.S. 448 (1962).

185. North Carolina v. Pearce, 395 U.S. 711 (1969).

186. Brady v. Maryland, 373 U.S. 83 (1963).

In the area of economic regulation and taxation, the Court almost invariably sustained the state classifications. With regard to taxes, invalid discrimination was generally rejected.[187] The only major tax case in which the taxpayer prevailed on grounds of improper classification was one imposing a tax at a different rate on domesticated foreign corporations.[188] The Court sustained a regulation of sale of eyeglasses by opticians that was inapplicable to over-the-counter sales of ready-to-wear glasses.[189] The Court held valid direct-action statutes against insurance companies,[190] and a state law prohibiting sales below cost even to meet competition.[191] Sunday closing laws did not violate the Equal Protection Clause,[192] which brings to mind Holmes's dictum in *Otis v. Parker*[193] in 1902: "The Sunday laws, no doubt, would be sustained by a bench of judges, even if every one of them thought it superstitious to make any day holy."

A ban on "debt adjustment" except by lawyers was also held proper.[194] California's legislation discriminating against Florida avocados was also held valid,[195] as was a full-crew law for railroad trains.[196] The single sport was *Morey v. Doud*,[197] in which the Court held that Illinois could not clas-

187. Walters v. St. Louis, 347 U.S. 231 (1954); Allied Stores v. Bowers, 358 U.S. 522 (1959); Youngstown Sheet & Tube Co. v. Bowers, 358 U.S. 534 (1959).

188. WHYY, Inc. v. Glassboro, 393 U.S. 117 (1968).

189. Williams v. Lee Optical, Inc., 348 U.S. 483 (1955).

190. Watson v. Employers Liability Assurance Corp., 348 U.S. 66 (1954).

191. Safeway Stores, Inc. v. Oklahoma Retail Grocers Ass'n, 360 U.S. 334 (1959).

192. McGowan v. Maryland, 366 U.S. 420 (1961); Two Guys v. McGinley, 366 U.S. 582 (1961); Braunfeld v. Brown, 366 U.S. 599 (1961); Gallagher v. Crown Kosher Market, 366 U.S. 617 (1961).

193. 187 U.S. 606, 609 (1902).

194. Ferguson v. Skrupa, 372 U.S. 726 (1963).

195. Florida Avocado Growers v. Paul, 373 U.S 132 (1963).

196. Firemen v. Chicago, R.I. & P.R. Co., 393 U.S. 129 (1968).

197. 354 U.S. 457 (1957).

sify American Express along with the United States Post Office and Western Union instead of with currency exchanges in the issuance of money orders. This case can be understood only as an expression of personal opinion by the Justices or a requirement that categories be spelled out in descriptive terms rather than by proper names.

The exclusion of Raphael Konigsberg from the California bar because of his personal history was held offensive to the principles of equal protection.[198] But the exclusion of out-of-state lawyers was sustained.[199] And, if *Griffin v. Illinois* stands for the proposition that government cannot discriminate between rich and poor, the Court in sustaining the federal reclamation acts nevertheless held it proper to distinguish between large landholders and small ones.[200]

In important decisions, the Court held that the Equal Protection Clause prohibited a legal distinction between legitimate and illegitimate children for purposes of wrongful death statutes.[201] And residence requirements for welfare recipients were also held to be an invidious discrimination.[202] The bulk of the cases in which the clause was used to invalidate legislation concerned the exercise of the elective franchise.

Racial designations on ballots were prohibited by *Anderson v. Martin*.[203] So, too, with a law prohibiting military personnel from registering as resident voters.[204] The poll tax was invalidated in one of the Court's shakiest opinions, again resting on distinctions between rich and poor.[205] The Court found that access to a position on the ballot was unduly re-

198. Konigsberg v. California State Bar, 353 U.S. 252 (1957).
199. Martin v. Walton, 368 U.S. 25 (1961).
200. Ivanhoe Irrigation Dist. v. McCracken, 357 U.S. 275 (1958).
201. Giona v. American Guarantee Co., 391 U.S. 73 (1968); Levy v. Louisiana, 391 U.S. 68 (1968).
202. Shapiro v. Thompson, 394 U.S. 618 (1969).
203. 375 U.S. 399 (1964).
204. Carrington v. Rash, 380 U.S. 89 (1965).
205. Harper v. Virginia, 383 U.S. 663 (1966).

stricted in three cases.[206] Only two challenges on equal protection grounds were not accepted in this field. A prisoner's right to an absentee ballot while in the penitentiary was held not to be justified by the Constitution.[207] And the power of a legislature, even a malapportioned one, to choose a governor after none of the candidates had secured a majority of the popular vote was upheld.[208]

These decisions under the Equal Protection Clause do not, however, reveal the extent of the egalitarian influence on that Court's opinions. But these were more than sufficient to call forth Professor Cox's judgment that, after the demand for racial justice, which he did not include in the egalitarian influence, "Egalitariansim thus became the second powerful factor shaping current constitutional decisions."[209]

A great deal more of the Court's business reflected this factor. For, as Cox also said in a frequently quoted remark: "Once loosed the idea of Equality is not easily cabined."[210] In part this may due to the amorphous nature of the substance of equality. It is, therefore, not always recognized, even when it is seen. In part its expansionist tendency may be due to its use as rhetoric rather than as an idea. And the rhetoric is subject to use, if not capture, by anyone on any side of the question.

Other constitutional provisions besides the Equal Protection Clause command equality. And the Warren Court also enforced these commands. The Fifteenth Amendment cases,[211] not least *Gomillion v. Lightfoot*,[212] in which Mr.

206. Williams v. Rhodes, 393 U.S. 23 (1968); Hadnott v. Amos, 394 U.S. 358 (1969); Moore v. Ogilvie, 394 U.S. 814 (1969).
207. McDonald v. Bd. of Election Comm'rs, 395 U.S. 802 (1969).
208. Fortson v. Morris, 385 U.S. 231 (1966).
209. Cox, THE WARREN COURT 6 (1968).
210. *Ibid.*
211. South Carolina v. Katzenbach, 383 U.S. 301 (1966); Gaston County v. United States, 395 U.S. 285 (1969). See Fiss, *Gaston County v. United States: Fruition of the Freezing Principle,* 1969 SUPREME COURT REVIEW 379.
212. 364 U.S. 339 (1960). See Lucas, *Dragon in the Thicket:*

Justice Frankfurter, in spite of himself, ignited the powder-keg of reapportionment, are in this category. The construction given the Citizenship Clause of the Fourteenth Amendment seems to preclude any distinction between native-born and naturalized citizens,[213] except, I suppose, with regard to eligibility for the presidency. As I have suggested at length elsewhere, the decisions under the religion clauses of the First Amendment also compel equality.[214] The Twenty-fourth Amendment, banning the condition of a poll tax for voting in federal elections, has an egalitarian flavor that the Court adopted for its own when it struck down Virginia's poll tax.[215] Certainly, too, the destruction of state power and the centralization of authority in the national government are part of this trend in seeking a uniform rule to govern all.[216] Even the void-for-vagueness cases[217]—which I prefer to denominate the vague-for-voidness cases—are essentially in this category, for they in effect hold that the legislative classification is overbroad. The *Aptheker* case[218] rested specifically on that proposition, and most of the cases concerned with Communists and subversives are not different in their constitutional question—that is, can these groups as defined be treated differently?

A Perusal of Gomillion v. Lightfoot, 1961 SUPREME COURT REVIEW 194.

213. Schneider v. Rusk, 377 U.S. 163 (1964).

214. See KURLAND, RELIGION AND THE LAW (1962); Kurland, *The Regents' Prayer Case: "Full of Sound and Fury, Signifying . . . ,"* 1962 SUPREME COURT REVIEW 1; Torcaso v. Watkins, 367 U.S. 488 (1961); Engel v. Vitale, 370 U.S. 421 (1962); Arlan's Dep't Store v. Kentucky, 371 U.S. 218 (1962); School District of Abington Township v. Schempp, 374 U.S. 203 (1963); Sherbert v. Verner, 374 U.S. 398 (1963); Chamberlin v. Public Instruction Bd., 377 U.S. 402 (1964); and the cases cited *supra* at note 192.

215. Harman v. Forssenius, 380 U.S. 528 (1965).

216. See chapter 3.

217. See, *e.g.,* cases cited *supra,* at note 152 and Tussman & tenBroek, *The Equal Protection of the Laws,* 37 CALIF. L. REV. 341 (1949).

218. Aptheker v. Secretary of State, 378 U.S. 500 (1964).

What must quickly become apparent is that all government processes necessarily involve the problem of classification and can be analyzed in terms of the propriety of these classifications. They are all subject to measurement against the demands of the Equal Protection Clause. And the Court seems more and more ready to address them in just those terms.

Some bases for classification are clearly forbidden or at least are highly suspect because of explicit terms of the Constitution: race is one, religion is another. But for the most part the test is the same as that which was put forth under the Due Process Clause. Is it reasonable for a governmental body to classify in this way? It is not surprising that we see an appeal to the Court to engage in the development of "substantive equal protection." For "substantive equal protection" is but another name for "substantive due process." Each will do as well as the other as a means of limiting or destroying nonjudicial government authority.

Nor is "substantive equal protection" a novel concept. It was utilized, for example, by the Taft Court in *Truax v. Corrigan*,[219] where the Court held that the Equal Protection Clause invalidated a state law that forbade injunctions in labor cases because injunctions remained available as a form of relief in other kinds of cases. The decision, like so many others that we have seen, was rendered by a Court divided five to four. Holmes and Brandeis were among the dissenters. Among other things, Holmes, in keeping with his judicial philosophy, said: "Legislation may begin where an evil begins. If, as many intelligent people believe, there is more danger that the injunction will be abused in labor cases than elsewhere I can feel no doubt of the power of the legislature to deny it in such cases."[220]

I invoke the example of *Truax v. Corrigan* at this time for two reasons. First, as a reminder of the fact that what we

219. 257 U.S. 312 (1921).   220. *Id.* at 343.

167

are talking about is the allocation to and use of power by the Court as an institution. As with the presidency, the individuals change but the power accrued by the institution remains, until taken away from it. I do not know, but I can guess, how those anxious for Mr. Warren and company to have this discretionary power may be more wary of giving it to the Nixon Court, especially as it blossoms with new personnel.

The second reason is to suggest that the notion of equality is multifaceted. Conformity and uniformity are also parts of equality. But even if we were to accept the egalitarian goal as contemporarily stated, we should be wary of making it our prime value. The modern definition, as I see it, I borrow from an Englishman, for England has the same forces to confront, even if it lacks a Supreme Court with which to do it: "The more nearly the citizens of a country resemble one another in the amount of money they spend, the goods they own, the education they acquire and the social deference they receive, the more nearly perfect that country will be."[221]

Yesterday, the exponents of this doctrine urged that the Supreme Court be the institution to determine its applicability to the social, economic, and political scene in the United States. Tomorrow they may regret this power in any governmental body, including the Supreme Court. As Geoffrey Gorer wrote:

> If mobilized public envy and resentment begrudge any social deference or conspicuous success outside the power hierarchy, then the way is being prepared for a single-value society. To the extent that the obverse of a desire for social justice is envy of, or resentment at, conspicuous success, rather than pity for conspicuous unsuccess, to that extent is the striving for a just state likely to result in a state where all power is concentrated in a single hierarchy, where all that will remain

221. GORER, THE DANGER OF EQUALITY 63 (1966).

of a democracy will be a ritual whereby members at the top of the power hierarchy will exchange political positions among themselves at irregular intervals. Democracy depends on a multiplicity of values; if only a single value is emphasized democracy cannot survive.[222]

Those too young to remember what happened to Europe immediately prior to World War II, as country after country fell under the thrall of equality, may yet find the allegory of Orwell's *Animal Farm* instructive and frightening.

222. *Id*. at 71.

5

Problems of a Political Court

OBVIOUSLY THE SUPREME COURT is more than the nine individuals gowned in black and ensconced in the marble palace in Washington. Like the presidency and the Congress, the Court must be viewed as an institution separate and apart from those who temporarily occupy the offices. It is important to examine the Court's actions and to evaluate its use of power not just for today. To paraphrase Maitland, one must take a deep account of yesterday in order that today not paralyze tomorrow.

The ardent advocates of enhancement of presidential power when John F. Kennedy occupied the White House seem to have lost most of their ardor during the more recent tenures of Presidents Johnson and Nixon. Those prepared to have the congressional role in foreign affairs and the Senate's power to review treaty commitments bypassed for more efficient methods have begun to recognize the values inherent in such checks on the executive will, as the Vietnam tragedy becomes ever more tragic. And now, with a radical change of personnel on the Supreme Court already begun, there must be at least some advocates of judicial power prepared to think in more institutional terms.

Just as the power flowing to the national government from the states became irreversible at some point in our history; just as the accretion of executive authority and the reduction of legislative authority has become intractable; so, too, the authority that any Court might assert—and the manner of its assertion—could become fixed for use by future Justices.

I do not mean that any of these trends could not be reversed. Certainly, they might be. But only at the cost of weathering a constitutional crisis with all its correlative consequences and dangers.

The proper question about the Court today—before the crisis is upon us—is not whether we should reverse the flow of authority but whether it should be slowed or speeded. The question is whether the essential function that the Court performs will be strengthened or weakened by further quick movements of the Supreme Court along the road that it has recently traveled.

We have it on very high authority that the Supreme Court's functions should be expanded and legitimized.[1] Adolf Berle tells us that withdrawal from power, apparently like withdrawal from drugs, would have most unpleasant consequences:

> A corollary to the first law of power (that it always replaces chaos) is an implacable rule. Power cast aside without provision for its further exercise almost invariably destroys the abdicating power holder—as, for example, Shakespeare's King Lear found out when he improvidently abandoned his power, and was promptly crushed. Conceivably, the Supreme Court might have avoided assuming the power position in the first place— but it cannot renounce it now. It has entered, created, and accepted a field of responsibility. Elements in that field might wreck the Court were it now to desert the function it has assumed.[2]

I do not know whether Lear's kingdom would have been better off had he remained in authority. Nor do I know that the Congress and the president are properly analogized to Goneril and Regan or their husbands. After all, we have seen that the administration of the realm of civil rights, if far from perfect, has been more effective when Congress and

1. BERLE, THREE FACES OF POWER (1967).
2. *Id.* at 51.

the executive have taken a hand than when it is solely the concern of the judiciary. In any event, the proper question is not abdication, but how the Court's authority should be exercised.

I suggest that we ask whether, as the Warren Court has moved toward the legislative mode and away from the judicial mode of carrying on its business, it has endangered the capacity to perform its peculiar function. A truly legislative body, as the Court itself has frequently said, must be directly responsible to the expression of majority will. The single institution in our system created for the purpose of protecting the interests of minorities—assuming that is what the Constitution is about, at least in part—is the Supreme Court. Its essentially antidemocratic character keeps it constantly in jeopardy of destruction. But that characteristic is both its principal virtue and its primary limitation. The question is, Do we secure more of what we need or want by turning the Supreme Court into a third legislative chamber or by retaining it as a judicial body?

I suggested at the outset that the Court has never been either purely judicial or purely legislative in its work. I should like, however, to examine some of its processes to determine whether it has in recent years been moving toward the legislative pole. I reject the notion that this is determinable simply by examining its conclusions and deciding whether the Court has made new law. If the Supreme Court did not make new law, it would be hard to justify its existence. Fixed principles are as readily applied by lower federal courts and by state courts as by the nine berobed men in Washington. The issue is rather how that new law is made and why, and what effect it will or should have.

Some political scientists and some self-styled realists among the lawyers would say that the Court is in fact already a legislative body, or is not different from a legislative body in its function. Indeed, Professor Berle's recent tantalizing if unconvincing little book opens with the proposition that "ultimate legislative power in the United States has come to rest in the Supreme Court of the United States."[3] But this position, it seems to me, rests on an oversimplified notion of how the legislative function differs from the judicial. I submit that the difference does not lie in whether one or the other has a lawmaking power. There may be some—even in this day—who are unwilling to recognize that courts make law. But our legal heritage derives from the great tradition of the common law which originated at a time when the courts were the prime lawmakers and the legislature was new to the function. And I am assured by Professor Kalven that, as he surveys developments in the field of tort law, he is more convinced that the common-law courts are as creative today as they ever were. At least since Holmes's day, we have recognized judicial lawmaking as a conscious process of creation not discovery:

> In substance the growth of the law is legislative. And this in a deeper sense than that what the courts declare to have always been the law is in fact new. It is legislative in its grounds. The very considerations which judges most rarely mention, and always with an apology, are the secret root from which the law draws all the juices of life. I mean, of course, considerations of what is expedient for the community concerned. Every important principle which is developed by litigation is in fact and at bottom the result of more or less definitely understood views of public policy; most generally, to be sure, under our practice and traditions, the unconscious result of instinctive preferences and inarticulate convictions, but none the less traceable to views of public policy in the last analysis. And as the law is administered by able and experienced men, who know too much to sacrifice good sense to a syllogism, it will be found that, when ancient rules maintain themselves . . . new reasons more fitted to the time have been found for them, and that they

3. *Id.* at 3.

173

gradually receive a new content, and at last, a new form from the grounds to which they had been transplanted.

But hitherto this process has been largely unconscious. It is important, on that account, to bring to mind what the course of events has been. If it were only to insist on a more conscious recognition of the legislative function of the courts, as just explained, it would be useful.[4]

The distinction that I am seeking to draw here between the juridical mode and the legislative mode is a distinction between two rule-making processes. When I suggest that the Warren Court has moved closer to the legislative form than most of its predecessors have done, it is not because it has made new law but because in making new law it has come closer to emulating the legislative process than did its predecessors. But I should emphasize that the Court still has a long way to go before identity of the processes will have occurred. For, I would repeat, one essential difference between the two systems lies in their respective constituencies. The legislature represents that combination of groups and individuals that makes a majority on that issue; the Court has peculiar obligations to discrete minorities. The majority is an ever present threat to the Court's authority and must be taken into account for that reason. And no one suggests openly that where the majority will is expressed through legislation, it is the Court's function to thwart it or prevent it. The exception is where the legislature imposes on individuals or minorities in so fundamental a fashion as to necessitate invoking the safeguards of the Constitution.

Comparing the role of the common-law judge to that of the legislator, Cardozo, in the Holmes tradition, had this to say:

My analysis of the judicial process comes then to this, and little more: logic and history, and custom, and utility, and the accepted standards of right conduct, are

4. HOLMES, THE COMMON LAW 31–32 (Howe ed. 1963).

the forces which singly or in combination shape the progress of the law. Which of these forces shall dominate in any case, must depend largely upon the comparative importance or value of the social interests that will be thereby promoted or impaired. One of the most fundamental social interests is that law shall be uniform and impartial. There must be nothing in its action that savors of prejudice or favor or even arbitrary whim or fitfulness. Therefore in the main there shall be adherence to precedent. . . .

If you ask how he is to know when one interest outweighs another, I can only answer that he must get his knowledge just as the legislator gets it, from experience and study and reflection; in brief, from life itself. Here, indeed, is the point of contact between the legislator's work and his. The choice of methods, the appraisement of values, must in the end be guided by like considerations for the one as for the other. Each indeed is legislating within the limits of his competence. No doubt the limits for the judge are narrower. He legislates only between gaps. He fills the open spaces in the law. How far he may go without traveling beyond the walls of the interstices cannot be staked out for him upon a chart. He must learn it for himself as he gains the sense of fitness and proportion that comes with years of habitude in the practice of an art. Even within the gaps, restrictions not easy to define, but felt, however impalpable they may be, by every judge and lawyer, hedge and circumscribe his action. They are established by the traditions of the centuries, by the example of other judges, his predecessors and his colleagues, by the collective judgment of the profession, and by the duty of adherence to the pervading spirit of the law.[5]

It is important to recognize that both Holmes and Cardozo were talking essentially about common-law courts where the analogy to legislation is closer and easier. For one thing, if

5. CARDOZO, THE NATURE OF THE JUDICIAL PROCESS 111, 112–14 (1921).

175

the common-law courts legislate interstitially, they also legislate only temporarily. If the legislature chooses a different rule from that pronounced by the courts, in the common-law world the legislative will would be dominant. This is the point made by J. R. Lucas in differentiating the English high court from the Supreme Court:

> The example of the Supreme Court of the United States of America shows that if we want to keep politics out of the administration of justice, we must deprive the officials who administer justice of all discretion which might be influenced by political considerations. Else there will be an incentive for politicians to attempt to "pack" the courts with their own partisans. But where the ultimate authority is a non-judicial court or assembly, all we need to ensure when selecting people to be judges is that they shall faithfully apply the laws enacted by the Legislature in all cases to which they clearly apply. It was not necessary to pack the English Bench because the same judges who decided the Taff Vale case could be relied upon, whatever their political opinions or private views, to apply the provisions of the Trades Disputes Act, which reversed the Taff Vale decision. Provided the judges, like reeds, will bow to political winds in due legislative form, there is no reason for them not to exercise, in the absence of a clear directive from Parliament, their own judgment on what is equitable and just. All that we do demand is that where Parliament has given a ruling, judges should follow it, even against their own judgment, not because Parliament is wiser, more equitable or more just than the judges, but . . . because it is expedient to concentrate all political discretion in Parliament, where, though wrong may be done, it will be done openly.[6]

It was this deference to legislative supremacy—and it should be recalled that eighteenth-century Americans were

6. LUCAS, THE PRINCIPLES OF POLITICS 217–18 (1966).

176

tutored by Coke's *Institutes*[7]—that was expressed, if inappropriately, by Marshall in *Osborne v. Bank of the United States*,[8] when he wrote: "Judicial power is never exercised for the purpose of giving effect to the will of the Judge; always for the purpose of giving effect to the will of the Legislature; or, in other words, to the will of the law." The equation of the will of the legislature with the will of the law is more interesting than the self-deprecation with which the sentence begins.

This supremacy of the legislature is missing in constitutional litigation. And thus there is an additional important distinction between common-law judicial legislation and that kind indulged by the Supreme Court of the United States. Common-law issues, by definition, are problems submitted for resolution by the judiciary in the absence of statutory attempts at resolving them. Constitutional adjudication, on the other hand, never takes place at so early a stage in the search for a solution to the social, political, or economic problem presented. It is not until one of the other branches of government has faced the problem and exercised or refused to exercise its lawmaking powers that the judiciary is called in to decide a constitutional issue. It is this factor of prior rule-making by legislative or executive decision that inheres in constitutional cases and is absent from the intangibles listed by Holmes and Cardozo in their descriptions of judicial legislation.

Indeed, it is this factor that has really brought forth the charge that the Warren Court has improperly become a legislature. That charge is, in effect, that the Court did not give adequate weight to the conclusions reached by other branches of government, branches that are at least equally appropriate bodies for ascertaining proper public policy. And Professor Berle's claim that the Court has become a super-legislature

7. See Thorne, Dunham, Kurland & Jennings, The Great Charter 53, 54, 57 (1965).
8. 9 Wheat. 738, 866 (1824).

is a claim to the power to disregard the judgment of other governmental authorities in deciding what rule is best. In essence, the attack is that the Court has failed to subscribe to the Thayer thesis about judicial review as stated in his biography of John Marshall:

> To set aside the acts of such a body [a legislature], representing in its own field, which is the very highest of all, the ultimate sovereign, should be a solemn, unusual, and painful act. Something is wrong when it can ever be other than that. And if it be true that the holders of legislative power are careless or evil, yet the constitutional duty of the court remains untouched; it cannot rightly attempt to protect the people, by undertaking a function not its own. On the other hand, by adhering rigidly to its own duty, the court will help, as nothing else can, to fix the spot where responsibility lies, and to bring down on that precise locality the thunderbolt of popular condemnation. The judiciary, to-day, in dealing with the acts of their coördinate legislators, owe to the country no greater or clearer duty than that of keeping their hands off these acts wherever it is possible to do it. For that course—the true course of judicial duty always—will powerfully help to bring the people and their representatives to a sense of their own responsibility. There will still remain to the judiciary an ample field for the determination of this remarkable jurisdiction, of which our American law has so much reason to be proud; a jurisdiction which has had some of its chief illustrations and its greatest triumphs, as in Marshall's time, so in ours, while the courts were refusing to exercise it.[9]

Certainly if the few cases of invalidation of national legislation are to be taken as the test,[10] the validity of the charge that the Court has improperly legislated in the area of con-

9. THAYER, HOLMES, & FRANKFURTER, JOHN MARSHALL 87–88 (Phoenix ed. 1967).
10. See chapter 2, *supra.*

stitutional review is debatable. Even with reference to review of state action, for the most part the Warren Court has been concerned not with determinations by legislatures but with those made by police officials and courts, who cannot speak with the same voice of the sovereign that Thayer so readily attributes to a legislature. Moreover, the Court's actions have occurred primarily in the area where Thayer's theory of enhanced legislative responsibility will not work. For the protection of minorities is not yet so popular that failure by the legislatures to afford it results in a "thunderbolt of popular condemnation." In any event, we have come too far along the road to national supremacy to suggest that the Court weigh the judgment of these state agencies as heavily as it would their national counterparts before promulgating new legislation.

There are other complaints about the Court's judicial legislation at the constitutional level. One is Mr. Justice Black's that the Court frequently does not justify its legislation by any command of the Constitution. In essence this is a rejection not only of constitutional judicial legislation but equally of that kind described by Holmes and Cardozo. Toward the end of the last Term of the Warren Court, Mr. Justice Black, in dissent, expressed his attitude in this manner:

> The latest statement by my Brother HARLAN on the power of this Court under the Due Process Clause to hold laws unconstitutional on the ground of the Justices' view of "fundamental fairness" makes it necessary for me to add a few words in order that the difference between us be made absolutely clear. He now says that the Court's idea of "fundamental fairness" is derived "not alone . . . from the specifics of the Constitution, but also . . . from concepts which are part of the Anglo-American legal heritage." This view is consistent with that expressed by Mr. Justice Frankfurter in *Rochin* v. *California* that due process was to be determined by "those canons of decency and fairness which express the notions of justice

179

of English-speaking peoples. . . ." 342 U.S. 165, 169. In any event my Brother HARLAN's "Anglo-American legal heritage" is no more definite than the "notions of justice of the English-speaking peoples" or the shock-the-conscience test. All these so-called tests represent nothing more or less than an implicit adoption of a Natural Law concept which under our system leaves to judges alone the power to decide what the Natural Law means. These so-called standards do not bind judges within any boundaries that can be precisely marked or defined by words for holding laws unconstitutional. On the contrary, these tests leave them wholly free to decide what they are convinced is right and fair. If the judges, in deciding whether laws are constitutional, are to be left only to the admonitions of their own consciences, why was it that the Founders gave us a written Constitution at all?[11]

The Justice asks what is certainly a basic and difficult question. And he states as well as anyone another meaning of the charge of judicial legislation. One cannot really answer his question, except by questioning the alternative that he suggests. Is it worse for the Court to read commands inhibitory of government from amorphous phrases that were put there by the Constitution's authors, as Harlan would do, than for it to read the same commands into specific language that can accommodate them only with more difficulty, as Black would do? What is the meaning to be given to such loose phrases as "due process of law" in the Fifth Amendment, or "republican form of government" in the Fourth Article, or "privileges and immunities" as used in the Fourth Article, or "equal protection of the laws" as in the Fourteenth Amendment? How can a strict constructionist, so-called, like Black have acquiesced in the reapportionment cases? The answer to Black and others voicing this same criticism can be found in the description of judicial legislation in the quo-

11. Sniadach v. Family Finance Corp., 395 U.S. 337, 350–51 (1969).

tations above from Cardozo and Holmes. Frankfurter, against whom Black leveled this attack again and again, has said:

> It may be that responsibility for decision dulls the capacity of discernment. The fact is that one sometimes envies the certitude of outsiders [as well as some Justices?] regarding the compulsions to be drawn from vague and admonitory constitutional provisions. Only for those who have not the responsibility of decision can it be easy to decide the grave and complex problems they raise, especially in controversies that excite public interest. This is so because they too often present legal issues inextricably and deeply bound up in emotional reactions to sharply conflicting economic, social, and political views. It is not the duty of judges to express their personal attitudes on such issues, deep as their individual convictions may be. The opposite is the truth; it is their duty not to act on merely personal views. But "due process," once we go beyond its strictly procedural aspect, and the "equal protection of the laws" enshrined in the Constitution, are precisely defined neither by history nor in terms. . . .
>
> No doubt, these provisions of the Constitution were not calculated to give permanent legal sanction merely to the social arrangements and beliefs of a particular epoch. Like all legal provisions without a fixed technical meaning, they are ambulant, adaptable to changes of time. That is their strength; that also makes dubious their appropriateness for judicial enforcement. Dubious because their vagueness readily lends itself to make of the Court a third chamber with drastic veto power. This danger has been pointed out by our greatest judges too often to be dismissed as a bogey. Holding democracy in judicial tutelage is not the most promising way to foster disciplined responsibility in a people.[12]

12. THAYER, HOLMES, & FRANKFURTER, note 9 *supra*, at 156–57.

On the other hand, it might be said that "holding democracy in judicial tutelage" is the only way that has yet been devised for preventing the "tyranny of the majority," as J. S. Mill termed it,[13] from imposing on the minority. This aspect of what Frankfurter's good friend Lord Radcliffe called "the problem of power"[14] remains the central problem of American life, not merely with reference to judicial problems but also because of those created by the executive and the legislature in their exclusive spheres of authority.

Yet, it must be conceded to Mr. Justice Black and others that, to the extent the Court's discretion has become less and less fettered by the judgments of its coordinate branches of the national government, by the decisions of various state agencies, by the language of the Constitution and federal statutes, it is behaving more and more like a legislative body and less and less like a court.

To the extent, too, that the Court's lawmaking is not justified by well-reasoned opinions, it is indulging a privilege that belongs more to the legislature than to an appellate court. The Supreme Court's own rules impose on federal trial courts an obligation to justify their judgments by stated findings of fact and conclusions of law.[15] Rule 52 has two functions. One is to make the trial court more aware of the problems that it is confronting. The other is to justify its result to a reviewing tribunal. But as Mr. Justice Jackson was fond of reminding his brethren, the reason that the Court does not have to meet this same obligation of justifying its results is only that there is no other court which can hold it responsible. "We are not final because we are infallible, but we are infallible only because we are final."[16]

Strangely, the defenders of the Court do not tend to argue that the opinions are well reasoned, but rather that they are

13. See MILL, ON LIBERTY 68 (Everyman ed. 1910).
14. See RADCLIFFE, THE PROBLEM OF POWER (Comet ed. 1958).
15. Rule 52, Federal Rules of Civil Procedure.
16. Brown v. Allen, 344 U.S. 443, 540 (1953).

no worse than John Marshall's classic judgments. The defect was put in these terms by Professors Bickel and Wellington of the Yale Law School:

> The Court's product has shown an increasing incidence of the sweeping dogmatic statement, of the formulation of results accompanied by little or no effort to support them in reason, in sum, of opinions that do not opine and of per curiam orders that quite frankly fail to build the bridge between the authorities they cite and the results they decree.[17]

The defense is not that the Court should not do better, but that it has sometimes been as bad in the past as in the present. Again, we are on the border of legislative prerogative to create rules without the need for justifying them.

Worse, however, is that this kind of opinion writing has led to the evils that disturbed Mr. Justice Cardozo when he was faced with the same kind of behavior by the majority of the Nine Old Men with whom he sat. The problem of which Cardozo wrote is endemic in American society, but one looks to the Court for higher standards than those of the hustings or of Madison Avenue. In *Snyder v. Massachusetts*,[18] Cardozo wrote:

> A fertile source of perversion in constitutional theory is the tyranny of labels. Out of the vague precepts of the Fourteenth Amendment a court frames a rule which is general in form, though it has been wrought under the pressure of particular situations. Forthwith another situation is placed under the rule because it is fitted to the words, though related faintly, if at all, to the reasons that brought the rule into existence.

17. Bickel & Wellington, *Legislative Purpose and the Judicial Process: The Lincoln Mills Case*, 71 HARV. L. REV. 1, 3 (1957). See also Handler, *The Supreme Court and the Antitrust Laws*, 1 GA. L. REV. 339 (1967), for further documentation.

18. 291 U.S. 97, 114 (1934).

Certainly the per curiam decisions that followed hard on the heels of *Brown*,[19] fit the description that is contained in the quotation from Cardozo. And this derives, I would suggest, from the notion that the judgment of the Court is not a resolution of a case or controversy but rather is an edict no different in form or consequence from a statute.

The old theory was that a court resolves a particular case that has been submitted to it. Its judgment is binding on all who were parties to the litigation. Indeed, it is said to be unconstitutional to bind those who were not parties to the litigation.[20] In form, the Court's judgments do not purport to control the behavior of any except those who were brought under its jurisdiction. At the same time, the opinions form an ample basis for prediction so that they meet Holmes's test, at least, of the meaning of law: "The prophecies of what the courts will do in fact, and nothing more pretentious, are what I mean by the law."[21]

Legislation, on the other hand, is premised on the proposition that it is directed to the entire population within the domain, or such portion of it as falls within the ken of the statute. Even if the executive or judicial power may be necessary to enforce it, the obligation is created by the statute. The distinction I have in mind may be revealed by pointing out the differences between the desegregation judgment in *Brown* and its coverage and the obligations created by the Civil Rights Acts of more recent vintage. The former, however clear its implications for those subjected to further litigation, created no duties except on those parties to the lawsuit. The Justices recognized this limitation on their power during oral argument in the case.[22] The statutes imposed

19. Brown v. Bd. of Educ., 347 U.S. 483 (1954); see chapter 3, notes 83–89; Wechsler, *Toward Neutral Principles of Constitutional Law*, 73 HARV. L. REV. 1 (1959).

20. See, *e.g.*, Supreme Tribe of Ben-Hur v. Cauble, 255 U.S. 356 (1921); Walker v. City of Hutchinson, 352 U.S. 112 (1956).

21. HOLMES, COLLECTED LEGAL PAPERS 173 (1920).

22. See FRIEDMAN, ed., ARGUMENT: THE COMPLETE ORAL ARGU-

duties on all within their ambits. And yet, as revealed in *Cooper v. Aaron*,[23] the Court seemed to assume the same scope for its decision as the statute could claim. We are told, not only by the opinion signed by every single Justice, but in the separate opinion of Mr. Justice Frankfurter as well, that the Court's decisions are the "law of the land." Frankfurter wrote:

> The duty to abstain from resistance to "the supreme Law of the Land," U.S. Const., Art. 6, ¶ 2, as declared by the organ of our Government for ascertaining it, does not require immediate approval of it nor does it deny the right of dissent. Criticism need not be stilled. Active obstruction or defiance is barred. Our kind of society cannot endure if the controlling authority of the Law as derived from the Constitution is not to be the tribunal specially charged with the duty of ascertaining and declaring what is "the supreme Law of the Land.". . . Particularly is this so where the declaration of what "the supreme Law" commands on an underlying moral issue is not the dubious pronouncement of a gravely divided Court but is the unanimous conclusion of a long-matured deliberative process.[24]

I am not quarreling with the result that the Court reached in *Cooper v. Aaron*. Indeed, I applaud it. Certainly interference with the effectuation of a decree of a federal court, whether by a governor of a state or a president of a union or a civil rights marcher, is intolerable and cannot be condoned. My question goes only to the elevation of Supreme Court decisions to inclusion in the Supremacy Clause of the Constitution.

Among other problems that such a conclusion raises is that of the immutability of constitutional decisions. If *Plessy*

MENT BEFORE THE SUPREME COURT IN BROWN V. BOARD OF EDUCATION OF TOPEKA 254, 407, 505 (1969).

23. 358 U.S. 1 (1958).   24. *Id.* at 24.

v. Ferguson[25] was the law of the land imposed on one and sundry, I expect it was, as many have contended, binding on the Supreme Court as well. If a Supreme Court opinion remains the law of the land until it is overruled, it becomes difficult to raise the question so that it might be subject to reconsideration. More, if Supreme Court decisions are the law of the land, there are frightening conclusions to be reached from what I earlier called derelicts of constitutional law. For example, most recent major legislation enacted by Congress would fall afoul of the ban on delegation of legislative powers. Last I heard, neither the *Schechter* case[26] nor *Panama Refining*[27] had been overruled. A Supreme Court opinion, whatever its merits, cannot seriously be treated as the equivalent of a statute for purposes of the Supremacy Clause. Nor have they been so treated, however highly the Supreme Court itself may regard some of them.

Indeed, the high mortality rate among Supreme Court judgments not only supports the conclusion just stated but suggests still another analogy between Supreme Court and legislative processes. Congress is, of course, not bound to adhere to decisions that it has made at earlier times. It can reverse itself as often as a majority thinks it appropriate to do so, without being called to account for its inconsistency. So, too, apparently with the Warren Court. It has paid less heed to stare decisis—one of the features that Cardozo pointed out as distinguishing legislative legislation from judicial legislation—than any Supreme Court in history. It started by overruling *Plessy v. Ferguson* and ended by destroying *Palko v. Connecticut*.[28] And between these, a very large number of constitutional landmarks[29] that once were

25. 163 U.S. 537 (1896).
26. Schechter Corp. v. United States, 295 U.S. 495 (1935).
27. Panama Refining Co. v. Ryan, 293 U.S. 388 (1935).
28. 302 U.S. 319 (1937).
29. *E.g.*, United States v. Reese, 92 U.S. 214 (1876); Weeks v. United States, 232 U.S. 383 (1914); Wolf v. Colorado, 338 U.S. 25 (1949); Irvine v. California, 347 U.S. 128 (1954); Colegrove v.

"the law of the land" were made into artifacts for the study of historians. Nor did it make a difference that some of the overruled cases were venerable while others were creatures of the Warren Court itself.

If a few of these features of the legislative process to which the Warren Court adhered had also been indulged, if to a lesser degree, by earlier Courts, the next analogy to which I would call your attention was totally novel to the Supreme Court. The United States reports are full of statements suggesting a distinction between legislation and judicial lawmaking in terms of the prospective or retrospective application of the resultant rules. For examples: Mr. Justice Brewer once said: "One often-declared difference between judicial and legislative power is that . . . the one construes what has been; the other determines what shall be."[30] Mr. Justice Pitney asserted: "Legislation consists in laying down laws or rules for the future."[31] And Mr. Justice McKenna wrote: "Statutes are addressed to the future, not the past."[32] The theme is constantly reiterated. They did not say that legislation could never be retroactive. "There is no constitutional inhibition against retrospective laws. Though generally distrusted, they are often beneficial, and sometimes necessary."[33] But nowhere was there any hint that judicial decisions could be solely prospective in their nature.

Green, 328 U.S. 549 (1946); Betts v. Brady, 316 U.S. 455 (1942); Darr v. Burford, 339 U.S. 200 (1950); Adams v. Tanner, 244 U.S. 590 (1917); Twining v. New Jersey, 211 U.S. 78 (1908); Adamson v. California, 332 U.S. 46 (1947); Feldman v. United States, 322 U.S. 487 (1944).

No less an authority than Marshall's Brown v. Maryland, 12 Wheat. 419 (1827), was mortally wounded if not destroyed by Youngstown Co. v. Bowers, 358 U.S. 534, 552–53, 561 (1959).

30. I.C.C. v. Brimson, 154 U.S. 447, 155 U.S. 3, 9 (1894).

31. Mitchell Coal & Coke Co. v. Pennsylvania R.R., 230 U.S. 247, 272–73 (1913).

32. See Winfree v. Northern Pac. Ry., 227 U.S. 296, 301 (1913); Nichols & Co. v. United States, 249 U.S. 34, 38 (1919).

33. Blount v. Windley, 95 U.S. 173, 180 (1877).

It was the Warren Court that initiated the practice of imitating the legislature by providing that its decisions in certain criminal cases, where it avowedly changed the meaning of the Constitution, would have only prospective effect. The genesis of the rule is of some interest. In 1932 the Supreme Court rejected the complaint that a state by making its judicial rule prospective had violated the Constitution. In *Great Northern Ry. v. Sunburst Co.*,[34] the state court had held that while it would apply the old rule to the case before it, from that point on a different rule would be applicable. It was Mr. Justice Cardozo who wrote the opinion rejecting the proposition that this procedure impaired a "federal right":

> Adherence to precedent as establishing a governing rule for the past in respect of the meaning of a statute is said to be a denial of due process when coupled with the declaration of an intention to refuse to adhere to it in adjudicating any controversies growing out of the transactions of the future.
>
> We have no occasion to consider whether this division in time of the effects of a decision is sound or unsound application of the doctrine of *stare decisis* as known to the common law. Sound or unsound, there is involved in it no denial of a right protected by the federal constitution. . . .
>
> We think that the federal constitution has no voice upon the subject. A state in defining the limits of adherence to precedent may make a choice for itself between the principle of forward operation and that of relation backward. It may say that decisions of its highest court, though later overruled, are law none the less for intermediate transactions. . . . On the other hand, it may hold to the ancient dogma that the law declared by its courts had a Platonic or ideal existence before the act of declaration, in which event the discredited declaration will be viewed as if it had never been, and the reconsidered declaration as law from the beginning.[35]

34. 287 U.S. 358 (1932).   35. *Id.* at 363–65.

The *Sunburst* case, of course, said nothing about the potential use of the prospective overruling process by the federal judiciary. What it did suggest was that there was no constitutional inhibition on such action, for if that judicial behavior did not violate the Due Process Clause of the Fourteenth Amendment, it is hard to see how that kind of action would be a violation of the Due Process Clause of the Fifth Amendment. On the other hand, it must be remembered that many opinions of the 1932 Supreme Court have carried very little weight with its successors.

In any event, nothing was done toward this possibility until Mr. Justice Frankfurter's concurring opinion in *Griffin v. Illinois*.[36] (It should be noted that the utilization of this process would not be important except to a Court dedicated to the revision of its old constitutional precedents.) In the field of criminal procedure, *Griffin* was an early antecedent of the major changes that the Warren Court was to bring about.[37]

Frankfurter's concurring opinion in *Griffin* was joined by not one other Justice. He joined the conclusion of the Court, but advocated the adoption of the prospective overruling procedure:

> The Court ought neither to rely on casuistic arguments in denying constitutional claims, nor deem itself imprisoned with a formal, abstract dilemma. The judicial choice is not limited to a new ruling necessarily retrospective; or to rejection of what the requirements of equal protection of the laws, as now perceived, require. For sound reasons, law generally speaks prospectively. . . . In arriving at a new principle, the judicial process is not impotent to define its scope and limits. Adjudication is not a mechanical exercise nor does it compel "either/ or" determinations.
>
> We should not indulge in the fiction that the law now

36. 351 U.S. 12, 20 (1956).
37. See chapter 3, *supra* at notes 107, 139, 142, 143, 148, 149.

announced has always been the law and, therefore, that those who did not avail themselves of it waived their rights. It is much more conducive to law's self-respect to recognize candidly the considerations that give prospective content to a new pronouncement of law. That this is consonant with the spirit of our law and justified by those considerations of reason which should dominate the law, has been luminously exposed by Mr. Justice Cardozo, shortly before he came here and in an opinion which he wrote for the Court. See Address of Chief Judge Cardozo, 55 Report of New York State Bar Assn., 263, 294 *et seq.,* and *Great Northern R. Co.* v. *Sunburst Oil & Refining Co.* . . . . Such a molding of law by way of adjudication is peculiarly applicable to the problem at hand. The rule of law announced this day should be delimited as indicated.[38]

I have suggested that the watershed case in the development of the new constitutional doctrines applicable to state criminal procedures came with the overruling of *Wolf v. Colorado*[39] by *Mapp v. Ohio.*[40] It was in the aftermath of *Mapp* that the seed planted by Frankfurter began its extensive growth. Starting with *Linkletter v. Walker,*[41] the Court has followed this practice of creating nonretroactive doctrines over and over again.[42]

I do not propose to enter the controversy over the desirability of the practice. Its problems have been fully elucidated by Paul Mishkin in a manner I cannot hope to improve upon.[43] All that I would emphasize here is that once again the Warren Court's behavior has been assimilated to that of a legislature.

38. 351 U.S. at 25–26.
39. 338 U.S. 25 (1949).   41. 381 U.S. 618 (1965).
40. 367 U.S. 643 (1961).   42. See chapter 3, *supra.*
43. Mishkin, *The High Court, the Great Writ, and the Due Process of Time and Law,* 79 HARV. L. REV. 56 (1965); see also Kitch, *The Supreme Court's Code of Criminal Procedure: 1968–69 Edition,* 1969 SUPREME COURT REVIEW 155.

There are still other ways in which the legislative process was imitated by the Warren Court. One of them relates to the practice of amicus curiae briefs. Frederick Bernays Wiener, the reporter for the Supreme Court's committee on the revision of its rules, revisions effected in 1954, has written on the subject in a way that reveals the issue:

> That the presentation of briefs *amicus curiae* had become a problem was evidenced by the 1949 amendment to old Rule 27(9). In fact, such briefs were no longer presented only by parties with cases or interests similar to or identical with those actually before the Court; they had become a vehicle for propaganda efforts. Far from affording assistance to the Justices, on occasion they did not even mention the decisive issue on which the case turned and which divided the Court. Instead their emphasis was on the size and importance of the group represented, or on contemporaneous press comment adverse to the ruling of the Court. Certainly there were multiplying signs after 1947 that the brief *amicus curiae* had become essentially an instrumentality designed to exert extrajudicial pressure on judicial decisions.[44]

The stringent rule adopted in 1949 was continued by the 1954 rules.

Despite the stringency of the rule, however, and in no small part owing to pressure by Mr. Justice Frankfurter,[45] the practice was relaxed. The Warren Court has been inundated with exactly the kind of amicus curiae briefs described by Wiener. What we have come to see is the development of a lobbying practice more decorous than the ones used in the legislative halls but directed to the same ends. The Court instead of squelching the practice has encouraged it.

There is still another aspect of the amicus brief that is a

44. Wiener, *The Supreme Court's New Rules,* 68 HARV. L. REV. 20, 80 (1954).
45. *Ibid.*

191

reminder of the legislative process. I have suggested elsewhere that no major congressional legislation has been forthcoming except at the request or direction of the president.[46] It is not that the legislation necessarily takes the form that the president desires. It is rather that the executive's views must be taken into account before the legislative decision is reached. The same is becoming true in the Supreme Court. The views of the solicitor general's office have been offered or requested in almost all the major litigation that has come before the Court in recent years and in a good deal of litigation that cannot qualify as important.[47] The effect of the solicitor general's amicus briefs, for example, is well known with regard to such cases as *Brown* and *Baker v. Carr*.[48] Whether the executive branch of government, which is also the chief litigant before the Court, ought to act in such an advisory capacity in cases in which it has no direct interest is a question that has not been raised. I do not offer an answer here. Again, I emphasize only the trend toward the legislative process that has come about in the conduct of the Warren Court's business.

Two more such analogies and I am done with them. Neither may seem important. Both display imitation of congressional behavior by Justices of the high court. The first is the multiplying occasions on which the Justices have taken to the hustings in defense of their opinions or in anticipation of those that they have not yet written. Supreme Court Justices

46. See Kurland, *The Impotence of Reticence,* 1968 DUKE L.J. 619.

47. In the final Term of the Warren Court, for example, the United States appeared as amicus curiae in the following cases: Universal Interpretive Shuttle Corp. v. WMATC, 393 U.S. 186 (1968); Hunter v. Erickson, 393 U.S. 385 (1969); Allen v. State Bd. of Elections, 393 U.S. 544 (1969); Hadnott v. Amos, 394 U.S. 358 (1969); *In re* Herndon, 394 U.S. 399 (1969); Zenith Radio Corp. v. Hazeltine, 395 U.S. 100 (1969); Daniel v. Paul, 395 U.S. 298 (1969); Utah Pub. Serv. Comm'n v. El Paso Natural Gas Co., 395 U.S. 464 (1969); Lear, Inc. v. Adkins, 395 U.S. 653 (1969); Benton v. Maryland, 395 U.S. 784 (1969).

48. 369 U.S. 186 (1962).

have always been in demand as speakers for bar associations and law schools. But they used to restrain themselves both in the number of occasions on which they would speak and in the subject matter that they were willing to address. This is all changed. In his Carpentier Lectures at Columbia University, Mr. Justice Black explained why he was willing to use the public platform in defense of his own views:

> In agreeing to deliver the Carpentier Lectures I was not unaware that many good people think that judges, more particularly Supreme Court justices, should never discuss legal questions beyond the requirements of particular cases which come before them. But in a country like ours, where the people have a voice in their government, public lectures about the Constitution and government can doubtless stimulate, and even help to clarify, discussion of vital constitutional issues that face our society. Under these circumstances, I cannot say that judges should be completely disqualified from participating in such discussions.[49]

What we have received, however, is not merely restatement of the Court's decisions, but commitments to positions made in advance of argument and hearing on cases that were to come before the Court. For example, Mr. Justice Douglas delivered a talk in which he indicated the evils of television cameras in the courtroom.[50] This was later utilized by the Chief Justice in writing an opinion for banning the use of television in criminal trials.[51] Mr. Justice Douglas's position on federal aid to parochial schools was the subject of a book,[52] and his position on the lawsuit that will come before him will certainly not be expected to differ from the stance he has already taken. Mr. Justice Black anticipated his posi-

49. BLACK, A CONSTITUTIONAL FAITH xvi (1968).
50. Douglas, *The Public Trial and the Free Press,* 46 A.B.A.J. 840 (1960).
51. Estes v. Texas, 381 U.S. 532, 569 n. 25 (1965).
52. DOUGLAS, THE BIBLE AND THE SCHOOLS (1966).

tion in the *New York Times* case[53] in a paper published in a law review.[54] The very language of Mr. Justice Goldberg's Madison Lecture[55] showed up in his later opinion in *Bell v. Maryland,*[56] without the benefit of attribution.

Nor do the Justices speak only prospectively. There is also their indulgence in rewriting or explaining their own opinions. The law review article is then utilized as authority for the meaning of the opinion, though the brethren whose acquiescence in the opinion was necessary for its promulgation did not participate in the rewriting. That, I submit, was the case with Mr. Justice Brennan's restatement of the *New York Times* case in his *Harvard Law Review* article.[57] One Justice even responded by published letter to the editor in defense of his opinion against charges made in an editorial.[58]

Once more, I am not concerned here with the desirability of the extracurricular activities but only with the parallel to the actions of political officers who also take their causes to their constituents in this manner.[59]

My final parallel between the Court and the legislative process relates to the crisis that develops at the end of each of their respective terms. Both the Court and Congress have the tendency to put off decision of their most important problems until adjournment is in the offing. Then we have

53. New York Times Co. v. Sullivan, 376 U.S. 254, 293 (1964).

54. Cahn, *Justice Black and First Amendment "Absolute": A Public Interview,* 37 N.Y.U. L. Rev. 549 (1962).

55. Goldberg, *Equality and Governmental Action,* 39 N.Y.U. L. Rev. 205 (1964).

56. 378 U.S. 226, 286 (1964).

57. Brennan, *The Supreme Court and the Meiklejohn Interpretation of the First Amendment,* 79 Harv. L. Rev. 1 (1965).

58. See Casper, *Jones v. Mayer: Clio, Bemused and Confused Muse,* 1968 Supreme Court Review 89, 99 n. 48.

59. One might find another coincidence between judicial and congressional behavior in overseas junkets by members of the Court at the behest and expense of the State Department.

what has appropriately been called "decision by deadline." One has but to glance through the reports of the Warren Court to discover that the month of June in each year is the time when vast constitutional revisions are most likely to take place. Whether this is conducive to the kind of opinions that such important problems deserve is a question that should arouse great concern. Congress has some reasons for decisions close to adjournment. It is not a continuing body and adjournment is necessary for congressmen to return to their electorate for the determination of whether they shall be returned to office. Then, too, budgets are annual matters with pressures unmatched by those on the Court. The Court's Term, on the other hand, is a totally artificial construct. There is no necessity for adjournment in June. And there is no reason why argued cases have to be decided before the June adjournment takes place. The latter is simply a holdover from the days when Chief Justice Hughes was trying to prove that the Court could remain current with its docket against a charge by President Roosevelt that the superannuated Justices were too old to perform efficiently.

Let me turn then to the problems that would be faced by a political court, some of which already exist. First, however, let me say that I do not mean to use the adjective in any pejorative sense. A political court is one that is given or assumes the function of making national policy. Since the Court is already engaged in that task, to a degree, we must be concerned with the expansion or contraction of the Court's competence and a recognition by the Court and the public of the role it is really playing in contemporary American government. Indeed, if the Court is to become a truly political institution, its competence would have to be recognized by the other branches of the national government as well.

The first problem with entrusting large areas of public policy to the Court for ultimate decision is that it is still, despite the changes that have been brought about, restricted to the judicial form. As an institution it still cannot act until a problem is presented to it by way of an adversary proceeding in the form of a case or controversy. This means, for one thing, that the Court cannot initiate the appropriate policy until the proper question is presented to it. I recognize that the Court has found ample excuse in some cases to speak to issues far beyond the cases presented. And I recognize, too, that in this day of the professional litigating organizations, many questions that would never have come before the high court will now be brought to it. But the extension in these areas is not sufficient to make the Court into a prime legislating agency.

The adversary process brings with it additional burdens. The Court's decisions have to rest on the evidence and materials brought before it by the litigants or such similar information as may be garnered by its very small staff from already existing published data. The Court, because it is a court, lacks machinery for gathering the wide range of facts and opinions that should inform the judgment of a prime policy-maker. This was recognized many years ago by Ernst Freund, as Dean Allen has recently made clear:

> "When interests are litigated in particular cases, they not only appear as scattered and isolated interests, but their social incidence is obscured by the adventitious personal factor which colors every controversy. If policy means the conscious favoring of social above particular interests, the common law must be charged with having too much justice and too little policy. It has fallen to the task of modern legislation to redress the balance." Freund's general point is a valid and important one: the kind of law that is made depends significantly on the kind of law-making agency that is employed. The courts are well adapted to weight the competing claims of individual litigants; but they are poorly equipped to resolve broad issues of policy involving, for example, the reallocation of resources

among large social groups or classes. Judicial law making in the latter areas is confronted by a dual peril: it may ignore considerations relevant to intelligent policy formulation, or, in taking them into account, it may inspire doubts about the integrity of the judicial process.[60]

Even Professor Berle, in his outspoken advocacy of the Court's assumption of the role of prime legislator in the national government, recognizes the difficulty:

Courts are organized and staffed and judges are trained to resolve cases and controversies, and decree remedies in individual cases. But where in doing that they are expected to enunciate rules applying to multitudinous situations at the same time—that is, to legislate—the problem of collecting data and arriving at a solution certainly goes far beyond their ordinary function. It is unfair as well as unwise to expect from courts legislation reorganizing county and state governments, rearranging school districts, directing school superintendents how their schools should be administered, determining whether the education given is sufficiently uniform to constitute "equal protection of the laws."[61]

Berle, it will be noticed, is speaking only about the problems with which the Court has already purported to deal. Obviously, there will be other problems of social policy that may be even more recalcitrant than those he mentioned. He would resolve the difficulty by providing the Court with a research arm, patterned, he said, after the Council of Economic Advisers—God save the mark!—which he would call the Constitutional Council. And he would also limit the Court to the resolution of major social problems that the other branches of government failed to resolve, whether from lack of interest or lack of capacity. (He does not tell us how

60. Allen, *Preface,* in FREUND, STANDARDS OF AMERICAN LEGISLATION xxiii–xxix (Allen ed. 1965).
61. BERLE, note 1 *supra,* at 67.

these questions will get to the Court but assumes, as recent history suggests he might, that someone will bring them there.)[62] Thus:

> This is what a Constitutional Council of the kind suggested could do. If legislation were proposed or in progress, that fact could be suggested to the courts. Abstention to get away from a problem is one thing. Abstention to permit orderly resolution of the problem (other than of individual rights in the situation) is quite different, and perhaps justifiable. If in a case the Supreme Court had to make a decree, it would have the equivalent of a committee report, presumably rendered after research of the relevant material. If, on the other hand, the Council reported that the matter was in ordinary legislative process, there would seem to be honorable reason for the courts, possibly retaining jurisdiction, to stand aside and leave the remedy to Congress, or perhaps to the state in question, as the case might be. Specifically, it would provide a method for recommending questions essentially legislative in character to the institutions presently in existence to deal with them, backed by the political processes of the United States, and after an appropriate dialogue carried on before the Constitutional Council or the joint congressional committee.[63]

The Constitutional Council—certainly a body of wise men—would consist of "professors of law, men with judicial experience, men with legislative experience, and men with social awareness,"[64] to be "appointed by the President by and with the advice and consent of the Senate." I find the scheme to be of questionable feasibility. Presumably the Constitutional Council would work in the manner of a Warren Commission, a Kerner Commission, or—as is the cur-

62. One way is suggested in FRIENDLY, THE DARTMOUTH COLLEGE CASE AND THE PUBLIC-PRIVATE PENUMBRA 9 (1969).
63. BERLE, note 1 *supra,* at 68–69.
64. *Id.* at 61.

rent fashion—a presidential "task force." Experience teaches me that this kind of body, like the Council of Economic Advisers, is not an efficient or effective means of discovering the facts needed for the best resolution of the problem, assuming there is a resolution of the problem.

Certainly, however, if this power is to be added to those already exercised by the Court, some program will be necessary—Berle's or another—to provide the Court with adequate data on which to base such momentous decisions.

The second deficiency of a political court goes to the absence of a means of supervising or enforcing the decrees that it promulgates. It can issue an order, it can use marshals and lower federal courts to bring about what it has commanded. But its tools are very limited indeed. One need but recall the response of President Jackson to Marshall's judgments in the Georgia Indian cases,[65] or Lincoln's response to the Court during the Civil War,[66] or even Eisenhower's phlegmatic response to the *Brown* case and its subsequent events, to realize that it takes more than an ipse dixit by the Court to make its decrees realities, even for those who were before the Court and certainly no less for the nation at large. With all appropriate acknowledgment of the intractability of the problems with which the Court has recently dealt, neither its desegregation principles nor its ban on school prayers nor its revision of police practices through the exclusionary rule can be said to have yet been enforced beyond their effect on particular litigants. It can chalk up a success in the reapportionment cases. But in the absence of public acquiescence it will need more clout than it now has to perform the more exalted function that is being wished on it. For all the talk of the famous decision in *Hobson v. Han-*

65. See Worcester v. Georgia, 6 Pet. 515 (1832); 4 BEVERIDGE, JOHN MARSHALL 511 (1919).

66. See *Ex parte* Merryman, 17 Fed. Cases 144 (No. 9487) (C.C. D.Md. 1861); ROSSITER, THE SUPREME COURT AND THE COMMANDER IN CHIEF 25 (1951).

sen,[67] the schools in the District of Columbia are more segregated today than they were at the time of the *Brown* decision. Hobson's choice indeed. Nor can one point to a single successful resolution of a major social or economic problem by the Court. The tragedy of *Dred Scott*[68] remains a ghost of terrifying proportions. Enough for me, however, to point to the problems of a political Court without naysaying those who have the wisdom and the courage to find solutions for them.

There is a third major difficulty with what Professer Berle appropriately terms "the Supreme Court's new revolution." On the subject of revolutions, I concede Professor Berle's expertise, since he was a coauthor of another peaceful revolution that succeeded better than many have been prepared to admit.[69] Nonetheless, I would point out that those who would expand the authority of the Supreme Court, like other contemporary self-styled revolutionaries, assume that the power to be given to it will be readily surrendered by those who now possess it. This must be based on the claim of the moral superiority of the revolutionaries. In this case, however, the change does not even have a base of "participatory democracy" to support it. More important, perhaps, is that competition for power is seldom resolved by claims of moral superiority.

The power that the Supreme Court would secure would have to come from the legislative and executive branches of the national government. Insofar as such power purports to come from the states, the Court would be grasping at no more than a mirage. In fact, since it is the presidency that now dominates the policy-making scene, it would be that branch from which the Supreme Court would have to capture its authority. It is clear, I submit, that in a contest be-

67. 269 F. Supp. 401 (1967); BERLE, note 1 *supra,* at 65–66.

68. Dred Scott v. Sandford, 19 How. 393 (1857).

69. See EINAUDI, THE ROOSEVELT REVOLUTION (1959); TUGWELL, THE BRAINS TRUST (1968); MOLEY, THE FIRST NEW DEAL (1966).

tween the president and the Court or between the Court and the Congress, the Court is not likely to enhance its power; it is much more likely to see it reduced. Wise Courts, in the past, have enlarged their ken insidiously, not by direct confrontation. Every direct confrontation has found the Court engaged in a strategic retreat. To this extent, at least, Hamilton was right when he suggested that "the least dangerous" branch has "neither FORCE nor WILL, but merely judgment" at its command.[70] The Court's capacity to express whatever will it has is entirely dependent upon the support of public opinion. Without it, as Tocqueville told us long ago, the Justices are impotent. As of now, the Court's hold on the public is weak indeed. This would not be so if it were true, as some of us like to think it to be, that the attitudes expressed in academe are representative of the best thought in society. It may be that these academic attitudes are the best that American society can produce—though I have my doubts. What is abundantly pellucid is that they are not necessarily representative of the thinking of anyone except those in these sheltered groves.

Let us assume, however, that ways and means can be found for enhancing the Court's prestige and power. The question then comes, how to staff such an institution. With the Court's duties no greater than they are, the problem has proved exceedingly difficult. For example, two judges whose views of the Supreme Court's proper role cannot be called expansionist stated the job specifications. Judge Learned Hand once said:

> I venture to believe that it is as important to have a judge called upon to pass on a question of constitutional law, to have at least a bowing acquaintance with Acton and Maitland, with Thucydides, Gibbon and Carlyle, with Homer, Dante, Shakespear and Milton, with Machiavelli, Montaigne and Rabelais, with Plato, Bacon,

70. THE FEDERALIST, No. 78, at 523 (Cooke ed. 1961) (Hamilton).

Hume and Kant, as with the books which have been specifically written on the subject. For in such matters everything turns upon the spirit in which he approaches the questions before him. The words he must construe are empty vessels into which he can pour nearly anything he will. Men do not gather figs of thistles, nor supply institutions from judges whose outlook is limited by parish or class. They must be aware that there are before them more than verbal problems; more than final solutions cast in generalizations of universal applicability. They must be aware of the changing social tensions in every society which make it an organism; which demand new schemata of adaptation; which will disrupt it, if rigidly confined.[71]

That was written in 1930. And, unfortunately, Judge Learned Hand had never discovered by personal experience the demands made on Supreme Court Justices by their offices. In 1954, fifteen years after he ascended the high court, Mr. Justice Frankfurter spoke to the same question:

Human society keeps changing. Needs emerge, first vaguely felt and unexpressed, imperceptibly gathering strength, steadily becoming more and more exigent, generating a force which, if left unheeded and denied response so as to satisfy the impulse behind it at least in part, may burst forth with an intensity that exacts more than reasonable satisfaction. Law as the response to those needs is not merely a system of logical deduction, though considerations of logic are far from irrelevant. Law presupposes sociological wisdom as well as logical unfolding. . . .

A judge whose preoccupation is with such matters should be compounded of the faculties that are demanded of the historian and the philosopher and the prophet. The last demand upon him—to make some forecast of the consequences of his action—is perhaps the heaviest. To pierce the curtain of the future, to

71. HAND, THE SPIRIT OF LIBERTY 81 (Dilliard ed. 2d ed. 1953).

give shape and visage to mysteries still in the womb of time, is the gift of imagination. It requires poetic sensibilities with which judges are rarely endowed and which their education does not normally develop. These judges, you will infer, must have something of the creative artist in them; they must have antennae registering feeling and judgment beyond logical, let alone quantitative, proof.[72]

You can readily see from these two quotations that at least these men thought the task of a Supreme Court Justice an awesome one. More, however, they also show that each man's notion of the ideal Supreme Court Justice is garnered from what he sees in his mirror each morning, however idealized and unrelated to the truth the image might be. The essential difficulty is that those making and confirming the Justices who take their place on the high bench—attorneys general, presidents, and senators—do not see in their respective shaving glasses anything like what Hand and Frankfurter described.[73] And it is their images that are reflected in the actual appointments. The results have been what they have been largely for this reason. It takes something of the romantic or the pedantic to appoint great Supreme Court Justices. These elements are—fortunately or unfortunately—missing from the makeups of most of those who appoint Supreme Court Justices. And so the question remains, Are we willing to entrust the power that belongs to nine Platonic Guardians to men of lesser capacity? If the response is affirmative on the ground that the executives and legislators who exercise the power now are no better qualified, I would suggest only that they are without life tenure—just think how you would shudder today at the thought of life tenure for presidents—and they are politically responsible directly to the people. As Learned Hand said more than once: "For

72. Frankfurter, Of Law and Men 35, 39 (Elman ed. 1956).
73. Cf. Baker, Observer: Up from Nonentity to Nixonia, New York Times, 9 September 1969, p. 40.

myself it would be irksome to be ruled by a bevy of Platonic Guardians, even if I knew how to choose them, which assuredly I do not. If they were in charge, I should miss the stimulus of living in a society where I have, at least theoretically, some part in the direction of public affairs."[74]

There are other difficulties in expanding the political power of the Court, including that of securing adequate time to perform its functions,[75] with "the unhurried deliberation which is essential to the formulation of sound constitutional principles."[76]

There are few strong personal beliefs that I have about the Supreme Court. The first is that the Court is not a democratic institution, either in makeup or in function. This should be seen for what it is, even at the cost of that grossest of contemporary epithets, "elitist." It is politically irresponsible and must remain so, if it would perform its primary function in today's harried society. That function, evolving at least since the days of Charles Evans Hughes, is to protect the individual against the Leviathan of government and to protect minorities against oppression by majorities.

Essentially because its most important function is anti-majoritarian, it ought not to intervene to frustrate the will of the majority except where it is essential to its functions as guardian of interests that would otherwise be unrepresented in the government of the country. It must, however, do more than tread warily. It must have the talent and recognize the obligation to explain and perhaps persuade the majority and the majority's representatives that its reasons for frustrating majority rule are good ones.

The Warren Court accepted with a vengeance the task of protector of the individual against government and of minor-

74. HAND, THE BILL OF RIGHTS 73 (1958). But see Rostow, *The Democratic Character of Judicial Review*, 66 HARV. L. REV. 193 (1952).

75. See Kurland, *The Court Should Decide Less and Explain More*, New York Times Magazine 34 (9 June 1968).

76. Williams v. Rhodes, 393 U.S. 23, 63 (1968).

ities against the tyranny of majorities. But it has failed abysmally to persuade the people that its judgments have been made for sound reasons. Its failure on this score is due to many causes, of which I can catalog but a few. One is that its docket is so overcrowded with lesser business that it cannot concentrate its efforts on the important constitutional questions that come before it. Second is that its communication with the public must come through the distortions of the news media, who will not invest the time, effort, or space to the careful job that is necessary exactly because the Court has no power base of its own. A third reason for the failure, if I may say so, is a judicial arrogance that has refused to believe that the public should be told the truth instead of being fed on slogans and platitudes. The fourth problem is even less soluble. It is that many of the Justices are incapable of doing better. They have fooled not only the public but themselves.

There is need for intelligence and integrity on the bench that go far beyond an average IQ and a distaste for venality. The Court, in performing what is, by definition, an unpopular task, is nonetheless dependent on popular support to keep it a viable institution.

If the Court's primary substantive function is impaired by these defects, so too is its important symbolic office:

> A gentle and generous philosopher noted the other day a growing "intuition" on the part of the masses that all judges, in lively controversies, are "more or less prejudiced." But between the "more or less" lies the whole kingdom of the mind; the differences between the "more or less" are the triumphs of disinterestedness, they are the aspirations we call justice. . . . The basic consideration in the vitality of any system of law is confidence in this proximate purity of its process. Corruption from venality is hardly more damaging than a widespread belief of corrosion through partisanship. Our judicial system is absolutely dependent upon a

popular belief that it is as untainted in its workings as the finite limitations of disciplined human minds and feelings make possible.[77]

And here again the Warren Court has failed us. What Arthur Schlesinger has described in his recent book as a crisis of confidence clearly extends to the Supreme Court. The restoration of that confidence is vital to the continuance of the rule of law in this country. For above everything else, the Supreme Court is symbolic of America's preference for law over force as the ruling mechanism in a democratic society. If it fails, the vital center disappears, and we "must ultimately decay either from anarchy, or from the slow atrophy of a life stifled by useless shadows."[78]

The Nixon Court has awesome tasks before it: To match the Warren Court attainments in the protection of individuals and minorities that today justifies the Court's existence; to restore the confidence of the American public in the rule of law. One or the other is not enough.

77. KURLAND, ed., FELIX FRANKFURTER ON THE SUPREME COURT 78 (1970).
78. WHITEHEAD, SYMBOLISM, ITS MEANING AND EFFECT 104 (1928).

Index